STAND OUT

STAND OUT

A SIMPLE AND EFFECTIVE
ONLINE MARKETING PLAN
FOR YOUR SMALL BUSINESS

Aaron N. Fletcher

TURNER

200 4th Avenue North • Suite 950 Nashville, Tennessee 37219
445 Park Avenue • 9th Floor New York, NY 10022

www.turnerpublishing.com

Stand Out: A Simple and Effective Online Marketing Plan for Your Small Business

Cover design: Gina Binkley
Book design: Glen Edelstein

Library of Congress Cataloging-in-Publication Data

Fletcher, Aaron N.
 Stand out : a simple and effective online marketing plan for your small business / Aaron N. Fletcher.
    pages cm
 Includes bibliographical references.
 ISBN 978-1-61858-072-6
 1. Small business marketing. 2. Internet marketing. I. Title.
 HF5415.1265.F575 2013
 658.8'72--dc23
                                    2013005077

Printed in the United States of America
13 14 15 16 17 18 19—0 9 8 7 6 5 4 3 2 1

For my wife, Elizabeth: Thanks for who you are, all you do, and how you make me—

and every being you encounter—feel.

ACKNOWLEDGMENTS

To my son, Parker, daughter, Maddy, and "TBD" baby number three (in the oven). Every day you fill my heart with joy and pride. I extend an eternal thank you to my sister Felicia for your love and sacrifices. And to the rest of my family: Nikki, Selley, Beth, Benny, Scott, and John for your love and support. And a warm thanks to my new "San Diego family," Mike, Colleen, Jeanne, and Kevin, for welcoming me with open arms into your wonderful family.

Thanks to Rusty Fisher for helping me transform an unorganized mass of marketing passion into a focused outline and book proposal that made sense. A very humble thanks to my agent, Jill Kramer at Waterside Productions, for helping *Stand Out* become a reality. And to my incredibly talented editor, Christina Roth, at Turner Publishing for your guidance, perspective, confidence, and toughness. I am extremely honored to be part of the Turner family.

A special "Mahalo" to Domenic and Colin for opening up your home to our family and providing the quiet Hawaiian paradise where much of this book was written. Me ka aloha pumehana.

Special thanks to my colleagues, mentors, and friends who have always pushed me to continually dream, learn, and grow: Jason Phillips, Greg Roden, Baron Cox, Earl Butler, Tom Foley, Amanda Bellerby, Vishal Shroff, Paula Glaser, Dan Haight, Rolando Luarca, Dave Fairbarn, Tyler Smith, Tim Stanley, Andy Cohen, Mark Goines, Cesar Gracie, Jake Shields, and Lance Hale.

I must also acknowledge all of my valued clients for your trust and willingness to be my "marketing guinea pigs," especially the following: Terry Doyle, Peggy Mehiel, Danny Quintero, John O'Connor, Domenic Lombardo, Amanda Powers-Sellers, Jenna Finkelstein, Noah Fardo, Brian

Lee, Scott Needleman, Len Mondschein, Len Shober, Jason Wischmeyer, Beth Roth, Dave Ford, Lynn Glazier, Paris Lee, Harry Margolis, Mark Miller, and Curtis and Krystal Jackson.

The marketing strategies in this book have been developed, tested, and refined as a result of years of trial and error, combined with relentless study with, and of, mentors, authors, and thought leaders. While assembling an exhaustive list would be nearly impossible, the following marketing ninjas had a major influence on this work:

Pat Flynn, James Schramko, Dean Jackson, Joe Polish, the late Gary Halbert, Tim Ferriss, Frank Kern, Steve Garfield, Dan Kennedy, David Meerman Scott, Jeff Walker, Trent Dyrsmid, AJ Kohn, Brian Clark, Sonia Simone, John Jantsch, Chris Brogan, John Wuebben, Joe Sugarman, Michael Port, Michael Masterson, Corbett Barr, Darren Rowse, Michael E. Gerber, Andy Jenkins, Tim Conley, Jason Van Orden, Jeremy Frandsen, Matt Wolfe, Nate Rivers, Anthony Robbins, Dan Sullivan, Chris Ducker, Laura Roeder, Michael Stelzner, Ann Handley, and Lee Odden. Seeking and studying anything produced by any of these folks would be among the best ways to spend your time.

CONTENTS

PART 5: NEXT STEPS FOR **STAND OUT** MARKETERS   289

INTRODUCTION

Why did I write this book?

Simple. Because, in my eighteen-plus years of helping thousands of small business owners get more customers through smart marketing and advertising, I realized a few constant truths.

These are the kind of truths that apply to businesses in all cities—from New York to Los Angeles, from Miami to Branson. Truths that hold steady across all business categories—law firms, restaurants, nursing homes, and even bowling alleys:

▶ Small business owners (like you) are the backbone of America, responsible for 90 percent of the nation's workforce.

▶ These business owners are highly skilled technicians at their respective crafts, so much so that these skills provided the opportunity and inspiration to make the exciting leap from employee to entrepreneur.

This laser focus on technical skills almost always comes at a steep price: a complete lack of skills and know-how in effective marketing.

▶ Virtually all of the new advancements in technology and marketing-information, tools, and resources never make their way down to the local level, leaving small business owners behind. Those business owners who realize this and seek out marketing knowledge and expertise are almost certainly stopped dead in their tracks by confusion resulting from two factors: There are way too many options, i.e., small business marketing books, websites, blogs, and consultants, and most of the options are either too technical (making them inconvenient), too basic (making them ineffective), or too outdated (making them useless).

Now more than ever, small business owners need a simple, easy to understand roadmap for effective online marketing.

WHY IS THIS BOOK FOR ME?

Answer the following questions:

▶ Are you a successful small business owner looking for more business online?

▶ Do you have a website but aren't satisfied with the traffic and leads generated?

▶ Do you know you need to do something to increase your Internet presence and show up higher on search engines, but aren't sure where to start?

▶ Are you busy running your business, with little time to spend on online marketing?

▶ Are you spending money on the yellow pages or print ads and seeing fewer and fewer results?

▶ Are you having a hard time tracking your marketing and ensuring that every dollar you spend produces a return-on-investment?

▶ Are you getting contacted by literally dozens of salespeople and websites, each offering to "get your business more Internet visibility," "increase your SEO," or "optimize your website"—all offering expensive solutions to help you, but leaving you confused in the process?

▶ Do you know that more and more of your ideal clients are looking online for services every day?

▶ Do you want to capture a piece of this current massive migration from traditional media (magazines, radio, and TV) to online media (Google, Facebook, Twitter), but just aren't sure how?

If any or all of the above describes you, and you're looking for a simple, proven, and easy-to-follow system to increase your online visibility, get more traffic to your site, become the dominant authority in your local niche, generate way more leads, and grow your business, then STAND

OUT is for you! STAND OUT provides not just a road map, but your own personal tour guide to help you down the road.

HOW HUGE AN OPPORTUNITY ARE WE TALKING ABOUT?

To get just a taste of what's been happening while you were busy starting, running, and growing your company, here are some blast-tastic stats about the great online migration:

▶ Every American spends sixty hours a month online.
▶ 55 percent of Americans use the Internet every day.
▶ 70 percent of American Internet users participate in social networking.
▶ The world spends 36 percent of its Web time using email, engaging in commerce, and performing searches.[1]

In addition, nearly everyone uses Google[2] to find what they're looking for—and for good reason (when's the last time you used the yellow pages to look for a dentist or order a pizza?).

Your fish are moving to a different pond.

WHY ARE WE ALL USING THE INTERNET TO FIND LOCAL BUSINESSES, ANYWAY?

The Internet provides us with an incredible amount of current information, giving the Web several distinct advantages over traditional media:

▶ **Relevance:** Because search engines produce results based on the specific terms and phrases we specify, we (usually) only see information related

---

[1] *The Huffington Post* (http://www.huffingtonpost.com/2010/06/22/Internet-usage-statistics_n_620946.html).

[2] http://www.karmasnack.com/about/search-engine-market-share/

to our specific query. We can assume that information found online is fairly current, at least more so than that in printed publications.

▶ **Interactivity:** The Internet gives us access to user-generated reviews, comments, and feedback related to the local products and services we're looking for. Access to peer validation greatly aids in the decision-making process, whether for a simple decision like which Mexican restaurant to dine at or a very serious one like selecting a surgeon for a knee replacement.

▶ **Convenience:** After a few keystrokes and a single click, we can find virtually every piece of information we could possibly need related to local services, from directions and distance to pricing, photos and videos, and reviews.

WHAT ABOUT US ADVERTISERS?

As new to online marketing as you may be, this new playing field has given us several amazing tools that our predecessors never dreamed possible:

▶ **Relevance:** Yes, this is the same number-one benefit consumers enjoy, and for the same reason. The fact that consumers can type in a few key words and get specific results means that you can target consumers who are only looking for the specific services you provide. No more "spray and pray," spending thousands on advertising aimed at the masses while hoping to reach a few folks looking for your products and services.

▶ **Engagement:** The Internet allows us to reach and deliver our message to our target audience in ways never before possible, going far beyond the simple text and photos that print media provide. We can use our websites to engage visitors with compelling videos, audios, and other multimedia elements, creating an experience instead of a one-dimensional sales pitch.

▶ **Measurement:** The digital nature of the Internet and online marketing provide the great advantage of measurement. By looking at a few simple metrics related to our online presence, we can discern which marketing programs are making money and exactly how much.

Of course, there's a carrot and stick element at play here. The "carrot," of course, is that the Internet has spawned huge, never-before-seen opportunities for small business owners.

The "sticks" to contend with are fear-based, "or else" reasons to take action ASAP:

▶ Nearly 80 percent of Americans are online looking for nearly everything, including local products and services.

▶ These folks demand more information, continually researching before making nearly every purchasing decision.

▶ They expect you to have a website (and online presence) for credibility.

▶ People use social validation (peer reviews) as a primary factor in deciding where to spend their money.

The fact is, to grab the carrot and avoid the stick, you have to adapt to this changing landscape or risk getting left behind. Enter STAND OUT.

THE STAND OUT PROCESS

The STAND OUT FORMULA is a simple, five-part system that's designed to take even the most tech-challenged business owner through an easy-to-follow process, from building a solid foundation through measuring your online marketing return-on-investment (ROI):

▶ **Part One—The STAND OUT Marketing Foundation:** Before spending another minute (or dollar) on online marketing, it's critical that you understand and implement the "5M" strategy: Forming the right marketing *mindset,* targeting the right *market,* crafting your unique *message,* selecting the best *media,* and tracking critical *metrics.* Part One also covers the basic Online Marketing Funnel and how it applies to your small business. This section will also reveal what you need to know about Google, serving as a great primer on online marketing and how search engines work.

► **Part Two—The STAND OUT Web Design Strategy:** Learn how to launch a simple but powerful WordPress website that creates an ideal user experience and builds trust with your visitors. Part Two starts with choosing a domain name, CMS, and hosting provider and takes you all the way through best practices in converting more visitors into qualified leads.

► **Part Three—The STAND OUT SEO Strategy:** This section covers a no-nonsense "Google 101" crash course in how search engines work, a step-by-step guide for optimizing your website, and steps to increase your online visibility by spreading your message across the Web. Part Three also reveals simple tools and strategies for measuring your online marketing, allowing you to trim the fat and do more of what's working.

► **Part Four—The STAND OUT Content Strategy:** This section reveals a simple game plan for education-based marketing, creating highly valuable blog posts, videos, and other forms of compelling content that speak directly to your clients' needs, quickly establishing you as the clear authority in your niche and generating a whole mess of traffic along the way.

► **Part Five—Next Steps for STAND OUT** Marketers: The final part of this book is all about becoming a "digital citizen," revealing several simple tools to help you leave the comfort of your own website and join the discussion, connecting with your audience wherever they hang out online.

That's it: five simple steps to establishing a STAND OUT business, so that you can start reaching more of your target audience, engaging them with great content and compelling them to contact you right now, growing your sales in the process.

HOW TO USE THIS BOOK

Due to its promise of providing you with a simple, effective, and easy-to-digest-and-implement road map for online success, this book is *not* a technical manual, taking up pages of space with screen shots, graphs, charts, and images of out-of-date websites. Each of the concepts, strategies, tips, and resources are the most effective and current available—selected through thousands of hours and dollars worth of testing by hundreds of business owners.

This book should be read in sequence cover to cover, as each chapter builds on the previous one, covering the key concepts associated with each topic and ending with specific step-by-step instructions, resources, and mistakes to avoid. I have also provided additional resources for each topic, allowing you to pursue any of them further if you wish.

Each chapter in this book is presented in a very consistent and logical format, providing you with the following elements:

- ▶ **KEY CONCEPTS:** a clear and concise description of fundamental material covered and why it's important to you and your business
- ▶ **RESOURCES:** links to additional tools and resources related to the subject matter
- ▶ **CHAPTER CHECKLISTS:** outlines of the specific steps required to implement the action items covered in each chapter

WHAT'S THE CATCH?

Timothy Ferriss, bestselling author of *The 4-Hour Workweek* and *The 4-Hour Body,* told me at a recent event in San Francisco, "Nearly all diets work. The diet isn't the problem. The problem is in the motivation to actually follow the diet."

So what's the problem with your "marketing diet"? Regardless of the specifics, the solution is the same: *You have to actually do the work.*

I understand that you have enough work on your plate already, starting a new small business or running an already established one, designing new products, getting them to customers on time, etc. Although the English proverb states, "You can lead a horse to water, but you can't make it drink," the good news is, my role as your "Internet Yoda" isn't just to show you the well, but to help you drink!

The well of online happiness has been laid out before us; now let's get drinking . . . or clicking!

PART ONE

THE STAND OUT

MARKETING FOUNDATION

ONE

USE THE "5M's" OF MARKETING TO BUILD A SOLID FOUNDATION

"The aim of marketing is to know and understand the customer so well the product or service fits him and sells itself."

—*Peter Drucker*

Before you can launch a killer lead-generating website, shoot to the top of Google, reach every last person on the Web who might be a candidate for your business, and build an online empire that's sure to generate copious amounts of wealth for years to come, we have some groundwork to do. It's critical that you obtain a solid foundation in marketing fundamentals, as this will help you get more out of your marketing, make better decisions, and realize a higher return-on-investment.

OVERHAUL YOUR CURRENT MARKETING PLAN

Every change begins with an overhaul.

You change your living room, what's the first thing you do? Tear down the wallpaper and rip up the floors, right? Maybe reupholster the couch and stain the coffee table; or throw it all out and start fresh with a whole new grouping?

If you're trying to get in shape, you typically tend to give your sedentary lifestyle a complete overhaul by joining a gym, buying all new sweats and sneaks, and downloading the Rocky theme onto your iPod.

Why should your marketing be any different? The fact is, it isn't; your marketing plan—if you even have one—is in desperate need of an overhaul, which, once completed, will leave you feeling refreshed, rejuvenated, and ready to tackle the task that most companies barely address, let alone feel the need to change.

The first step on the path to marketing success is to understand and use a system we call "The 5 M's of Marketing." The 5M Marketing Strategy is an incredibly simple, yet powerful system that addresses each of the essential components of any small business marketing program:

1. **Mindset:** how to think more like a marketing-focused business owner and understand the need for and value of getting more involved with your marketing
2. **Market:** how to ensure that you understand exactly who your target clients are and precisely what their needs are
3. **Message:** how to determine the single most important benefit your business offers clients, which separates you from your competitors
4. **Media:** how to determine where you are most likely to reach your ideal clients, at exactly the right time
5. **Metrics:** how to know which of your marketing efforts are working and, more important, which ones aren't.

Together, these 5M's make up a successful marketing strategy for any size company, from Mom & Pop's Market to Microsoft. Each of the 5M's builds upon the other, and together they form the rock-solid foundation you need for effective marketing.

MINDSET

The primary mission of your small business is to reach and secure customers. Providing your products and services to them is impossible without first reaching them. You must build marketing skills that rival your technical skills.

Before you can start using the 5M Process to help your business reach its full potential, there's one more thing we need to discuss.

The primary reason most business owners find themselves in roughly the same financial position two, five, or even ten years after starting their business is because of one painfully obvious fact: their marketing stinks.

Your spouse may not have told you. Your employees, advisors, mentors, suppliers, customers, friends, cousins, and definitely your enemies have all failed to clue you in one this single most powerful of truths. Maybe they thought you knew what you were doing. Maybe *you* thought you knew what you were doing!

But you, and I, know better. Per Hans Christian Andersen's title, "The Emperor's New Clothes," it's hard to admit (and for others to tell you) that your marketing stinks. But unfortunately, because of poor marketing, most small businesses spend money on advertising without measuring the results, buy expensive websites before planning how the site will reach and engage new customers, pay ridiculous fees to "SEO experts," and write blog posts that few people find or read.

Bad Marketing = Bad Internet Marketing

In most cases, the culprit is the lack of an effective marketing system. And you can't implement a marketing system without marketing knowledge. What's more, you can't obtain marketing knowledge until you do two critical things:

1. **See the need to obtain it.**
2. **Create the time to obtain it.**

And this is where the golden nugget lies: Until now, you've been too busy running your business to effectively run your business.

BUSINESS OWNER 2.0: YOUR NEW MARKETING MINDSET

What do you really do for a living? Are you a dentist? Divorce attorney? Housekeeper? Think again.

Most business owners answer the universally uninspired cocktail party question—"what do you do for a living?"—by answering with the products and services they provide.

But herein lies the problem, and the gigantic need for a dramatic shift in your mindset: **You are not what you sell!**

So, what are you? Well, first of all: Congratulations—you just got a promotion! You're no longer a dentist; you own a dental practice. You're not a lawyer; now you own your own law practice; you aren't a housekeeper—you are the proud founder of a housekeeping business!

And you are solely responsible for the one central task of every business owner:

Getting. Your. Next. Client.

But I have "Someone Else" who handles that!

This is an all-too-common reaction I get from busy business owners. And it makes sense on the surface: stick to your core competencies and outsource all the menial, repetitive, or "unimportant" tasks, looking for opportunities to automate, consolidate, and eliminate costly tasks.

This is also why most business owners run into problems with marketing: they select a Web designer when they have no idea what questions to ask or what an effective website (in terms of actually generating leads) looks like. Or they hire a blog/content writer without reading the content he or she has crafted before or understanding which content strategy will attract and engage their audience.

Marketing, by definition, is a core element of every business. In fact, **marketing is *the* core element of your business.** And that's simply too important to farm out!

Of course, you can outsource repetitive tasks within your marketing system (such as someone to physically bring the postcard mailers down to the post office or post the tweets you write), but only **after you've gained a complete understanding of the process,** or at least enough to monitor the quality of these vendors' work. You can't monitor quality control if you don't know what "quality" in online marketing looks like. From now on, you must take complete ownership of marketing your business. If you're a dentist, you might hire a hygienist, but by that time, you're already quite knowledgeable about teeth.

The New Marketing Mindset Checklist:

▶ You're in the business of marketing your services, not just providing them.

▶ You should spend as much time gaining tools and knowledge related to marketing your business as you can.

▶ Your marketing and your website are your reputation and they are too valuable to outsource until you understand them in detail.

▶ You must become a provider of valuable content that helps people understand their options as they relate to the products or services you provide.

▶ You must pay close attention, as often as you can, to basic metrics related to your marketing.

RESOURCE: For more on the three personas of a small business owner and a great road map for work *on* your business instead of *in* your business, read *The E-Myth* by Michael Gerber. This is the second book I recommend to small business owners.

How do your marketing skills stack up to your legal/dental/accounting skills? If you've identified the need to add more feathers to your marketing quiver—and fast—then the rest is simple, as long as you've got the right mindset.

MARKET

The second "M" of Marketing is all about understanding who exactly your target clients are and what exactly they need.

Market research—and specifically defining your target market—is the most important element of any marketing strategy, period. Why? Because all the best ads, Web designs, special offers, promotions, landing pages, postcards, and flyers add up to squat if they don't speak to the right audience.

Every component of your marketing strategy points back to this step. And sadly, this is also the step that most small businesses fail to understand or implement.

The Four Steps of Short-Lived Entrepreneurship

Many small businesses use the *Field of Dreams* philosophy when starting a business: "Build it and they will come." This assumption is a dangerous—if not deadly—one.

You've probably heard the way-too-often-quoted statistic: "90 percent of small businesses fail in the first 3 years." Have you wondered why this is? Surely the pizza didn't taste *that* bad, did it?!

Most small businesses adhere to the following steps when starting out:

1. **Develop a passion or skill.**
2. **Start the business.**
3. **Develop products and services.**
4. **Find customers to sell these products and services to.**

As common as this start-up sequence may be, it's flawed and extremely risky. By skipping over the first and most critical step of market research, many small business owners gamble with their already meager budgets and often perish as a result.

The irony here is that most of the risk associated with starting and running a small business can be avoided by adding just a light dose of market research up front.

A better approach to starting a small business:

1. **Clearly identify a specific target market.**
2. **Ask them what they want.**
3. **Build what they want.**

The Importance of Identifying a Single Target Market

Until you know exactly who your small business should be catering to, you can't possibly craft an effective message that resonates with them. This means, no matter how much you spend on marketing, Web design, direct mail, brochures, or bus benches, you'll be broadcasting bland messages that resonate with no one.

Whenever I ask a small business owner which city he or she serves, the answer that follows sounds like a nervous fourth grader who forgot to study the night before, just after being called upon in Geography class ("Cleveland, Akron, Gainesville, Ohio, Buffalo, Nebraska, Earth, The Shire . . . !"). We want to sell our services to anyone and everyone who will buy.

In doing so, we push out bland messaging that fails to grab or resonate with any one specific group of people. But we must understand one powerful and sometimes painful truth about marketing:

"If you aim to appeal to everyone, you appeal to no one."

This means that people resonate with messages that speak directly to them. Not "them" as in humans. Not "them" as in Americans, Females, Truckers, Soccer Players, or any other label that can be pluralized. Them as in:

"Larry, the busy accountant with 3 kids who lives 11 miles from your store and is concerned about finding an affordable suit that looks great and can be tailored quickly!"

Your target customer is one person.

Sound like this could put you out of business? It won't. The most effective way to approach targeted marketing is to go deep before you go wide. Learn to effectively identify with and market to a small niche (the smaller the better) successfully and then do the same for additional niches.

Pretend you are a forty-year-old professional male who enjoys riding your Harley Davidson on the weekends. While going for a ride last weekend, you were rear-ended by a text-messaging pizza delivery guy at a stoplight, causing several serious but not life-threatening injuries.

You need a lawyer and fast! You hobble to your computer, jump onto Google, and search for "injury lawyer who handles motorcycle accidents in Dallas," or one of many potential search queries. After just a few seconds, you see the following websites listed among the top search results:

- ▶ DALLAS INJURY LAWYER
- ▶ DALLAS AUTO ACCIDENT ATTORNEY
- ▶ DALLAS MOTORCYCLE ACCIDENT LAWYERS
- ▶ THE DALLAS HARLEY DAVIDSON INJURY LAWYER

Which of these options do you think would resonate with you enough to click through to the lawyer's website and learn more? This specificity is true for any type of business. You should be the gym for busy professionals, the cake shop for corporate events, the burger joint for budget- and health-conscious students, or even the website designer for residential real estate agents.

Once you understand, approach, and become the authority on one niche, you can start to market to the next and so on.

How targeted an audience is too targeted? If you aren't known as the authority in a niche, your target is too large. If you can't earn a living, it's too small (think "the best Italian restaurant for albino poker players").

Focus Your Message: Create a Target Customer Profile

Which segment of your market are you targeting? To identify your market, create a Word document and list the following elements as they apply to your business:

QUESTIONS FOR IDENTIFYING YOUR TARGET MARKET

1. **What are the demographics of my market? What are the measurable statistics that I know about my market such as age, income, or occupation, and how many of these people are in the area that I service?**

2. How often do they purchase services like the ones I offer, and what quantity of these services do they purchase?

3. What are the psychographics of my market? What are the lifestyle preferences of my market? Are they all music lovers, golfers, or condo owners?

4. Is this a group I enjoy working with and/or find fascinating? If I have to spend a lot of time with this group will I be bored or repelled by its members?

5. What kind of connection do I have to this market so I know it well? Am I part of the market myself or have I been part of it in the past? Do I have family and friends that are part of it?

6. What are the professional organizations, clubs, or activities that my target market frequents? I want to be able to find my market and talk to them directly. Do I know where to go?

7. What newspapers, magazines, or websites does my market enjoy? If I want to stay in touch with the market on an ongoing basis then I need to know what this group is reading.

8. Do I understand the problems that my market faces? Will my product or service solve a problem for the members of this market?

9. Do I know the language that this market uses? Knowing the vocabulary of my market gives me more credibility.

10. Do I know what attracts this group? How do I let this group know about my product or service? What will get their attention?

11. Do I know who influences this group? Who are the people that this group respects? What are they advocating, and can I align my product or service in some way with them and their message?

Your answer to the last question can be very helpful in terms of how you can best serve the needs of your target market, and it will inform the way you interact with the rest of our 5M System.

Doing strong market research before making big moves helps you merge the needs of that market with your own reasons for going into business, so that you'll succeed in that business long after your non-market-research-doing competitors have shuttered their doors for good.

MESSAGE

Now that you know exactly who you're trying to reach (your ideal customers) and what their most pressing needs are, you can craft a unique message that engages them and positions your business as the obvious choice.

The whole point of any marketing activity is to get the right message to the right people (your target audience) in the right place (your target media) at the right time (right when they're looking and in need!). If the message is off, everything else crumbles.

Most marketing gurus refer to your unique marketing message as a Unique Selling Proposition (USP). What you choose to call it isn't important; that you create and use one effectively is not only important but absolutely *critical* to your business! In this digital, overly plugged-in age, we all have short attention spans when it comes searching for things online. When someone arrives at your website for the first time, they already have their mouse over the dreaded back arrow, spending just seconds subconsciously deciding, "Is this site the right place to get my need filled?"

IT'S NOT ABOUT YOU

Look at a few dozen small business websites and you'll be remiss to find more than one or two who meet visitors with a message that addresses their needs. This is especially true for us providers of professional services (consultants, lawyers, doctors, real estate agents, etc.). These sites are the worst offenders when it comes to self-centered, ineffective messaging:

"Over 20 Years of Successful Litigation." "CPA, DDS, PHD, BLAH BLAH BLAH." Most small business websites just talk about what the business does, not what the business does differently.

As Michael Mastersen stated in his great book on starting and running a successful business—*Ready, Fire, Aim*—"Your customers don't care about your company. They care about finding a solution to their current need."

Let's head back over to Google and revisit the page of "injury lawyer who handles motorcycle accidents in Dallas" (which you had opened after your recent Harley accident). After a quick scan of the top few results, you decide to click on two sites. Each has a large, bold headline on the home page:

▶ Site One: "Biggest Injury Law Practice in Dallas, We Have Six Lawyers and a Super-Huge Conference Room!"
▶ Site Two: "If You've Been Injured on Your Harley, Get the Answers and Compensation You Need Fast."

Which would make you stick around, at least for a few seconds, to learn a bit more?

Crafting and deploying a powerful unique selling proposition can be a game-changer for your business. Multi-million-dollar companies and franchises have been built on powerful USPs alone. Check out these powerful examples of companies taking the time to identify their clients' primary needs and answering them in a simple and consistent fashion:

Domino's Pizza:
▶ Primary customer need: "I am frustrated with how long it takes to get a pizza delivered."
▶ USP: "You get fresh, hot pizza delivered to your door in 30 minutes or less—or it's free."

FedEx:
▶ Primary customer need: "I need to make sure this package gets there tomorrow."

▶ USP: "When your package absolutely, positively has to get there overnight"

M&M's:

▶ Primary customer need: "I love delicious chocolate candy but am tired of chocolate-covered messy hands."
▶ USP: "Melts in your mouth, not in your hand"

THE SIMPLE WAY TO DEVELOP YOUR UNIQUE SELLING PROPOSITION

To craft your unique marketing message, combine the answers to these three questions into one simple, powerful, and effective message:

1. **What is the primary need of your customers that your business fills?**
2. **Who, exactly, are your customers?**
3. **What is the *one unique thing* that sets your business apart?**

Your goal is to ensure your message will ring out everywhere people encounter your business: on your website, in direct mail, on your menus, in your store or office, and on your business cards. The good news is that you'll almost certainly and quickly see increased response from your marketing campaigns, as crafting a great USP can transform your company from another "me too" business in a crowded sea to a "market of one" who serves a specific niche like no other can.

MEDIA

The advent of the Internet has made selecting the right places to advertise your business both easier and more difficult: easy because the digital age provides us with never-before-experienced abilities to track and measure virtually every aspect of online marketing, difficult because this limitless number of sources and measures often leaves us paralyzed and unable to see the forest through the trees when it comes to making sound marketing decisions.

Therefore, it's this step—determining where to reach these elusive clients of yours—that makes all the difference in the world. In order to reach marketing success, you have to deliver the right message to the right people in the right place(s).

The cool thing about the Internet is that it allows for an incredibly high level of targeting, both in demographics (age, sex, income, location) and psychographics (interests and lifestyles). This targeting gives small business owners the remarkable ability to focus marketing dollars to your exact audience.

COMMON PLACES TO REACH YOUR AUDIENCE ONLINE

Before we talk about the best places to reach your audience online and put together your online marketing strategy, let's look at a laundry list of eight common online channels that can be used to increase your online visibility:

▶ **Your Website:** Your site is the "hub" of your online marketing. This means that many, if not most, people who find your business online end up going to your site, either for further information regarding your services, or to validate your business. Understanding this common user behavior is critical when putting together your online marketing plan. This is why most successful businesses use other channels like social media, online directories, and paid advertising to drive visitors back to their websites.

▶ **Search Engines:** These include Google and "the other ones." Getting your business visible on search engines is critical to your online marketing success. Two primary ways to get found on search engines are in both the natural (organic) and the paid search results (PPC).

▶ **Social Media Sites:** Facebook is at more than a billion users per month and counting. Twitter and many other social sites are gaining popularity at record speeds, and Google is placing ever-increasing emphasis on social factors when ranking Web pages. Social media sites will be an important aspect of your marketing strategy.

▶ **Online Directories:** The Web has many business directories. Some are general online directories (Yahoo business), while others focus on location (Google+ Local) or type of business (Lawyers.com).

▶ **Multimedia Sites:** Owned by Google, YouTube is the second largest search engine in the world. Video and other multimedia (photos, slides, audio) are gaining popularity and thus showing up much more frequently in Google search results.

▶ **Industry Sites and Blogs:** Following the goings-on in your industry, these allow users to "join the discussion," which is important for any small business looking to gain trust and an online following.

▶ **Joint Ventures and Partnerships:** If you're a residential house painter, do you partner with carpet cleaners, window replacement companies, or landscaping providers? Partnering with other professionals who share your target market is a powerful method for reaching more customers.

▶ **Offline Sources:** Let's not forget direct mail, advertising, and events (trade shows, seminars, etc.). These "offline" sources will always be very effective vehicles for reaching your target audience. Many small businesses use direct mail and print ads to drive people to their websites to purchase a product, fill out a Web form for a free download, or respond to some other offer.

For each of these, there are a few basic but important techniques to ensure you're doing the right things—both in terms of connecting with people (your customers) and in terms of showing up in search engines. We'll cover the "how to" on these techniques in Chapter 8.

METRICS

The fifth and final "M" of marketing is the most important. Most local businesses lose thousands of dollars and potential clients each year by simply not paying enough attention to the performance of their marketing. Marketing without metrics isn't marketing at all.

If you think about it, the success of nearly every aspect of our lives is determined by metrics. The effectiveness of an education is measured by grades. The measures of any successful diet or fitness program include pounds lost, change in blood pressure, increase in bench press weight . . . the list goes on!

The quality of any business process, from baking bread to manufacturing microchips, is determined by careful and concise measurement. And marketing is no exception! In fact, as a small business owner, you must be extra metrics-minded, as you have less margin for error than do larger companies. Yet most small business owners I talk to cannot answer even the most fundamental questions related to their marketing metrics, such as:

▶ How many visitors are coming to your site each month?
▶ What percentage of them convert to leads (via phone or Web forms/email)?
▶ What is the average lifetime value of a new customer?
▶ Which of your marketing channels are producing a positive ROI?

If you can't answer each of these, fear not—soon you'll be able to rattle off the answers faster than an auctioneer on a 5-hour Energy drink.

KEY MARKETING METRICS FOR YOUR BUSINESS

▶ **Measure your online marketing funnel.** In the next chapter, we'll introduce you to a simple, three-step online marketing funnel that can be used to evaluate and improve every aspect of your marketing. One of the great benefits of using this simple funnel is that we can segment each phase into meaningful and easily digestible measures:
  • **REACH:** Search engine rankings, visits to your website
  • **ENGAGEMENT:** page views, bounce rate, and social "shares" of your content
  • **CONVERSION:** phone calls and lead forms resulting from traffic to your site

▶ **Measure your advertising spending and ROI.** Given the limited marketing and advertising budgets of most small businesses, it's critical to measure which campaigns and expenses are bearing fruit and which should be minimized or eliminated. In Chapter 9, we'll delve into a few essential marketing metrics that'll ensure you're getting the most out of your budget.

▶ **Measure your competition.** In *The Art of War,* the great Sun Tzu said, "If you know your enemies and know yourself, you will not be imperiled in a hundred battles; if you do not know your enemies but do know yourself, you will win one and lose one; **if you do not know your enemies nor yourself, you will be imperiled in every single battle**." This famous quote is especially applicable to marketing. The more you know about your competition—the where, when, what, and how of their methods for reaching and acquiring new clients—the more clear the path to out-marketing them will become! Every metric you apply to your business should be used to scrutinize your competitors.

In order for you to really use and reap the benefits of a marketing metrics program, the program must be simple, requiring little time to update, and insightful, helping you to keep your fingers on the pulse of your marketing strategy. The end goal is to create a simple dashboard that will reveal the key metrics you need to be watching and acting upon to STAND OUT online and elsewhere.

CHAPTER CHECKLIST

✔ **Get into the Right Mindset**
  • You're in the business of marketing your services, not just providing them.
  • You should spend as much time gaining tools and knowledge related to marketing your business as you can.
  • Your marketing and your website are your reputation and are too valuable to outsource (at least until you understand them in detail first).

- You must become a provider of valuable content that helps people understand their options.
- You must pay close attention to basic metrics related to your marketing.

✔ **Identify Your Target Market**
- Pinpoint the geographic territory your business will service.
- Create a customer persona.
- List the demographics of your target clients.
- Determine how often your typical customer utilizes services like yours.
- Find out how your competitors find new clients.

✔ **Craft Your Unique Marketing Message (Value Proposition)**
- What is the primary need/concern of your clients that your business/services fill?
- Why do your customers choose you over the competition?
- What is the one unique thing that sets your business apart?

✔ **Identify the Best Media to Reach Your Customers**
- List which media your target audience consumes.
- Determine which media your competitors use to find new business.

✔ **Measure Your Marketing**
- Ensure that every dollar you spend on marketing or advertising can be tracked.
- Implement metrics to measure your basic online marketing funnel.

TWO

UNDERSTAND THE BASIC ONLINE MARKETING FUNNEL

"That's been one of my mantras—focus and simplicity. Simple can be harder than complex: You have to work hard to get your thinking clean to make it simple. But it's worth it in the end because once you get there, you can move mountains."

—*Steve Jobs*

Now that we have laid the groundwork for a solid, 5M marketing foundation, it's time to discuss the second critical component of your small business online marketing foundation: understanding the basic online marketing funnel.

Most small business owners are confused by the myriad of terms, acronyms, and technical jargon associated with online marketing. This leaves them unsure of how to evaluate or understand the growing number of available options, much less communicate with and order services from marketing consultants and Web design companies ("Yes, I'd like some SEO and PPC, with a side of backlinks and tweets please . . ."). However, **your entire online marketing program and goals can be broken down into three primary phases:**

▶ **Reach:** getting your business and message in front of the right people (your target customers) in the right places
▶ **Engagement:** implementing best practices in Web design and content creation (blogs, videos, etc.) to build trust and authority with the folks you've reached
▶ **Conversion:** ensuring that the maximum percentage of the people

who are engaged with your brand are taking the specific actions you desire (e.g., calling or emailing you, signing up for a newsletter, or downloading an e-book)

This basic Reach-Engagement-Conversion funnel is used, in some form, by virtually all of the largest high-tech marketing companies and agencies. Only the level of detail and complexity of tools used differ between them.

Before we dissect each of the three phases, let's first examine why we use the analogy of the funnel and why it's critically important to categorize and manage your marketing programs this way.

BENEFITS OF USING THE SIMPLE ONLINE MARKETING FUNNEL

According to Wikipedia, a funnel is ". . . a pipe with a wide, often conical mouth and a narrow stem." Your goal in marketing is to reach your target audience—the wide mouth or opening of the funnel—and move them through a series of narrowing steps—the phases of the funnel—all the while controlling and measuring how many drop off along the way, ultimately leaving you with many more new customers at the bottom of the funnel.

Using the basic online marketing funnel provides several powerful benefits to your business:

▶ **Simplicity:** Because the funnel consists of only three phases, it's very simple to understand and manage—every activity associated with your marketing and advertising can be categorized into one of the phases.

▶ **Time Savings:** Using the simple online marketing funnel allows you to spend less time on deciphering and managing your marketing and more on what really matters—running your business and getting more customers!

▶ **Cost Savings:** This simplicity saves you time and money, providing you with a simple and clear view of what's happening with your marketing. This measurement also provides clear insight into what's working in your marketing—and what's not.

▶ **Continuous Improvement:** Each of the funnel's phases provides a clear point to measure and improve upon. For example, if your website gets 500 visitors per month (REACH), but only 5 leads (CONVERSIONS), you know that you have some work to do in ensuring more of your visitors are prompted to contact you.

THE SIMPLE ONLINE MARKETING FUNNEL EXPLAINED

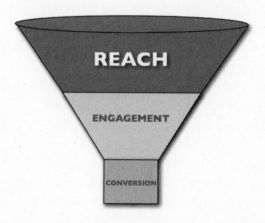

Figure 1: The Basic Three-Step Online Marketing Funnel

REACH

Reach is defined as someone (ideally, in your target audience) coming into contact with your brand. Reach includes every activity (or channel) that allows your business to get in front of the eyeballs of your target customers. This can include any place your business is listed, advertised, or mentioned, both online and offline. Reach can be accomplished via both free (SEO or Social Media) and paid (Yellow Pages or Google PPC Advertising) sources.

Putting in place a great online reach strategy is critical to your success. Reach is the first phase, the "mouth" of your marketing funnel. You must effectively get your message in front of the right people, in the right places, or nothing else you do afterwards matters. Picture a Ritz Carlton in the middle of the Mohave Desert. It doesn't matter how soft the mattress, stellar the service, or tasty the bisque if you have no customers to offer them to.

This "5-star hotel in the middle of the desert" analogy represents exactly what most small business owners do when it comes to online marketing: spend most of their limited time and money on expensive Web designs, resulting in the unavoidable disappointment that sets in over the following weeks and months of virtual tumbleweeds that follow.

It's critical for you to understand that you have to go and get your visitors, not sit around waiting for them to appear. To this end, we will later explore the most commonly utilized channels for reaching customers online.

The last important concept related to the REACH phase of the online marketing funnel is measurement. You must have in place simple and frequently updated metrics related to your reach.

Examples of reach measures include:

▶ **Search engine rankings:** where your site ranks on Google and other search engines with your targeted search terms
▶ **Website traffic:** how many visitors come to your website and social media sites each month
▶ **PPC impressions:** the total number of people exposed to your ad(s) online
▶ **Email open rates:** if you're using a list, the total percent of people who open (and presumably read) your message

In Chapter 9, we'll cover specific tools to measure your online reach in detail.

ENGAGEMENT

The second phase of the Online Marketing Funnel occurs when someone interacts with your brand, content, or media. The goal of engagement is to get your visitors to "stick around" for a while, checking out your website, reading your articles, or watching your videos. Engagement is critical because we are all easily distracted when it comes to browsing the Internet, searching for answers to our questions or looking for local services. The average website user visits a site for just sixteen seconds! This means that you have an extremely small window of opportunity to make a first "virtual" impression and show each finicky visitor that they have "come to the right place" and should stick around awhile, learning more about your company and the services you provide.

It is a shame to spend significant time and money increasing your online REACH, only to have dozens or even hundreds of potential new clients arrive at your website and quickly decide "this isn't for me."

There are specific psychological and emotional "triggers" that have been proven to establish trust and authority with new website visitors, so you must implement a specific plan consisting of best practices in engaging Web design and content creation. In Chapters 4 and 10, we will dive deeply into the elements of the creation of engaging Web design and small business content.

And lastly, we can't forget engagement metrics. Online engagement can be best measured by looking at the following metrics (most of which can be analyzed using Google Analytics, a free tool from Google which is covered in Chapter 9):

▶ **Bounce rate:** measures the number of website visitors who, upon arrival to your site, click their "back button"—a negative measure of engagement

▶ **Time on site:** measure of how long the average visitor stays on your website—a critical way to gauge engagement, as more time on your site equals more trust and confidence in your brand, and a higher likelihood of contacting you eventually and thereby becoming a lead (CONVERSION)

▶ **Page views:** the number of pages visitors look at while on your site—more pages equals greater engagement
▶ **Social "Likes" and "shares":** people who interact with your website or content via social media are showing a clear sign of engagement, taking action and letting you and others know they've found value in your content

CONVERSION

A conversion happens when your target customers (visitors) take a pre-determined desired action. For E-commerce sites—websites that sell products and services directly online like eBay, Zappos, and Amazon—a conversion is measured in the number of actual purchases (physical transactions). For the typical small business owner like yourself, a conversion is defined by the generation of a qualified lead (via Web form or phone call), or the acquisition of a new newsletter subscriber (often called an opt-in) or new social media fan/follower.

Just like the other two phases of the online marketing funnel, conversions must be closely measured. Conversion metrics are the most black and white of the entire marketing process, as they can be easily quantified by asking one important question: how many qualified leads were generated? The key with conversions is to ensure that your inbound leads and other measures of conversion are accurately tracked and measured. The most common conversion measures include the following:

▶ Incoming phone calls
▶ Web forms (one on every page of your site)
▶ Emails
▶ Newsletter subscriptions or downloads

NOTE: Measuring the volume and quality of inbound leads is critical in every area of marketing and advertising. Whenever you pay any entity for advertising, don't fall victim to common sales tactics from "advertising experts," including their avoidance of specific numbers. When you invest in marketing, you have the right to reports and trackable metrics associated with your ads. Although there are secondary benefits to most marketing channels (links to your website, "branding," and exposure), you must refine any paid relationship down to five metrics:

1. **How many leads were generated in a given time frame?**
2. **What did you pay for each lead (total spent, divided by number of leads)?**
3. **How many of these leads became clients?**
4. **How much was the average client worth (total sales divided by number of clients)?**
5. **What was the ROI for this lead source (amount spent, divided by new sales)?**

CHAPTER SUMMARY

Looking at your online marketing campaigns, strategies, and metrics within the context of a simple, three-step funnel provides even the busiest of small business owners great insights into every aspect of online marketing. Using this funnel to examine every Web page, blog post, video, and online promotion you launch will ensure maximum results for your online marketing efforts. The STAND OUT Online Marketing Strategy works so well because it ensures that everything you do to promote your business is optimized to reach, engage, and convert your target audience.

CHAPTER CHECKLIST

✔ **Understand the Basic Online Marketing Funnel**
   • Reach: getting your business and message in front of the right people (your target customers) in the right places
   • Engagement: implementing best practices in Web design and content creation (blogs, videos, etc.) to build trust and authority with the folks you've reached

- Conversion: ensuring that the maximum percentage of the people who are engaged with your brand are taking the specific actions you desire (e.g., calling or emailing you, signing up for a newsletter)

✔ **Measure Each Phase of the Online Marketing Funnel**
  - Reach: search engine rankings, website traffic, PPC impressions
  - Engagement: your website's bounce rate, time on site, and page views
  - Conversion: what percentage of visitors turned into leads (conversion rate)

PART TWO

THE STAND OUT
WEB DESIGN STRATEGY

THREE
CHOOSE THE RIGHT DOMAIN NAME, CMS, AND HOSTING PROVIDER

"In today's information age of Marketing and Web 2.0, a company's website is the key to their entire business."

—*Marcus Sheridan*
Nationally acclaimed marketing speaker

In this section we'll start with a blank page (or screen) and guide you through the steps required to launch a basic but powerful site that's easy to use and update and includes current best practices in engagement and lead conversions.

Your website is the core of your online presence. Regardless of how potential customers find you—whether searching on Google, noticing an ad you placed on Facebook, or browsing reviews on Yelp—today's savvy online consumers *will* check out your site as part of their vetting process when seeking out products or services.

In today's ultra-digital landscape, even offline marketing and advertising efforts drive prospects to business websites. For example, the last time you received a postcard for a teeth cleaning, I'll bet you at least checked out the dentist's website and online reviews before letting her start going to work in your mouth with shiny metal objects.

Yet most small business websites are "online brochures": uncompelling, seldom updated, text-filled "digital sales flyers" that fail to either reach and engage visitors or serve as effective tools for lead generation.

In their bestselling book *Inbound Marketing*, Brian Halligan and Dharmesh Shah (co-authors and co-founders of HubSpot) say the following of online "brochureware" websites:

The history of the company website began with the paper brochure that was handed out at trade shows and stuffed into envelopes for mailing to unsuspecting prospects. When the Internet came into play, this same brochure was handed to a Web Designer who turned it into a beautiful website. This made sense at the time; brochures were static, the Web was new and mostly static, and companies had spent lots of money to have these brochures designed. However, having a "brochureware" website is where the trouble starts for many businesses today.

Does your current website fall into the "online brochure" category? Even if you have a modern, frequently updated site that's generating some leads, I'm willing to bet your site is missing several elements of an effective lead generation engine.

Most small business owners start the website creation process by paying a chunk of money to a Web designer who was not screened with the right qualifying questions, giving them little guidance relating to the purpose and goals of the website. And those few business owners who do assume an active role in the design and functions of the site often focus way too much time and energy on aesthetics rather than on the broader strategy required for online success.

SIX SIMPLE STEPS TO LAUNCHING A GREAT WEBSITE

Now, let's look at six simple steps that will get you to a live, basic yet effective website in nearly no time!

Step 1: SELECT A GREAT DOMAIN NAME

Now it's time to select a domain name. This is a very important decision, as your domain name should and will become synonymous with your brand more and more as the Internet becomes an increasingly significant part of your business.

Selecting a great domain name is the first of many Search Engine Optimization activities we'll be doing along our path to launching an awesome website. Although we'll cover a series of lessons on SEO later, it's imperative that you get a preview right now, and selecting a Google-friendly domain name is an important step toward online success.

Just as with other aspects of online marketing, it's important to balance branding with SEO: choosing a domain that resonates with your audience—a memorable and user-friendly domain that people can easily type and remember—while factoring in the SEO benefits of keyword-rich domains. In the past, Google's algorithms placed great value on the inclusion of keywords in domain names, meaning that using your target search terms within your Web address would help your site rank higher on Google (this is why using the domain "ColumbusPizza.com" would help you rank for these keywords better than "LuigisPlace.com"). However, recently Google has turned down the signals on exact-match domains, as many low-quality websites were outranking more content-rich sites in search results.

Recall the 5M's of Marketing, where we stressed the importance of focusing your messaging on the needs of your target customers. This includes your website copy, printed materials, and most certainly your domain name! Your customers care less about you than they do about finding answers to their most immediate questions.

Tips for choosing a great domain name

- ▶ **Use relevant keywords.** Start by brainstorming the top five or six keyword phrases that relate to your business. For example, if you are a bankruptcy lawyer in Dallas, you may list the following keyword phrases: Bankruptcy, Lawyer, Lawyers, Attorney, Attorneys, Dallas.
- ▶ **Keep your domain short.** Users will be better able to remember your website address, and shorter addresses both display better in SERPS (search engine results pages) and fit better on business cards.
- ▶ **Use the ".COM" only.** Users often place more trust in ".com" websites and assume that extension most often when remembering a website URL. If you must make an exception and can't find any suitable ".com" domain names, you can go with ".net" or ".org"

only—avoid any of the new and weird ones (".biz," ".ca," ".tv").

▶ **Make your Web address easy to type.** Many small business sites contain terms that are often misspelled or don't make sense together (e.g., www.dealsyousave.com). Remember to balance search and branding—don't act on the temptation to use a keyword-rich domain at the expense of poor branding or usability ("ClevelandBakeryCoffeeAndCateringServices.com would be bad).

▶ **Avoid using hyphens or weird characters.** Resist the temptation to purchase and use "Atlanta-pet-sitting-services.com," for example. These domains are obviously unfriendly and don't provide much SEO value. More important, using hyphens can result in your hard-earned marketing and advertising budget working to drive traffic to your competitors ("If you'd like to learn more about our services, go to Atlanta, dash pet, dash sitting, dash services, dot com").

▶ **Save the abstract branding for the big companies.** Crafting your local business domain name may not be the best time to get ultra-creative—this isn't the time to invent new words or create a new online revolution. Zappos.com can get away with this but you'd be better off with www.denvershoestore.com. Again, you want to consider your brand, but not with complete disregard for keyword-rich SEO friendliness.

▶ **Make sure your domain describes what you do.** Many site owners make the mistake of generating the "wrong traffic," that is, attracting users that won't convert into clients. For example, a site called "www.freestockinfo.com" that offers a $500 investment course may discourage users and yield few, if any, benefits.

▶ **Length of time matters!** If you are starting a new site, be sure and register your domain for five years or more. Most small business owners fail to realize that Google and other search engines place more trust in domains with longer registration periods. This may act as a filter for short-lived spam sites. If you have a domain name that's been live for more than a year that you are unhappy with after reading this section, please see "What about my current domain" on page 36 to pass any "SEO juice" from your old domain to your new one.

▶ **Avoid tricks and shortcuts.** Many people try to capture misguided traffic in the form of misspelled domain names. Google (and people) have caught on to such practices and these tactics seldom pay off (buying "DenverHairSaloon.com" won't do any good nowadays).

▶ **Do not pay "cyber-squatters" for domain names.** Buying and selling domain names has blossomed into an extremely lucrative industry, based largely on small business owners paying too much for "aged" and "reserved" domains. Right around the time you start enjoying increased visibility and traffic to your site, you'll also start receiving more emails and phone calls from sales reps selling you an exhaustive number of things including domain names. In most cases, paying more than a couple hundred bucks for a domain name you really, really like isn't warranted. Keep searching for a great domain using the tactics outlined in this chapter and spend the money you've saved on marketing.

KEY CONCEPT: What to Do If All the Good Domain Names Are Taken

If you've already been searching for the perfect domain name, you're probably feeling a bit pessimistic and frustrated, as most of the good, keyword-rich ".com" domains have been taken. This is normal—you can't simply jump onto Godaddy, whip out your Amex, and throw down $12.00 to reserve "LosAngelesPizza.com." However, there are several techniques you can employ to find a great domain name that still supports both SEO and branding goals:

▶ Use a prefix like "the," "best," or "top": I have had great luck in finding powerful domains for my clients by simply adding "the" as a prefix, resulting in a killer domain from both search and branding perspectives (if I ever have to file for bankruptcy, I don't want any Orlando bankruptcy lawyer—I want "TheOrlandoBankruptcyLawyer"!).

▶ Swap the order of keywords in your domain: try using "TireRepairDallas" if "DallasTireRepair" has been taken. Your site will still make sense to people searching without sacrificing keywords.

▶ Try a short suffix that's simple and still makes sense to users: "hub," "services," and "info" are examples of commonly used suffixes if all of your ideal domain names are unavailable.

▶ Attract active buyers by adding a "buyer adjective": or add one that describes your unique marketing message to your domain (cheapdomains.com, fastdivorce.com).

RESOURCE: SEOmoz's 12 Rules for Choosing the Right Domain Name: http://www.seomoz.org/blog/how-to-choose-the-right-domain-name

Step 2: REGISTER YOUR DOMAIN NAME

Once you've clarified the ultimate domain name for your business, the next step is to register your domain with a reputable registrar. This is a pretty straightforward process: all you need to do is pay around $12.00 per year for domain registration. However, I do have a few tips for you to avoid potential headaches down the road:

▶ Whenever possible, register your domain(s) with the same company who handles your hosting (see the recommended hosting providers in the next section). This makes it easy to manage potential transfers and billing and to avoid letting renewals slip through the cracks.

▶ Register your domain for at least 3 years. Many SEO experts agree that longer domain registration periods act as a signal of trust in the eyes of Google. Prolonged registration also allows you to enjoy the peace of mind that comes with knowing your domain is protected for several years.

▶ Set your domain name to auto renew. As badly as most of us despise having companies auto-charge our credit cards, this is one case where doing so is in your best interest. This will help prevent accidental surrender of your domain name.

▶ Purchase the ".org" and ".net" versions of your domain name. Although you may never use these variations, owning them is a cheap and important measure toward protecting your brand.

What about My Current Domain Name?

There are several reasons you may want to start using a new domain.

The important thing when transferring domain names is that you're able to start using your new website address while preserving the authority and online mojo of your former one—especially if you've had it live for 2 years or more and have invested time and money increasing the site's Web presence via social media and/or SEO.

Don't let the fear of starting over or of technical barriers prevent you from upgrading to a better domain name. All you need to do is create what's called a "301 Redirect," which is geek-speak for a permanent change of address. Most hosting providers and domain name registrars allow you to do this right from your "control panel" without the need to access or make changes to your code. The cool thing about doing a 301 Redirect is that nearly all—98 percent, according to Google—of the "online mojo" in the form of links to your site, trust, or other quality factors in the eyes of Google, gets passed on to the new website!

Contact your domain name registrar for further guidance or read this article: http://blog.hubspot.com/blog/tabid/6307/bid/7430/What-is-a-301-Redirect-and-Why-Should-You-Care.aspx

Step 3: Use a Content Management System [CMS]

Now that we know who your website is trying to reach and what we want them to do, there's one more layer of groundwork to be laid: you must decide which foundation to build your site on.

Most small business websites are "Non-CMS" sites, designed using HTML, an acronym standing for "Hyper Text Markup Language" (http://en.wikipedia.org/wiki/HTML). All this means is that such sites were designed using code, including HTML, CSS, and/or additional programming languages.

There are numerous downsides to such sites, the most significant being that whoever owns and manages these sites can't easily access, manage, and update their own websites. In fact, many business owners actually pay monthly maintenance fees for a "Web master" to update and maintain their sites. If this is you, we're about to change that.

A Content Management System (CMS) is a platform that allows for even the most non-technical folks to log in to their own websites and perform numerous functions, all without knowing a lick of geeky code. There are literally hundreds of CMS platforms available, each with a unique set of features, popularity, cost structure, and intended use.

Three of the most commonly used CMS systems are WordPress, Joomla, and Drupal. I recommend you build or rebuild your site on WordPress. In fact, in my consulting business, we require that our clients move their non-WordPress sites over before we start working with them, for the same reason a SCUBA instructor requires professionally manufactured and calibrated regulator, mask, and fins: your success depends on it.

ADVANTAGES OF USING WORDPRESS TO BUILD YOUR WEBSITE

WordPress (http://wordpress.org/) is the largest, most powerful, and easiest CMS anywhere, period. According to Wikipedia, WordPress "manages 22 percent of all new websites. WordPress is currently the most popular CMS in use on the Internet" (http://en.wikipedia.org/wiki/WordPress).

Initially developed as a blogging platform, WordPress has since become the premier CMS for businesses of all sizes, functions, and categories. From the smallest of local businesses, all the way up to large entities such as eBay, Yahoo, Ford, and *The Wall Street Journal,* WordPress has become the de facto platform for building great-looking, stable, and well-performing sites.

Aside from the general benefits of any popular CMS, WordPress website owners enjoy several other powerful features and functions:

▶ **Ease of use:** Easily access, edit, publish, and manage content using a simple, non-technical interface. Performing these basic functions is as simple as updating your Facebook page.
▶ **Low cost:** Most CMS systems are free, open-source platforms that can be downloaded by anyone with a decent Internet connection. The base files are free, so your only expenses would be hosting and any premium themes or customizations you care to do. Additional savings also result from not having to pay high maintenance fees to your hosting company.

▶ **Support:** Like all popular CMS systems, WordPress is frequently updated to ensure ongoing security, performance, and reliability.

▶ **Large number of professional themes:** WordPress is supported by a large community devoted to creating powerful and elegant themes that require very little customization to give small businesses a modern and professional online presence. Instead of building a site from scratch, you can start with a general framework or "theme" that's been proven to work for other businesses in your niche, and have this site customized to your liking.

▶ **Performance:** CMS platforms are designed to reflect current best practices in SEO site speed and security, all of which greatly contribute to your overall success online.

▶ **Portability:** You can easily switch hosting providers or marketing advertising agencies without being tied to any proprietary CMS systems or paying lofty "data transfer" fees.

▶ **Thousands of free plugins:** Plugins are stand-alone modules that add a specific function to your WordPress site, including social media sharing, SEO, installing Google Analytics, contact forms, Web lead forms, and much more. We'll cover plugins later in this chapter.

Whether you're in the process of building your first site or considering an update or upgrade to your current one, we'll cover a simple process for ensuring that your new site meets your online marketing goals.

KEY CONCEPT: Even if you're planning to outsource maintenance of your site to someone else, you still need a CMS-based site like WordPress for site performance, security, support, and access to thousands of open-source plugins and add-ons. Using a well-established CMS such as WordPress allows for building better websites, with countless features and at a much lower cost than that of building a custom site.

The final benefit of working with WordPress is that it's easy to launch and upload, with "one-click installs" and a basic theme that you or a designer can customize.

Step 4: CHOOSE A HOSTING PROVIDER

Once you've chosen the best content management system for your website and registered your domain name, the next step is to choose the type of hosting and hosting company that will be best suited for your website and business needs.

In a nutshell, Web hosting is defined as a hosting Internet service provider (ISP) that provides you with a Web server, a physical machine that stores the files that make up your website. "Hosting" your site on such a Web server makes your site available to visitors on the Internet.

Every website has an IP (Internet protocol) address, which is simply the specific location or "virtual address" of the server on which your Web files (site) reside. This is an important concept to understand, as hosting companies offer low-cost "shared" hosting plans that require customers to share a single IP address.

The main factors you should take into consideration are cost, size, the functions of your site, and which of the four types of hosting you need: free, shared, virtual-dedicated, or dedicated server (explained below). Since many hosting providers provide similar services, the key for me is service. Nothing is more frustrating than being stuck with your website down, unable to reach your provider's technical support department for answers to simple questions. Along these lines, you want to host your site with a provider who offers extensive how-to tutorials (preferably videos) on their site as well.

Types of Website Hosting:

▶ **Free hosting** is becoming more common lately. But it is not recommended for small business owners because it involves a lack of technical support, the inability to use your own domain name, poor performance, and the inability to access and update your site. It's critical to use your own domain (rather than "yourbusiness. wordpress.com").

▶ **Shared hosting** is a very inexpensive and popular option for small business site owners. Shared hosting means that several websites share the same Web server. This may be the best option if you're on a budget (three to five dollars per month), but I must caution you to only utilize shared hosting from reputable companies like those listed on the following page, as it's important to avoid being associated with questionable or "spammy" websites (like adult or gambling sites).

▶ **Virtual Dedicated Servers,** also known a Virtual Private Server (VPS), is the next step up from shared hosting in both cost and quality. VPS hosting allows website owners to own a dedicated portion of "space" on a Web server, resulting in better performance (speed). VPS servers also allow fewer sites to share an IP address, which is better than shared hosting from a security perspective.

▶ **Dedicated hosting** is a hosting plan in which a website owner rents a whole "dedicated" server and enjoys increased flexibility, performance, and security. However, the cost of dedicated hosting makes it unappealing for the average small business site, thus making this form of hosting most suitable for large e-commerce sites with thousands or more visitors per day.

KEY CONCEPT: Get the Best of Both Hosting Worlds

Many hosting providers want you to purchase a dedicated IP address while using shared or virtual-dedicated hosting plans. This is a great option for hosting your website, as doing so provides both the lower cost of shared hosting and the increased trust and security of dedicated plans. Be sure and select a hosting provider that can offer a dedicated IP address and take advantage of this option. The additional cost is only around $30 per year.

WARNING: Don't Move Your Site to a Bad Neighborhood

When it comes to Web hosting, it's very true that you are the company you keep. Many low-cost hosting plans require you to share a server and IP address with dozens or even hundreds of sites. This can not only cause problems with performance (site speed and load times) but also with your online trust, as sharing an IP address with gambling or adult sites can reflect poorly on your site from the vantage point of search engine and spam filters. For this reason, spend the extra money on a dedicated or "virtual-dedicated" hosting service, as explained on the following page.

RECOMMENDED HOSTING PROVIDERS

There are tons of hosting providers out there. If you are using WordPress or a similar CMS-based platform, ensure that your provider has good reviews from members of the online community or people using the same platform. You should also look for a hosting provider who offers "one-click" installs for your CMS system.

Sound like a lot of research? No worries—here's my short list of high-quality hosting providers who provide great service and work great with WordPress and other CMS platforms:

▶ Bluehost (http://www.bluehost.com/)
▶ MediaTemple (http://mediatemple.net)
▶ DreamHost (http://dreamhost.com)
▶ HostMonster (http://www.hostmonster.com/)

Each of these providers would be a great fit, depending on your personal preference and budget ($4.95 - $50 per month, depending on the level of service).

Step 5: LAUNCH A BASIC THEME

Since you have all the prerequisites in place—you've selected your CMS, registered a strong name, and signed up for hosting with a trusted provider—you're about to see just how powerful and non-technical (and fun!) getting your virtual hands dirty can be.

You can register a domain and launch a basic website in five minutes or less with no technical knowledge. This won't be your "final" website, with all the best practices in Web design, usability, lead generation, and SEO implementation (Reach, Engage, Convert), but the goal now is to get your domain live, which serves you in two significant ways:

1. **Launching a site "starts the clock ticking" when it comes to Google's trust factors.**
2. **Having this basic site live on your domain name provides the "shell" or platform that you or your chosen Web designer(s) and programmer(s) will be working in.**

Just follow these simple steps:

1. **Choose a domain name.**
2. **Pick a hosting provider/domain registrar.**
3. **Decide which credit or debit card to use and sign up for hosting.**
4. **Click on the "one-click WordPress Install" from your hosting control panel.**
5. **Install WordPress on your new domain name.**

RESOURCE: **"How to Build a Blog in Less than 4 Minutes (and Write Your First Blog Post)"**

Pat Flynn of Smart Passive Income, a great blog which any small business owner would gain immense value from following, demonstrates the above process in the video, "How to Build a Blog in Less than 4 Minutes (and Write Your First Blog Post)" (http://youtu.be/wPwQvnar99w).

STEP 6: DECIDE TO HIRE A DESIGNER OR DO IT YOURSELF

Whether you have used the quick-step process we just covered to launch a "shell" or basic site, or you have an existing site that's already built on WordPress with another CMS platform, the next step is to customize your site to reflect best practices in each of three phases of the online marketing funnel.

Customizing and even creating your own website can be a simple, non-technical, cheap, and fun process! These days you can use very high-quality, professional-looking themes that allow you to add your own logo, branding (through colors and basic design elements), and content with virtually zero technical knowledge.

I am not suggesting that you spend the next year mastering Web development, programming, or graphic design, neglecting your business in the process. But by being more involved with the design of your site, gaining just enough knowledge in terms of reach, engage, and convert elements on your site, you'll save yourself a lot of heartache, time, and money. In other words, you need to know the basics before you pay anyone to work on your site.

There are three basic models for getting a great site designed:

1. **Outsource the process entirely.**
2. **Do the whole website yourself.**
3. **Use a hybrid approach: pick a theme that you can customize with some help from a hired programmer.**

As you've likely guessed, I strongly recommend the third method. The reason for this is that the hybrid approach to launching or re-launching a website provides the best of both worlds: You can gain way more control of the process and save a ton of time and money compared to either outsourcing the whole enchilada or applying the do-it-yourself method. The hybrid method lets you do the easy stuff, picking up valuable knowledge and skills in the process, while letting skilled pros handle the technical side on a much cheaper, pay-as-you-go basis.

Regardless of which path you choose, you'll find the following steps and resources extremely valuable.

WHERE TO FIND A GREAT WORDPRESS THEME

WordPress has become so popular among small business website owners, bloggers, and Internet marketers that an entire marketplace has been spawned from companies who create and sell ready-made "Themes," which are essentially highly customizable and affordable templates that can be used with any WordPress site with little more than a click of a mouse. Think of these themes as "shells," or foundations, upon which we'll be expanding over the next several chapters to meet the specific needs of your business.

WordPress themes range from free to $300. Several popular theme companies also offer "theme clubs," allowing you to pay one flat fee or monthly subscription for access to all available themes. This option may be useful if you have or plan to have several websites, or if you intend to test multiple themes over time.

TIPS ON CHOOSING A THEME:

▶ **Use a big-picture perspective when looking at themes.** Don't fixate on the colors, logos, or images—you're only choosing a theme based on the overall structure of the site, not the cosmetics.

▶ **Go with a reputable theme company.** WordPress is constantly being updated, releasing new functions and security measures. It's important to work with a theme that's large and stable enough to provide ongoing support and updates.

▶ **Look for theme portfolios.** Most theme providers offer galleries that display examples of real websites that were built using the providers' themes. These will help you to better envision what your site will look like once customized.

Popular WordPress Theme Companies

▶ **Studiopress.com:** StudioPress by Copyblogger.com is a great resource for professional-looking and well-performing themes. Each Studio Press theme functions on Copyblogger's Genesis Framework, which is simply a base theme that all of their other themes work with. The benefits of using a "framework" like Genesis include search engine-friendliness, security, and simple yet versatile customization

▶ **Elegant Themes** (http://www.elegantthemes.com): Just as with Studio Press, Elegant Themes work within their own "framework."

▶ **Woo Themes** (http://www.woothemes.com/): Woo Themes offers a great community and support structure, combined with nearly 100 unique, customizable themes, many serving specialized uses such as retail shops, video-based websites, and social media themes.

▶ **Themeforest** (http://themeforest.net): Many first-time visitors to this site find themselves overwhelmed by the vast selection of professional-looking themes, many at just $50 or less. Before buying a theme on this site, be sure and consider the ratings and popularity of the seller and theme.

▶ **Free Themes on WordPress.org** (http://wordpress.org/extend/

themes/): Wordpress.org offers more then 1,500 free themes for your unlimited use. Many look very professional and can be customized well enough to provide a basic yet professional site if you're in a hurry or on a shoestring budget.

Whichever theme you decide on, you'll need to upload and activate it on your site in order for the theme to display on your new site.

How to Add a WordPress Theme to Your Site

Once you purchase a new theme, you'll usually be able to immediately download it right to your computer. Since a theme is essentially a folder containing files, it's pretty simple to activate a new theme using one of two methods:

▶ **Upload the theme from your WordPress Admin Dashboard.** As long as the theme you're adding to your site is in compressed (.zip) format, you can easily upload and activate it by clicking on Appearance > Themes > Add New Theme. If you run into trouble, simply use YouTube to find videos on this or any other WordPress– related function. If you intend to use a free theme, you can simply download these from your Admin panel.

▶ **Use an FTP connection.** An FTP (File Transfer Protocol) is a simple application used to transfer files from one server to another over the Internet. Some functions, such as adding images or logos to your site may require the use of an FTP client. If you plan on performing these functions yourself, I recommend you use Filezilla (http://filezilla-project.org), as it's a very simple, trusted, and stable FTP tool that works very well.

If you've come this far, the next step is to seek the services of an expert who can help you customize the site and implement the Reach, Engage, and Convert elements covered in the next three chapters. Although many business owners will be able to meet their Web design goals using the "off-the-shelf," non-technical customization options offered by most themes, others will want a more personalized design that will require the skills of a WordPress designer. If you fall into this latter category, it's important to use a skilled, well-vetted contractor rather than learning advanced Web design skills yourself.

How to Hire a Great Website Developer for a Fraction of the Cost

As an entrepreneur and business owner, you probably already have a website that falls into one of the following two categories:

1. **A free or low-cost website that came along with a recent domain name or related online purchase, or**
2. **A way-too-expensive "designer" website that cost you an arm and a leg but has yet to generate more than the occasional lukewarm lead**

Either way, it's time to find and hire a great designer/developer who can complete the customizations you'll need, quickly and at a reasonable price, by using a reputable outsourcing site.

Outsourcing sites are simply online marketplaces which focus on matching customers (business owners like you) with qualified contractors who have agreed to perform specific skills for a fixed or hourly price. These sites make money by charging clients ("hirers") a small percentage of the fees paid to each contractor, usually around 10 percent—a small price to pay for the stability, trust, and ease of use provided.

Top Outsourcing Sites

▶ **Odesk** (http://odesk.com): Odesk is a great source for finding and hiring skilled contractors for both short- and long-term assignments. I've found Odesk to be better for technical work such as WordPress Programming and SEO, and not so much for writing, virtual assisting, or journalistic tasks.

▶ **Elance** (http://elance.com): Elance is a wonderful portal for finding writers, editors, and project management resources. While this site also boasts thousands of contractors skilled in technical areas, I've found better results using ODesk for the aforementioned tasks.

▶ **Guru.com** (www.guru.com/): This site is much like Elance and Odesk in that it is a very well-constructed, popular site offering experienced and skilled resources. I recommend you browse each of these three sites and test out one or two that you like best for ease-of-use and talent related to your needs.

▶ **99 designs** (http://99designs.com): This is a great site if you're looking for a fresh Web design, logo, brochure, or even a T-shirt for your business. Using 99 Designs is a simple and unique experience. Unlike most outsourcing, which is essentially hiring a contractor with a task-based fee structure, 99 Designs uses "crowdsourcing," where you agree to pay a fixed price for a task, and several contractors work to earn your business. You'll get to see designs from 10, 20, or more designers and pick the one you like best, or you can ask for a full refund if none of the designs are what you envisioned. 99Designs.com is great for design work but not for coding (creating an actual website from your design). The other sites listed are better for this kind of work.

▶ **Fiverr** (http://fiverr.com): If you haven't checked out Fiverr, you're in for a treat! Fiverr.com is a site comprised of folks who will do nearly anything for $5.00. Need a cheap graphic or logo designed? No problem. Want someone to do a professional voice-over or YouTube video intro for your business? Piece of cake. How about having someone film themselves singing "Happy Birthday" to your significant other, while riding a unicycle in front if the Eiffel Tower? Consider it done (seriously). Fiverr is a great concept and there are dozens of truly valuable services on there for you to experiment with.[3]

---

3 Although Fiverr.com is great for small, limited tasks, I do not recommend using this site for complete Web designs or other complex projects.

How to Pick the Best Contractor to Work on Your Website

A common and costly mistake made by outsourcing newbies is to jump the gun when hiring a contractor. Nothing is more frustrating than going through the exciting process of hiring someone to work on your website or marketing campaign, only to be met with severe disappointment soon afterward.

Because each outsourcing site may have hundreds or even thousands of contractors specializing in the skills you're looking for, it's critical that you have a quick process for sifting, sorting, and screening potential service providers:

▶ **Search for specific skills.** Each of the outsourcing sites allows you to search for a specific skill for which you're looking to hire. To start off on the right foot, be very specific in what you search for: typing in "WordPress programmer" is much more targeted than "Web Designer."

▶ **Filter based on location, quality, or price.** Narrow your list of potential candidates by filtering for service providers who are within your price range. If you want to hire a contractor located in a specific area or who speaks a specific language, filter by these criteria as well.

▶ **Check reviews and portfolios.** This will serve as an immediate indicator of whether you're dealing with the caliber or style that you're looking for. I recommend that you avoid brand-new contractors and stick with those who have a proven, verifiable track record of working with businesses similar to yours.

▶ **Start with a small test.** Never hire a freelancer for a large or high-paying task or project right off the bat—ask your top candidates to perform a very focused, small task at first. Doing so will provide you with immediate insight into the working relationship to come, and may help you avoid wasted time and money.

▶ **Communicate clearly.** When it comes to giving instructions to your new contractor, leave nothing to chance or interpretation. Provide as much detail and as many examples of what you want up front and you'll greatly reduce unnecessary back-and-forth communication resulting from a misunderstanding of your requirements. It's also important that your contractor speak and write your native language fluently. Lastly, use Skype, Google chat, or any other video/audio to clearly and efficiently communicate with your consultant(s).

WARNING: Be Aware of Potential Security Risks Associated with Outsourcing

By definition, outsourcing is temporary in nature. As such, certain security measures must be taken. In cyberspace, trust must be earned. It's important to limit access to sensitive data including website hosting and domain registrar logins and financial information. If you must grant rights to outsourced contractors, do so on a controlled and temporary basis. If you're unlucky enough to encounter fraud or illegal activity resulting from actions taken by a freelancer you've hired, recourse may be difficult or even impossible, particularly if the freelancer is overseas.

RESOURCE: For Longer-Term Outsourcing Needs, Check Out Virtual Staff Finder

If you're a more experienced or savvy online marketer, you may have identified a need for outsourced skills and bandwidth on a regular basis. You may want ongoing help with your SEO, Pay-per-click (PPC), Content Development, or Analytics, or even a virtual assistant to help you stay organized and free up your time to work on more profitable activities. If so, take a look at Virtual Staff Finder (http://www.virtualstafffinder. com/) (VSF), a reputable agency based in the Philippines whose sole focus is sourcing and screening long-term contractors. I have used VSF in hiring several full-time team members for our organization and have had great success with them. VSF charges a flat fee for their services and they guarantee their results.

VSF breaks down contractors into four main categories:

- ▶ Virtual Assistant (VA) ($450-$600 per month)
- ▶ Web Developer ($700-900 per month)
- ▶ SEO and Online Marketer ($500-$800 per month)
- ▶ Graphic Designer ($500-800 per month)

They don't recommend you assume any overlap, meaning you shouldn't expect a WordPress programmer to check your email.

CHAPTER SUMMARY

So there you have it—you've picked a client-grabbing, Google-friendly domain name that's sure to go to work for you for many years to come, possibly even leading your competitors to reconsider their chosen profession in the process! You have launched a basic site on your domain, using a cost-effective and solid hosting provider. You've also created the perfect springboard to customize this newly sprouted site and help it grow.

RESOURCES: WordPress Beginners

▶ WPBeginner (http://www.wpbeginner.com) is a great site to help you get started with WordPress.

▶ Lynda (http://lynda.com) offers simple, how-to training videos covering virtually every category of software, from basic Microsoft Office to advanced coding and graphic design applications. I highly recommend their WordPress tutorials.

▶ The WordPress Classroom (http://www.thewpclassroom.com) is another high-quality site offering members videos and training materials to help new users get the most out of WordPress.

CHAPTER CHECKLIST

✔ **Select the Right Domain Name**
- Use relevant keywords
- Keep your domain short.
- Use the ".COM" TLD only
- Make your Web address easy to type
- Avoid using hyphens or weird characters

✔ **Register Your Domain**
- Choose a reputable registrar

- Register your domain for a long period of time (three years or more)
- Set your domains to auto-renew to avoid losing them
- Choose the right content management system
- Pick a Hosting Provider
- Choose between free, shared, VPS, or dedicated hosting

✔ **Launch Your Basic Site**
- Use your hosting provider's "one-click install" feature

✔ **Hire a Qualified Designer or Choose a Basic DYI Theme**
- Use an outsourcing site to hire a designer
- Choose a great theme to customize from a theme provider

FOUR

DESIGN AN ENGAGING WEBSITE THAT BUILDS TRUST WITH YOUR AUDIENCE

"Bad design is smoke, while good design is a mirror."

—*Juan-Carlos Fernandez*

Online engagement can be defined as how well your website does at grabbing your visitors, enticing them to remain on your site for longer than the industry average of ten to thirty seconds.

We small business owners spend a great deal of our limited time and money trying to reach more clients and generate site traffic, only to have most of these new visitors immediately "bounce" (hit the dreaded "back button," leaving your site never to return) all too often. We use phrases like *"visit* us online," or, *"go to* my website" for a reason: each person who clicks a link to your site goes through the same sensory input, subconscious scrutinizing, and screening they would if they were walking into your office for the first time. Nowadays, arriving at an online destination engages the senses almost as vividly as actually being at a corresponding office or store in person.

Making a great first impression is even more crucial online. Without the burden of politeness, people arriving at your site won't hesitate to turn around and "walk right out the door" at the first feeling of uncertainty. Luckily, there are well-defined, proven techniques we can use to influence the level of comfort our visitors feel when visiting our sites for the first time.

Engagement is the art of doing everything we can to keep visitors on our sites, consuming our content. Engagement is the bridge between reach (traffic) and conversion (leads). Your ultimate success online hinges largely on how well your website and content grabs your visitors and establishes rapport, positioning you and your business as a suitable resource for the information, resources, or services your audience is searching for.

FIVE STEPS TO A MORE ENGAGING WEBSITE

Online engagement is truly about synergy, as each of the engagement elements we're about to cover work together, many of which on subconscious level, to result in increased time spent on your site. Every second a potential client spends on your site is an opportunity for a bond to be built between them and your brand, increasing the odds that they'll eventually contact you over your competitors when the need arises.

Step 1: FOCUS YOUR DESIGN AND CONTENT ON YOUR CUSTOMERS

The first step in designing a highly effective, non-brochure looking, lead-generating website is to ensure we know exactly who your site is supposed to be resonating with: your target customers, *and them only*. If you're a pizza place owner, your site should say "Hungry? Let's eat." If you're a bankruptcy lawyer, maybe your dome page should hint, "Ahhhh relief, a fresh start is around the corner."

In order to define your target customer, create a specific "user persona" for your website. Recall Part 1—all you need to do is clearly state who a typical user on your site should be (the more specific the better) and what they're looking for (cost of a divorce, closest dry cleaner, cheapest flowers).

DEFINE YOUR SITE'S IDEAL USER EXPERIENCE

Now that we have determined whom your site is intended to reach and connect with, we must ensure that the design of your site resonates perfectly with their goals and needs. Online marketing experts and Web designers refer to this step as a "user experience," which is a fancy way of saying "the experience someone has interacting with a brand, product, or service."

In the context of your website, we'll define user or visitor experience as the overall experience of each visitor to your site. This includes how well the design, layout and structure supports the needs of your visitors.

Elements to Consider in Your Overall Website User Experience:

▸ **Overall structure and design layout:** Remember that too many decisions results in indecision. Do you want a super, Zen-like simple home page or an "authority site" with dozens of links to articles, blog posts, videos and external resources? I recommend you start simple, incorporate each of the elements covered in this chapter, and go from there.

▸ **Colors:** Long before the Internet, much study had gone into the psychological effects of colors (http://www.1stwebdesigner.com/design/color-psychology-website-design/). For example, many psychologists and website usability experts agree that blue shades make us feel comfortable and secure, while reds conjure images of confidence, strength, or danger. Do the colors of your site reflect your brand and services your business provides?

▸ **Messaging:** Most sites are almost entirely focused on business owners and products/services, when your content should clearly address the visitors' needs.

DEFINE A CLEAR GOAL OF YOUR WEBSITE THROUGH A MISSION STATEMENT

Before we start tweaking and adding elements to your site, it's critical that we take a few moments to define the goals of your site. If you're thinking "the goal is to generate some darn leads," you're on the right track. Or as many of us marketing folks might say, the goal of marketing is to help our customers know, like, and trust us.

Now that you've gone through the exercises of defining your typical user persona and ideal user experience, let's combine them into a simple, powerful website mission statement. This easy exercise can really help you define and communicate your online marketing and website goals to staff, contractors and even customers.

For example a heath and fitness club may use the following website mission statement: "Busy families in the Denver area should come to www.denversportsclub.com to find answers to their health, diet, and fitness questions and see our business as a trusted resource, eventually contacting us to schedule a visit to our center."

Writing a mission statement for your website can benefit you and your business by:

▶ Ensuring that your staff and contractors (Web designers, marketing consultants) clearly understand and remain focused on the goals of your site.
▶ Allowing you to publish this statement on your website and in online and offline ad copy.
▶ Keeping you motivated to write content focused on the big picture.

Step 2: USE SIMPLE NAVIGATION

Navigation is the central guide on your site that shows your visitors which pages are available and how to get there. Usually found at the top or along the side (also called a "sidebar") of most websites, the navigation menu, often referred to simply as the "menu," should be clearly visible and located consistently in the same spot on all or at least most pages of your site.

The term "menu" could not be more relevant to the purpose of this website element, as it has one singular goal: to ensure that your visitors can quickly see what's available and get to the specific content on your site that they're looking for.

Poor navigation is a primary reason people bounce from websites— you can't expect a new visitor who's just arrived on your site to automatically be interested enough to invest the time and energy required to decipher how your website works and where to find what they need. You must keep it simple and easy to use.

"Don't make me think. I've been telling people for years that this is my first law of usability. And the more web pages I look at, the more convinced I

become. It's the overriding principle—the ultimate tie breaker when deciding whether something works or doesn't in web design."
                                            —*Steve Krug, author of* Don't Make Me Think!

Here are a few powerful tips to ensure your next website visitor pulls up a chair and sticks around for a while:

Follow the status quo. Setting up the navigation style of your website isn't the time to get creative. When browsing the Web, we expect things to be located in certain places, with little tolerance for the new and unusual. I am as big a fan of art, design, and creativity as the next guy, but when I'm browsing a website looking for a new dentist, I expect ease of use and a predictable navigation menu. Thus, place the main navigation of your site either horizontally across the top (above or below the header) of your pages, or within the right or left sidebar.

Keep it consistent. One of the top ways to keep visitors engaged is to maintain consistent, predictable navigation on every page of your website. This "persistent" navigation helps visitors get their bearings on your site and gives them the comfortable feeling that they understand the overall structure of your site without "re-learning" how to get around after each click to a new page.

Remember, we browse and search the Web with ultra-short attention spans. We arrive on a new site with a default level of skepticism. One of the best ways to combat fickle behavior is to eliminate surprises through the use of consistent navigation throughout your website.

Practice Zen-like simplicity. Limit the main navigation of your site to the three to five most important sections or specific pages you really want your potential customers to see. This is counterintuitive to most small business owners, as we often want first-time website visitors to learn all about our companies, our products, and us. However, you can't skip to the honeymoon before at least buying them (a drink) first. A "barrage" of options will usually result in a bounce. Just keep in mind that, quite often, too many decisions leads to indecision!

Prioritize contrast over camouflage. Make sure that each menu bar and navigation element used on your site clearly stands out. Many sites are seemingly designed more with the goal of winning design awards than of generating leads. But it's much more important that the navigation of your Web pages clearly present your visitors with compelling content.

Always go wide instead of deep. Most Web usability experts and online marketers agree that most websites should maintain a very "shallow" Web page hierarchy, meaning that no page on your site should be more than two clicks away from the home page. If visitors can't get to any page on your site within one or two clicks, the content is probably not important enough to be on your site.

Use action verbs. One of the most effective changes you can make to the navigation of your site is to change the "anchor text"— the specific words users click within your navigation—from the boring, canned text most sites use to action verbs that convey a sense of energy and action! Change terms like "About us | Services | Contact | Blog" to way more energetic, click-inducing action verbs such as "Read Our Story | See How We Can Help | Learn About Fitness | Schedule a FREE Visit.

Use breadcrumbs. As a wise man once told me while I was lost in Costa Rica: "You only need two pieces of information to navigate anywhere on the planet: exactly where you are now and exactly where you're trying to get to." Most small business websites place too much focus on the home page and not enough on the blog posts, content and other pages. This is a poor tactic, as most visitors landing on your site from Google will land on one of your content pages (also called "deep" or "inner" pages). Bread crumbs help users keep track of where they are within a website, by providing a path from the home page to the current page. For example:

Home > Blog > 10 Ways to Get Larger Biceps

Many CMS systems like WordPress automatically include bread crumbs as an option for most free and paid themes. Just make sure that you or your Web designer has enabled them.

One of the biggest mistakes small business website designers make is placing all their eggs in one basket when it comes to navigation, making it very simple to access all the content on your site from your home page but not from "deep" pages (your individual blog posts or pages). It's important to create navigation that allows your visitors to see a clear path to any page or section of your site from the page they are currently on.

Step 3: INCORPORATE SOCIAL PROOF AND TRUST

Have you ever decided not to dine at a restaurant after seeing only a handful of folks eating there? When you shop for a new book on Amazon.com or decide which movie to see on your next night out, do you base your decision on reviews from other book readers and moviegoers like yourself?

Regardless of the type of business you operate, nothing builds trust and confidence more quickly and effectively than evidence that many folks just like us have enjoyed a positive experience from using your products or services. In the marketing world, we call this *social proof*.

There are many powerful psychological factors at play when it comes to social proof, but all you need to know now is that you'll likely find an immediate increase in visitor engagement after you've implemented a few powerful social proof elements on your website:

Testimonials: This is the simplest and most direct type of social proof to implement. Ask your satisfied customers for written permission to publish an endorsed comment on your site. Including as few as one or two comments from happy clients on your home page and products/services pages can be the most effective piece of copy you add. Set a goal to obtain at least three testimonials from clients, including photos if possible. Videos are even better! Include a "Testimonials" tab or link right in your navigation.

RESOURCE: Website Trends: Testimonials Design

Here's a blog post revealing 5 great ways to incorporate testimonials into your Web design: http://www.noupe.com/how-tos/web-design-trends-testimonials-design.html

Social "Fan Boxes": Nothing says "you've come to the right place" like a Facebook fan box. These are simple "widgets" that display information related to your "fans" or "followers" on Facebook or other social sites.

RESOURCE: Three Simple Steps to Adding a Facebook "Like" Box to Your Site:

- ▶ Go to https://developers.facebook.com/docs/plugins/.
- ▶ Log in to your fan page.
- ▶ Go to the following URL: https://developers.facebook.com/docs/plugins/.
- ▶ On the left sidebar you'll notice a link that says "Add a Fan Box."
- ▶ Copy the "script" (simple piece of pre-generated code) and paste it on your site wherever you'd like the Like box to appear (usually in a sidebar or footer).

Trust Icons: When you head to your neighborhood grocery store, how conscious are you about which brands you buy? Do you prefer to fly on certain airlines over others? Virtually every purchase we make is driven by branding. Each year, companies spend billions of dollars building familiarity and trust in their flagship brands.

Like many components of a successful website design, the trust we feel occurs on a subconscious level. When we encounter familiar logos we have grown to trust (Visa, American Express, The Better Business

Figure 2: Example of a "Facebook Fan Box" used on my blog

Bureau), we experience increased feelings of security and confidence in the online destination where we've just arrived. The following types of trust icons should be implemented in your site to increase your business's trust factor.

1. Trust by Association. One of the easiest and most powerful techniques small business website owners can use is leveraging the trust of larger companies.

Best Types of Trust Icons to Use on Your Site

▶ **Associations and Memberships:** Logos from trade or business associations, such as the American Dental Association (ADA), and paid membership programs, such as the Better Business Bureau (BBB), are effective trust icons, especially when they are recognized by the consumer.

▶ **Certifications:** Any certifications that you, your employees, or your business hold that separates you from your competition make great trust icons. These include continuing education certifications that require a higher degree of skill in your field, or health and safety certifications.

▶ **Media Icons:** Has your business been mentioned in any online or print media? If you've ever been quoted, reviewed, or cited by local or national news outlets, you need to add these trust icons to your site, pronto! Few things can build instant trust faster than "As seen on *Oprah,*" or, "As seen on CNN."

▶ **Social Media and Reviews:** Although we've already talked a bit about using your social media "fan boxes" and sharing tools to increase your online engagement, there's a third, very powerful, use for social media in your engagement plan: celebrate your 5-star reviews (or at least 3.5 and above).

▶ **Security:** If you have taken the time to secure anti-spam or e-commerce security (SSL) for your site, be sure and include these icons prominently as well.

▶ **General Trust Icons:** Including Visa, MasterCard, and other payment provider logos is a great trust-building technique.

Figure 3: Sakkas, Cahn & Weiss, LLP makes good use of trust logos on their site (http://www.sakkascahn.com/).

WARNING: **Avoid Copyright and Trademark Infringement**

Every business entity maintains the right to control the distribution of its intellectual property, including logos, banners, and other proprietary graphics or images. Be sure and consult with any organization and confirm your right to publish icons on your site, preferably in writing.

KEY CONCEPT: **Don't Use Trust Icons to Impress Your Friends**

Many ego-driven industries like real estate, law, medical, and other professional services (what I call "face-driven" trades) focus too much on peer validation and not enough on the consumer (target customer). Don't make the common mistake of filling valuable space on peer- or industry-focused trust icons—make sure to use icons that your clients will recognize.

    2. Online Reviews: Online reviews are quickly becoming the currency of small business success. In decades past, marketing and advertising was centered on businesses telling us how great they and their products were. Nowadays, our ultra-connected online environment has transformed each of us into mini research analysts who look for, and expect to find, reviews for any product or service we're considering using.

Recent changes by Google, Bing, and Yahoo have also placed greater SEO value on reviews, making the tasks of reviews acquisition and promotion even more important in your online marketing strategy.

If your site is built on WordPress or another popular CMS platform, you can easily add "widgets" that will display your latest rating and reviews from Yelp and other popular online reviews sites.

Figure 4: J. David Ford Construction (www.eastbayretrofit.com) uses a Yelp reviews widget on his WordPress site.

RESOURCE: The Yelp Bar WordPress Plugin

This is a great free plugin that you can easily add to your site with a few mouse clicks (http://wordpress.org/extend/plugins/yelp-bar/). Once installed, the Yelp bar plugin will publish your business's number of reviews and its average rating, as well as a link to your Yelp business page.

3. Expert Endorsements: Another powerful but seldom-used form of social proof is expert endorsements. Many larger companies center their entire marketing and advertising budgets around paying for celebrity endorsements (Michael Jordan might wear Hanes underwear in real life, but you'll have a hard time convincing me that Shaq really drives a Chrysler—unless perhaps they removed the front seat).

Obviously the reason most small businesses don't use celebrity endorsements is that they don't have the budgets to hire talent of such caliber. However, you have in your possession one bargaining chip worth great value—your products and services! Offer them to local celebrities or figures of prominence at no charge in exchange for a published endorsement. If you run a bakery, send free cookies to the mayor. If you own a print shop, offer to print jerseys at no cost to your local pro or semi-pro sports team. Get creative and get your business out there—a little sweat up front can pay huge dividends when your website visitors see a figure they recognize raving about your business!

4. Client Lists: This tried-and-true technique has been employed by larger companies for centuries. If you're in the process of acquiring solid testimonials and have little or no online reviews, publishing a client list on your site can be a fast way to improve social proof.

LEARN MORE: See the article by Aileen Lee of TechCrunch: "Social Proof Is the New Marketing," at http://techcrunch.com/2011/11/27/social-proof-why-people-like-to-follow-the-crowd/

Step 4: MAKE YOUR CONTENT HIGHLY SHAREABLE

Now more than ever, it's very important to encourage your readers to share your content on social media sites, giving you increased exposure with each "Like," "+," or tweet. Each time an article you've published on your site gets shared via social media sharing icons, that article also gets shared with the reader's entire social network.

SOCIAL SHARING EXPANDS ONLINE REACH

Social sharing yields holistic benefits, helping you reach, engage, and convert.

Recently, Google has published the increased SEO value they are placing on social media sharing in their ranking algorithms, using real human editors to express which content they find useful via social sharing. One of the easiest ways to increase these social signals on your online content is to place social media sharing icons or widgets in your content, before, after, or even next to every page and blog post on your site, making it extremely simple for readers to share your content.

For your website, I recommend you use "floating social media widgets" (see following page). This is another case of "function before form" in online marketing and Web design, as many website owners may balk at the awkward appearance. Don't worry, the lift your site will experience in social media traction will change your opinion and make you a "fan."

RESOURCE: Use the Digg Digg Plugin on Your WordPress Site

One of the great benefits of using WordPress is the almost limitless library of pre-made "plugins" (http://wordpress.org/extend/plugins/) that perform countless functions, most of them at no cost. For social media sharing on WordPress sites, I recommend Digg Digg (http://wordpress.org/extend/plugins/digg-digg/), which allows you to easily add your choice of social media sharing icons before, after, or floating next to your content and Web pages. See appendix A for a list of recommended WordPress plugins.

Step 5: LEVERAGE MULTIMEDIA

"A picture is worth a thousand words" says it all when it comes to the exponential engagement power that images have compared with text alone. Written copy combined with images, photos, video, and other forms of multimedia are much more effective at connecting with readers/consumers than just text. Keeping in mind Web surfers' short attention span, it's critical to reach out and grab their attention with a visual aid.

Figure 5: Caring.com uses floating social widgets for increased sharing.

KEY CONCEPT: Never Publish Text Alone

Multimedia should play a role in your Web design and content publishing strategies. As a good rule of thumb, ensure that every piece of content you publish (be it a bio of yourself or a member of your team, blog post, or any other form of Web content) should include at least one photo, video, or other form of multimedia.

FORMS OF MULTIMEDIA

1. Photos and Graphics: Adding high-quality photos and graphics to your blog posts and Web pages has never been easier. The Web is filled with photo/graphic sharing and hosting sites, offering thousands of amazing images, many at no cost.

On each of these sites, you can do a simple search for the topic of your choice, resulting in a large selection of images to choose from.

RESOURCE: Free Stock Photo Sites
▶ Creative Commons (http://creativecommons.org/)
▶ Free Range (http://freerangestock.com/index.php)
▶ Stock Vault (http://www.stockvault.net/)
▶ Free Digital Photos (http://www.freedigitalphotos.net/)
▶ Flickr (http://www.flickr.com/)

WARNING: Avoid Being Sued for Image Copyright Violation
Doing a Google images search is not a good way to find photos. Recently, there have been many lawsuits over the unauthorized use of photos and other copyrighted media, including one from Getty Images, who sued several website owners for illegal use of their images.

Another copyright consideration: any time you take a picture or video of an individual and use it for commercial purposes—which includes your website—you must acquire a "model release" (information found at http://en.wikipedia.org/wiki/Model_release).

If you want to play it safe, use a paid image licensing site like iStock (http://www.istockphoto.com/), the Web's largest publisher of inexpensive, royalty-free images and video.

2. Online Video: Most small business owners cringe at the thought of this unknown, seemingly technical and expensive medium. However, the truth is that video has become extremely simple to create, edit, and publish online.

One of the measures of online engagement is "time on site," or how long the average person stays on your site during a typical visit. As you can imagine, video, with its unique ability to engage viewers' senses, is one of the most engaging forms of content.

Later in this book, we'll cover simple steps for creating your own videos. For now, there's a simple way for you to reap the online engagement rewards that using videos has to offer, with zero technical knowledge:

adding existing videos to your site. All you need to do is find a video that does a good job explaining or adding to the topic your article intends to cover and embed that existing video right into your blog post.

Top Video Hosting and Sharing Sites

- ▶ YouTube (http://www.youtube.com/)
- ▶ Vimeo (https://vimeo.com/)
- ▶ Flickr (http://www.flickr.com/)
- ▶ MetaCafe (http://www.metacafe.com/)
- ▶ DailyMotion (http://www.dailymotion.com/)

3. Slide Presentations, Audio, and Other Multimedia: Websites and services like Slideshare (http://www.slideshare.net/) and iTunes (http://itunes.com) have developed into their own formidable niches of multimedia, each with its own unique benefits and tools for increasing engagement on your site. In Part Three, we'll cover how to use several forms of media to help syndicate—that is, publish your content using these different platforms.

TAKE ACTION: Embed a Slideshare Presentation on Your Site!

Slideshare is a very cool and useful online destination, using its own form of media that's a cross between a PowerPoint presentation and a video. It's "the world's largest community for sharing presentations." With 60 million monthly visitors and 130 million page views, it is among the 200 most frequently visited websites in the world.

Let's explore this tool by finding a Slideshare presentation related to your business niche that would benefit your customers:

- ▶ Go to slideshare.net.
- ▶ Search for presentations that relate to your business niche (for example, if you own a pizzeria, a quick search for "pizza" would yield several pizza-related slide presentations).
- ▶ Choose a presentation that you think your audience might find valuable. The local maker of Italian pies may choose the following

presentation: http://www.slideshare.net/spatiallyrelevant/the-unconfirmed-history-of-pizza

▶ Next, click on the "embed" icon, located at the top of the presentation.

▶ Copy the provided embed code.

▶ Paste this anywhere on your site where you want your visitors to see it!

Adding multimedia is a great way to increase user engagement, keeping your visitors tuned in long enough to start forming a bond with you and your brand.

RESOURCES: Web Design and Usability Resources

WEBSITES

▶ http://www.usertesting.com/ and http://www.feedbackarmy.com/ are low-cost resources if you want unbiased feedback related to the experiences of your website visitors. You'll receive highly useful feedback related to where users get stuck, how well they understand the overall theme and purpose of your site, and a great amount of general feedback related to your site. UserTesting.com even gives you videos of testers making comments as they browse your site!

▶ http://whichtestwon.com is a super-interesting and fun site that publishes the results of usability and conversion testing, comparing two nearly identical landing pages and measuring how small elements in copy and design affect engagement and conversion rates.

▶ Personas: The Foundation of a Great User Experience (http://uxmag.com/articles/personas-the-foundation-of-a-great-user-experience)

BOOKS

▶ *Don't Make Me Think!: A Common Sense Approach to Web Usability* by Steve Krug and Roger Black
▶ *Neuro Web Design: What Makes Them Click?* by Susan M. Weinschenk

CHAPTER SUMMARY

You now have a completely different idea of what it takes to produce a high degree of engagement on a Web page, a specific blueprint that combines several consciously placed "engagement elements" to produce a synergistic effect, engaging your visitors on multiple levels of consciousness.

CHAPTER CHECKLIST

✔ **Ensure that the design and content of your website is focused solely on your target customers.**
✔ **Be sure that your site produces an ideal user experience that reflects your brand. Your overall design theme, colors, and messaging all support this ideal visitor experience.**
✔ **Use simple and consistent navigation that stands out, containing only the site content that is the most important for your visitors to see. Be sure that your navigation elements contain action verbs rather than canned phrases.**
✔ **Incorporate social proof and trust icons into your site:**
  • Publish testimonials from satisfied clients
  • Use at least four trust icons
  • Include online reviews from well-known review sites like Yelp and Google
  • Add a "Facebook Fanbox"
✔ **Make it easy for users to share your content by including social media sharing widgets and icons on every page.**

✔ Leverage the power of multimedia by incorporating at least one photo, video, Slideshare presentation, or audio clip to each piece of content.

FIVE

GENERATE MORE LEADS USING WEBSITE CONVERSION TRIGGERS

"There's a fine line between fishing and just standing on the shore like an idiot."
—*Steven Wright*

Conversion is the final stop on the route to marketing happiness. Conversion is the one measure of indisputable, ROI-producing proof that you are on the right track when it comes to managing your online marketing funnel.

Online conversion is also a grossly underused element of marketing for most small business owners—an untapped well of prosperity, in fact. But even the "newbiest" of online marketers can gauge how well he or she manages his marketing campaigns by asking him or herself one simple question: "What is the conversion rate on my website?"

WHAT IS A CONVERSION RATE?

A conversion is what occurs when a qualified lead—your target customer— takes a specific and measurable action that signifies interest in becoming a customer of your business.

The term "conversion rate" simply refers to the percentage of visitors who become qualified leads or perform a desired action. For example, if your website gets a thousand unique visitors each month and generates ten qualified leads, the conversion rate of your site is 1 percent.

KEY CONCEPT: Not All Conversions Are Made Equal

It's important to point out that the term *conversion* can have different meanings for different types of businesses:

- ▶ **Ecommerce sites:** usually define conversion as a purchase, someone actually going through the "checkout process" and buying product(s)
- ▶ **Online marketers:** use the term to signify an "opt-in" or subscriber, someone joining an online mailing list by giving their name and/or email address
- ▶ **Social media advertisers:** can refer to a conversion as a new "Like" or "Add," as the goal of such campaigns is often to increase the number of social media followers
- ▶ **Small business websites:** usually refer to a conversion as a qualified lead, with the end result being a website visitor calling the business or submitting an online lead form

KEY CONCEPT: Measuring Conversion Rates Goes Beyond Your Website

This chapter will focus on improving the conversion rates on your website; however, it's critical to measure conversion rates (and ROI) anywhere your business is listed. This includes paid directories, PPC and social media ads, and Yellow Pages and other offline channels—everywhere your business is exposed to your target audience.

FIVE WAYS TO GENERATE MORE LEADS ON YOUR WEBSITE

Implementing just a few simple best practices in conversion can make a huge difference in your bottom line. If you can increase your website's conversion from 1 to 2 percent, you will have doubled your number of qualified leads!

1. Use Landing Page Best Practices

A landing page is the first page of your website that a visitor arrives or "lands" on. Initially used in the PPC (pay-per-click) world, landing pages are designed for one thing: to get visitors to take specific action, whether buying a product, downloading an ebook, or "opting in" by joining an email list or filling out a lead form.

The art and science of designing and optimizing landing pages has evolved into an industry of its own, known as Conversion Rate Optimization (CRO). In order to achieve improved conversion rates, high paid CRO consultants and agencies use advanced software and tools to test and tweak every aspect of a landing page, from the copy, headline color, and font, to the shape and test of the call-to-action button. As you can imagine, improving the conversion rate by just .5 percent on a site that gets millions of unique visitors per month can result in a significant increase in sales revenue.

Figure 6: An example of a landing page used by Match.com (image source http://match.com)

TREAT EVERY PAGE AS A LANDING PAGE

A huge mistake often made by small business website designers is putting all their eggs in one basket, placing all the trust building, engagement, and conversion elements on the home page only. This costly oversight can easily be prevented if website owners and designers are made aware of one simple fact: Most first-time visitors to your site do not land on your home page.

The next time you look at your Google Analytics reports, check out the "Content > Landing Pages" report. This shows which specific pages on your site visitors landed on, ranked from most to least popular. Although your home page may be the most popular, it gets only a small percentage of your total traffic. This means that most of your visitors are entering your site on your content pages, which is why we must treat every page as a landing page. Each blog post you write must contain as many engagement and conversion elements as possible. Each page must stand alone in its ability to build trust with the reader, steering him or her toward action.

How to Make Your Web Pages Like Your Landing Page

▶ **Focus each page on a single topic.** Whether coming from Google, Facebook, or a yellow pages ad, your visitors arrive at your site expecting to find specific information that relates to the question or need that brought them there. It's critical to focus each page on your site on a very narrow topic and avoid the common, lazy, "kitchen sink" approach used on all too many sites. For example, if you're a bankruptcy lawyer, you should have separate Web pages for chapter 7, chapter 13, foreclosure, and chapter 11. If you're a pastry chef, you'd find great benefit in creating separate pages for cakes, pies, and croissants.

▶ **Reduce options, driving visitors towards conversion.** One of the core tenets of landing page optimization is to funnel visitors toward the call to action (Web form or phone number). This is best accomplished by limiting or removing other potentially distracting options that can cause visitors to "click away" from your calls to action, never to return.

▶ **Include conversion elements on every page.** Don't expect your visitors to seek out ways to reach you, clicking around your site looking for your contact form or phone number. Make it easy for them to take the next step by adding your Web forms and phone numbers to every page in "persistent" sections that don't change, like your header or sidebar.

2. Provide a Compelling Offer and Call to Action

According to businessdictionary.com, a call to action (CTA) is defined as, *"Words that urge the reader, listener, or viewer of a sales promotion message to take an immediate action, such as 'Write Now,' 'Call Now,' or (on Internet) 'Click Here.' A retail advertisement or commercial without a call-to-action is considered incomplete and ineffective,"* (http://www.businessdictionary.com/definition/call-to-action.html).

To the layperson, the call to action may seem unnecessary, intrusive, or even cheesy. No one wants to pressure their audience and risk being seen in a negative, infomercial-esque light. But every blog post you write, ad you place, or postcard you send must have a clear and compelling call to action. Otherwise, you are entering a sword fight with a spatula. An effective call to action adds a competitive edge to everything you print, post, or publish.

There exists no greater tragedy in online marketing than the all-too-frequent occurrence of a small business owner taking the time to write epic content that engages and builds trust with readers, only to have the visitors leave your site and find your competitor.

ELEMENTS OF AN EFFECTIVE CALL TO ACTION

A call to action must incorporate the following elements:

▶ **Who the reader is:** Nothing appeals to us more than contextualized or targeted communication that feels like it's speaking directly to us, whether we are:
  • "bay area road bikers"

- "families of 4 or more"
- "small business owners"
- "chicken farmers"

▶ **What they'll get:** In the form of a valuable offer or promise, tell your users or readers exactly what they'll get for taking action:
  - "to schedule your free consultation"
  - "to gain instant access to a FREE video"
  - "to reserve your spot"
  - "to make an appointment"
  - "to get a free soda"

▶ **How to take action:**
  - "call"
  - "click"
  - "press 0"
  - "come on in!"

▶ **Where to take action:**
  - "in the box below"
  - "the number above"
  - "at the front desk"

▶ **When to take action:** Adding urgency (limited time) and/or scarcity (limited supply) is a time-tested tactic:
  - "now"
  - "before September 28th"
  - "while supplies last"

▶ **Why to take action:** The "why" focuses on the benefit to the reader:
  - "to save time and money"
  - "to learn the secrets of fly fishing"
  - "so you can spend more time with your family"

TAKE ACTION: Write Your First Call to Action

For example's sake, let's assume you'll use your new CTA at the end of every new blog post you write. All you need to do is ensure that your offer addresses each of the six editorial questions every good call to action should answer: who, what, where, when, why, and how.

Using our "pizzeria owner" scenario from last chapter, let's say I wrote a blog article entitled, "How to make gluten-free pepperoni pizza." At the end of this article, I want to increase conversions by offering readers a coupon for a free pitcher of soda for any family of four or more who comes in for pizza.

Combining all six elements of a great call to action, here's how my offer might look:

▶ Love Pizza and Soda Together?
▶ Quench Your Thirst at No Cost! (WHY)
▶ Bring in your hungry family of 4 or more (WHO)
▶ Download (HOW) the Coupon Below (WHERE)
▶ Before April 21st, 2013 (WHEN)
▶ Get a Free Pitcher of Soda! (WHAT)

You can incorporate the six elements in any order—what matters is that you use all six, all the time, every time.

RESOURCE: 5 Real-Life Examples of Fantastic Calls to Action
http://blog.hubspot.com/blog/tabid/6307/bid/30691/5-Real-Life-Examples-of-Fantastic-Calls-to-Action.aspx

Use Your Calls to Action Everywhere You Can

As discussed, your target customers will encounter your business through many channels, including your website. Because you can never predict exactly how or where this "first contact" may occur, it's critical to include a strong call to action on every page of your website and elsewhere where your business is listed, online or otherwise.

▶ **Blog posts:** Once a reader has found your article and taken the time to read it in detail, coming to see you as an authority in your niche in the process, where do they end up? At the end of your blog post. What better time than to leverage the reader's heightened state of interest and focus than now?

▶ **In the header, sidebar, and footer:** One extremely effective measure is to make a call to action part of your site's DNA. By including a strong CTA in the header, sidebars, and footers of your site, you're helping to put conversions on autopilot, as your visitors can't help but be exposed to your offers on every page.

▶ **Online listings:** Each instance in which you list your business online is an opportunity to increase conversions—no one says leads have to come from your website alone!

▶ **Social media profiles and multimedia sites:** Whether consumers find you on YouTube, Facebook, Twitter, or any other social media community, they should be prompted to contact your business right then and there.

3. Use Simple Web Forms to Capture Leads

A Web form, or "lead form," is nothing more than a small area on a Web page containing fields. After users enter information into these fields, the information gets sent to a server for processing. Simply put, Web forms provide an easy way for visitors to contact you, much simpler than sending you an email or even picking up the phone.

Lead forms and their proper placement are a critical component of your conversion strategy. Remember, you have one singular goal when it comes to conversion: to measurably increase the percentage of your website visitors who convert into leads (which, again, means they contact you and express interest in your products or services).

Take a look at a few small business websites and the number of steps needed to get in touch with the corresponding businesses. On most sites, you'll see some form of a "contact us" page that may or may not have a contact form. This is bad for two reasons:

▶ Any time you require your visitors to click around to find something, your conversions will start to dwindle with each additional action they'll have to take before getting to the form.

▶ Burying your contact form on one page means that you're missing 90 percent of your opportunities to generate leads. This is like a grocery store with one checkout counter hidden in a backroom.

Lead forms are one of the most valuable tools in your conversion arsenal for several reasons:

▶ **Measurability:** Each form can be easily tracked (we'll cover this later) so that website owners can quickly and accurately measure the success of traffic-driving efforts all the way through conversion (lead forms filled out).

▶ **Familiarity:** These days, it's safe to assume your customers are used to interacting with and trusting online Web forms, for both business and pleasure.

▶ **Highly customizable:** There are dozens of companies who offer user-friendly, "drag and drop" Web form solutions, allowing you to quickly customize your forms to your needs and those of your visitors.

▶ **Portability:** As we'll see next, most Web form solutions allow you to place lead or contact forms just about anywhere on your site using a simple "copy and paste" code.

Types of Online Lead Forms

Before you bang your head against the wall or sell off your Facebook stock to hire a Web designer, hold your horses. If you can copy and paste, you possess all the technical skills required to add beautiful, powerful Web forms to your site. There are dozens of reputable products and entire companies dedicated to "drag and drop" Web forms and lead management.

Virtually all of these solutions work the same way, with two basic steps:

▶ Choose a Web form solution that works for the platform your site is built on. There are both free and paid solutions.

▶ Easily customize the form.

The one decision you'll need to make is what type of form you want to use, in terms of what happens to the information once a form has been filled out. There are two main categories to choose from:

1. **Simple email posted forms:** As the name implies, these forms simply capture the information gathered from form users and email this data to you and/or any other folks you specify. The pros of these forms is that they are very easy to use, and with off-the-shelf plugins available for many CMS systems, they're usually free.

    If you're using WordPress, you can install plugins right from your website. See this link for further details: http://codex.wordpress.org/Managing_Plugins

    For the copy and paste method, use one of the following Web form providers:
    *   Gravity Forms (http://www.gravityforms.com/)
    *   Formidable Forms (http://formidablepro.com/)
    *   Contact Form 7 (http://contactform7.com/)

2. **Database-driven forms:** These forms have the same front-end functions as simple email forms, with the added functionality of posting respondents' data directly into a lead nurturing database or email marketing system, both of which store your "Web leads" in one organized place, making it super-easy to build and follow up with your growing list of contacts via email marketing campaigns. These email marketing platforms are very useful:
    *   Aweber (http://www.aweber.com)
    *   MailChimp (http://www.mailchimp.com)
    *   Constant Contact (http://www.constantcontact.com/)
    *   Vertical Response (http://app.verticalresponse.com)

HOW TO USE LEAD FORMS FOR MAXIMUM CONVERSIONS

Be sure your forms are designed for maximum lead-generating effectiveness by following these Web form tips:

▶ **Make your forms as short as possible.** Many small businesses make the mistake of requiring too much information on their forms.

The problem with this is that a higher number of fields measurably reduces conversion. Shorter is better when it comes to lead forms. Try and challenge yourself to minimize the number of fields to as little as two or three. It's better to have less information from a hundred leads than to have more detailed information from only ten leads. Start with the following fields and measure your conversion rates:

- Name
- Phone
- Email (optional)
- Message

Make sure your lead forms gather the minimum amount of information you need to be able to follow up with your prospects. You can always ask more questions once you make contact.

▶ **Place at least one lead form on every page.** Most website owners miss a huge opportunity and lose countless leads each month by not properly positioning lead forms. You can't expect your visitors to have either the time or the attention span required to seek out a contact form—you must make it easy for them.

▶ **Place your lead forms in prominent places.** It's also critical that you place lead forms in places where your visitors are most likely to see and interact with them. Start with a form above the fold (viewable on users' screens without scrolling), on every page. The sidebar is a great spot since it shows up on all or most pages.

▶ **Make your form STAND OUT.** Many Web designers make the mistake of treating contact forms like any other design element, aiming to make them blend in with the aesthetics of the website. Don't do this. Your lead form should jump out and grab your reader's attention, clearly revealing the "next step," which is usually contacting you, stopping by your place of business, or downloading content.

▶ **Remember to include your call to action.** Most small business sites that do make use of Web forms do so without incorporating effective calls to action. A form with the header "Contact Us" is better than no form at all. To get the highest conversions from your lead forms, be sure to include an offer with a powerful call to action as we covered earlier.

▶ **Tell your visitors that spam's not an issue.** These days we're all hyper-resistant to handing out our personal information. The last thing any of us want is to have our email address sold and blasted by spammers. All the trust-building measures we've covered contribute to your visitors feeling comfortable enough to give up their coveted e-digits, but you should also underscore your anti-spam policy on the form itself.

4. Make the Phone Ring with Prominent Phone Numbers

The advent of fax machines, computers, mobile phones, and tablets may have provided new methods of lead generation, but none of these techy devices have yet displaced the undisputed heavyweight champion of lead generation: the telephone!

In fact, most advertising models used for online and mobile platforms involve driving users to the phone (as opposed to using lead forms alone). In terms of engagement, getting a phone call from a potential customer is much better than receiving a Web form. You, or your staff, are much more able to qualify leads on the phone, converting a higher percentage of them into appointments and customers.

There are a handful of easy things you can do with your phone number that are proven to result in more phone calls from qualified leads. Many of these best practices are the same as the ones we just covered relating to lead forms.

How to Double Your Phone Bill in Ten Minutes (In a Good Way)

▶ **Use a local number.** In many cases, 800 numbers have strategic advantages over their local counterparts, including making a business look bigger and increasing call-ins by paying for long-distance charges. But for small, local businesses, the use of toll-free numbers has been proven to lower call rates because most local consumers in search of a local business want to talk to someone local.

▶ **Place the number in the header on every page of your site.** The header is a great place to start. Just as with lead forms, don't make the mistake of expecting your visitors to seek out your phone number.

▶ **Make your phone number larger.** This is another issue that creates design and positioning conflicts. Few of us want to be perceived as "salesy" or "cheesy" in the way we and our businesses are portrayed online. For greater visibility, however, make your phone number two or three times as large as you'd normally feel comfortable with.

▶ **Pair your phone number with a call to action.** For increased results, tell the user exactly what to do and when, and what they'll get in return for doing so. And remember, the promise should speak to your customer, not your business. "Speak to one of our representatives" doesn't cut the mustard compared with "Discover How to Erase Your Credit Card Debt."

▶ **Track your phone calls.** One of the greatest advantages of online marketing is the complete transparency that it offers. Rather than just guess what's working or going by feel, you can—and should—discern, right down to the dollar and phone call, which lead sources are producing a positive ROI and which are falling flat. Utilize one of several services offering trackball trackable phone numbers (see the list provided in Chapter 9). These simple-to-use services allow you to purchase local numbers at very low rates (usually less than $5.00 per month) and assign them to specific advertising or marketing campaigns. Alternately, you can train your staff to keep a log of inbound calls, along with weekly reports detailing which sources generated inbound interest.

5. Say "Hello" with Popups and Toolbars

Aside from the staple tools of online lead conversion covered thus far, there are several ancillary elements, including online chat services, pop-up forms and Web toolbars, that, depending on your business goals and website design, may deserve a place in your lead-generation arsenal:

▶ **Popups and lightboxes:** Most of us hate "popups," especially those of us who were unfortunate enough to get attacked by the multiple simultaneous Christmas-light-adorned popups so common in the late '90s, which often prevented any further action, as the computer would freeze completely and indefinitely. Luckily in our current era, those abrasive popups have been toned down and transformed into vehicles to communicate important information that people find useful. If you're open to experimenting with this slightly more aggressive lead generation/conversion tactic, here's a list of simple-to-use popup and lightbox plugins for your WordPress (or other CMS) site:

- WordPress Popup (http://wordpress.org/extend/plugins/wordpress-popup/)
- Pippity (http://pippity.com/)
- Premium List Magnet (http://premiumlistmagnet.com/)

WARNING: Now Google Hates Popups Too!

Google's quality score is a set criteria that the search engine uses for PPC (pay-per-click) customers to measure the quality of Web pages. Quality score factors in a number of elements including your site's bounce rate, content quality, relevance, and a litany of other criteria. Using popups places a clear negative "ding" on your Google quality report card.

While you certainly should not use popups on pages you're driving Google AdWords campaigns to, you may still find great use for, and conversions from, tasteful popups. For more information, go here: http://support.google.com/adwords/bin/answer.py?hl=en&answer=2454010.

▶ **Web Toolbars:** This is the much less aggressive cousin of popups. Web toolbars are small, colored banner-like blocks that slide into view from the top or bottom of the page. Web toolbars can be customized to your liking and include either a hyperlink to the Web page of your choice or a complete mini-contact form.

Recommended Web toolbar solutions:

- **Hello Bar** (http://www.hellobar.com) is an awesome solution for increasing conversion rates. All you need to do is register, customize the bar using their simple drag-and-drop interface (selecting your message, colors, and target page to link to), download the Hello Bar plugin, paste some simple code when prompted, and . . . Hello! More leads are on the way! And, it's FREE to try for thirty days. I recommend that you start with a Hello Bar and monitor the results (difference in opt-ins or leads generated).

- **Viper Bar** (http://www.viperchill.com/viperbar/) is a great WordPress plugin that integrates with many Web form providers and allows you to launch a full-blown contact form within your toolbar. To add a Viper Bar to your site, simply download the Viper Bar plugin from your WordPress control panel.

6. Start Up a Conversation with Online Chat

An online chat window is a small box that appears on a Web page, offering visitors on-the-spot customer service. In my opinion, online chat windows can be more helpful to your visitors than not, providing an easily accessible format for folks to have their basic questions answered in real time. You must evaluate whether this fits into your site design and supports your online marketing goals.

There are two categories of live chat services available: self-managed and outsourced. The only difference is who does the "chatting"— someone you manage or an outsourced, full-service provider. Start with the outsourced version, as you're not in the live chat business and there's no sense setting up such infrastructure (even a simple one) before you test the results from using live chat in the first place.

▶ **Self-managed live chat:** With this option, your staff communicates with respondents via an "operator interface," which is simple software that allows whomever you designate to communicate with visitors. When your staff is out of the office or you're closed for business, your staff can simply "turn off" the live chat feature on your site. These services charge a modest monthly fee ($10-100), depending on the number of "operator" licenses you have.

- LiveChat (https://www.livechatinc.com)
- BoldChat (http://www.boldchat.com)
- Live Person (http://www.liveperson.com)
- Kayako (http://www.kayako.com)

▶ **All-in-one live chat solutions:** Just as the name implies, these providers offer complete solutions, meaning their staff responds to chat requests as representatives of your business. The top turnkey live chat providers are extremely good at what they do. Reps are trained to capture the respondents' contact information and redirect their questions to their meeting with you, either in-person or over the phone.

- Total Live Chat from Reach Local (http://www.reachlocal.com/live-chat)
- Answer Connect (http://www.answerconnect.com/services/webchat-services)

7. Entice Your Audience with Conversion Magnets

A conversion magnet is a tool—usually a piece of high-quality content—that's designed to offer something of enough value that it influences visitors' behavior.

In the context of your website, conversion magnets include e-books, downloads, tip sheets, white papers, videos, and coupons—anything that provides enough value to make your audience take action. Remember, Internet users are reluctant to give out personal details, so you have to offer something that's very relevant and of exceptional value to your audience.

The potential benefit of taking the time to put together a high-quality traffic magnet is a measurable increase in qualified leads. Keep in mind that most of your site visitors won't contact you—even if you have an incredible 5 percent conversion rate, ninety-five out of every one hundred visitors that come to your site will leave, usually never to return or contact you again. Conversion magnets are about reaching out to those folks who may be on the fence and grabbing them with an offer they can't refuse.

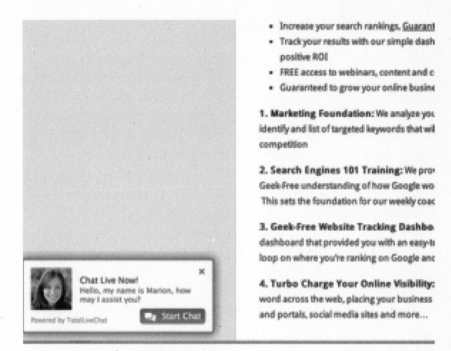

Figure 7: Example of online chat window used on a website

For example, let's say you're checking out websites of local assisted living communities, doing research for an aging parent or family member. The first two sites you visit both have contact forms and calls to action in prominent places. So far so good. But the two contact forms differ in one regard—one has a conversion magnet and the other does not:

▶ Website #1 lead form offer: "Contact us now for a FREE tour"
▶ Website #2 lead form offer: "FREE Download: The Smart Family's Guide to Paying For Senior Care: 10 Things You Must Know Before Selecting an Assisted Living Community"

Which of the above offers do you think would generate a higher conversion rate? The second offer is much more compelling, because it promises something of value in return.

TYPES OF CONVERSION MAGNETS

Regardless of format, the content of your conversion magnet should be focused on one thing: the top questions and concerns of your audience. All it takes is a quick look at your past several customer interactions to come up with a clear list of their most frequently asked questions. We'll cover how to create each of the following types of media later, but for now, look at this list and start thinking about which would best suit your audience and business goals.

▶ **Tip sheets:** The simplest to create, tip sheets are little more than sheets with tips on them. All you need to do is create a "Top 10 Things You Need to Know About/Secrets of/Tips to . . ." list in PDF format and place it on your site. Once a respondent fills out your website form, they will be directed to the Web page that contains your tip sheet.

▶ **Video:** Creating and uploading attractive, client-engaging and converting videos is as simple as point, shoot, click. How-to and Q&A videos are extremely popular on YouTube and other video sharing sites.

▶ **E-books:** Nothing builds credibility and trust with your audience like e-books. Easy and cheap to write, manage, and deliver (no printing or postage required), e-books are great conversion magnets—who wouldn't readily trade their name and email address for thirty to fifty pages of high-quality content that addresses their needs?

CHAPTER SUMMARY

The end goal of your website, content, marketing, and advertising efforts is to generate qualified leads and customers. Once members of your target audience come into contact with your brand and message (Reach), and consume your copy and read your content (Engagement), it's critical that you provide them with a well-lit path to the "next steps" (Conversion), while eliminating distractions that could lead them astray, never to return. Using the conversion strategies outlined in this chapter will go a long way toward a measurable increase in qualified leads and customers.

CONVERSION TOOLS AND RESOURCES

▶ **Google's "Website Experiments"** (formerly Website Optimizer) is a great tool built right into Google Analytics that allows you to test different design elements (copy, headlines, etc.) against each other to see which ones convert better. See this article from Entrepreneur for more details: http://www.entrepreneur.com/blog/223724.

▶ **Which Test Won** (http://whichtestwon.com) is a great site that compares versions of landing pages, letting users guess which test "won," or yielded the higher conversion rate.

CHAPTER CHECKLIST

✔ **Use Landing Page Best Practices for Every Page of Your Site:**
- Focus each page on a single topic
- Include your engagements whenever possible
- Reduce options, driving visitors towards conversion
- Include conversion elements on every page

✔ **Include a Strong Call to Action on Every Page of Your Site**
- Ensure that your CTA answers all six editorial questions: who, what, where, when, why, and how

✔ **Use Simple Web Forms to Capture Leads**
- Place a form in a prominent position on each Web page
- Keep the form short, requiring only two to four pieces of information
- Build trust with an anti-spam statement

✔ **Incorporate Best Practices in Telephone Conversion**
- Place your phone number in large type in a prominent position on every page
- Include a call to action with your phone number
- Use tracking phone numbers to measure results

✔ **Use a Conversion Bar or Popup Lightbox**

✔ **Experiment with Live Chat Services**
- Use a conversion magnet for increased response

PART THREE

THE STAND OUT SEO
STRATEGY

SIX

GOOGLE 101: HOW SEARCH ENGINES WORK

"If it isn't on Google, it doesn't exist."

—*Jimmy Wales*

This chapter is about understanding the online landscape and obtaining the minimum knowledge every business owner must possess to survive in the digital era. We're not talking about anything technical here, just simple insights into how Google works in terms of finding small business websites and "deciding" where they rank in search results—very important stuff to understand, as the difference between being number one or buried on page ten of Google is the difference between being seen online or not seen at all.

My chosen line of work puts me in contact with a large number of small business owners. During our conversations, I'm often met with a great number of questions regarding ranking on Google, getting "SEO'd," and the like. Most of these conversations contain at least some level of misinformation, anxiety, and perhaps even a bit of fear on the part of small business marketers. And for good reason. Most available sources of information related to search engine optimization (SEO) are too technical, geared more toward full-time marketers than small business owners in need of the "Reader's Digest" version of this subject matter.

Gaining a little basic knowledge about the functions of search engines is critical, as we can't possibly achieve positive results when it comes to increasing the visibility of our businesses online without being able to view our websites and marketing activities from Google's perspective—at least not in a fundamental way.

WHEN I SAY GOOGLE, I MEAN GOOGLE

I've intentionally written this section on Search Engines with strong emphasis on Google. Although there are several useful and popular search engines, I focus on Google for several reasons:

1. Google owns 70 percent of the global search market, with over three billion searches each day and annual sales exceeding $10 billion. Gearing your online marketing efforts toward increased visibility on Google makes sense (http://searchengineland.com/by-the-numbers-twitter-vs-facebook-vs-google-buzz-36709).

2. Other search engines use very similar algorithms to generate results, so well-designed, high-quality websites will rise to the top with these search engines, as well.

3. Pareto's Law (the 80/20 rule): you can't afford to launch and manage separate Bing! and Yahoo campaigns, so let's focus on the big Kahuna.

US SEARCH ENGINE MARKET SHARE

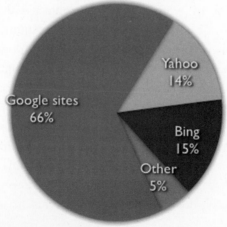

Figure 8: U.S. Search Engine Market Share

SEARCH ENGINE FACTS

▶ Google: 34,000 searches per second (2 million per minute; 121 million per hour; 3 billion per day; 88 billion per month, figures rounded)
▶ Yahoo: 3,200 searches per second (194,000 per minute; 12 million per hour; 280 million per day; 8.4 billion per month, figures rounded)
▶ Bing: 927 searches per second (56,000 per minute; 3 million per hour; 80 million per day; 2.4 billion per month, figures rounded)

In this section, you'll receive a quick and dirty, no-nonsense primer on SEO, how search engines work, and a few super-simple tools and resources to get you up to speed in rapid fashion.

A BRIEF HISTORY OF SEARCH ENGINES

Before Google, search engines based results largely on how many times the desired keyword(s) appeared on a Web page. For example, back in the days of Alta Vista or Lycos, the number-one search result for the keyword "shoes" was usually whichever site used the word "shoes" the highest number of times on its pages. This was extremely ineffective, as any website owner could "game" the search engines by adding tons of keywords to his or her site. This produced a poor "user experience," as people in search of information were often left with disorganized and irrelevant results.

What Google did differently from other search engines was to base search results on an algorithm that includes hundreds of factors that determine how search results are generated. This means that the Google search engine produces extremely relevant results—closely matching what the user is looking for. This "relevance" is Google's primary competitive advantage, both in paid (PPC or Google AdWords) and natural or "organic" search results (covered later in this book).

People use Google because they can expect the best results quickly. Most people have neither the need nor the desire to know about the complex processes and technologies used to make this happen, they just know it works. As a small business owner, you don't have this luxury. You need a basic understanding of the Internet from Google's perspective as well, if you want to drive more qualified leads to your website in an amazingly cost-effective and measurable fashion.

ANATOMY OF A GOOGLE SEARCH ENGINE RESULTS PAGE [SERP]

The first stop on Le Tour De Google is a quick and dirty overview of the typical search results page. Google's search engine results page (SERP) is an ever-changing organism comprised of several independent and often intermingling components, being generated on-demand for each person in real time as they type in one or more keywords and click "search" (called a search query). If this sounds confusing, don't fret—all you need to know is that Google displays several forms of content, each with the potential of being included in your online marketing strategy:

1. The Search Bar

The search bar is where people type in a query (often called search terms or keywords), based on the nature of the information they're looking for. Often within milliseconds, the user is met with "search results" that represent what Google deems the most relevant response. These "blended results" usually include resources in several forms including organic results, paid ads, videos, images, news, and more.

NOTE: A major part of your online marketing strategy will be to determine the best keywords to use, both within your website and elsewhere around the Web, to help you show up in the highest number of searches that would benefit your business. Keyword research is so important, we've devoted the next chapter to it, so stay tuned!

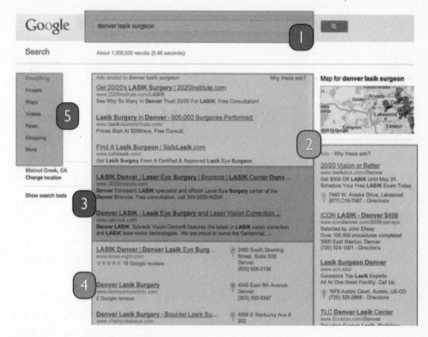

Figure 9: Anatomy of a Google SERP

2. Paid Search Results

This portion of the search results page is occupied by paid ads, purchased by businesses and agencies using Google AdWords.

BENEFITS OF USING GOOGLE ADWORDS

It is true that, despite their dominant position on the page, AdWords ads only generate 12 percent of the total traffic (defined by a user clicking from a link on the search results page to the advertiser's website). And unfortunately this low share of available clicks may lead you to "skip over" AdWords in search of the higher traffic numbers of natural search results, but don't discount paid ads so soon. Google AdWords may in fact be one of your most effective sources of targeted traffic and qualified leads, for three primary reasons:

▶ **Immediate results:** Unlike organic or natural search results (SEO) traffic, paid traffic can produce results in minutes—literally. AdWords customers can simply buy these paid positions using the AdWords "bidding system," based on CPC (cost-per-click), to determine where their ads are displayed on the search results page. This is a powerful option, often used by businesses with new websites or those in extremely competitive markets.

▶ **Measurability:** Unlike many forms of marketing and advertising, PPC campaigns can be easily and accurately measured, often using automated tools that calculate each ad's ROI in real time by calculating what percentage of clicks to your website convert into qualified leads or customers.

▶ **Ultra-targetability:** Google AdWords customers can exercise extreme selectivity in choosing when and to whom their ads are displayed. Using simple AdWords campaign settings, you can target people located within a specific radius of your business, looking for specific information or services (search terms) at specific times, on specific sites, using specific devices.

3. Organic Search Results

The organic or "natural" results are the Holy Grail of online visibility and a long-time staple traffic generator to websites in all categories. When geeks (like me) and laypeople (like you) talk about "SEO," "Search Engine Optimization," "getting to #1," and "website optimization," they are almost always referring to Google's organic search rankings.

Unlike with the PPC section of the typical Google results page, obtaining high organic rankings can be tricky, complex, and often daunting for most small business owners. However, doing so can result in a lot of new traffic, leads, and customers for your business. Organic results get around 80 percent of the clicks on SERPS. This means most people who do a Google search click on the top three organic results. Ranking below the top five or six spots can result in invisibility.

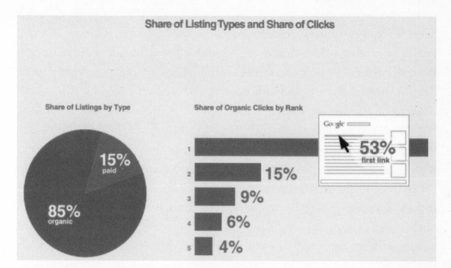

Figure 10: The first organic listing on Google gets 53 percent of clicks (source: Search Engine Watch http://searchenginewatch.com/article/2215868/53-of-Organic-Search-Clicks-Go-to-First-Link-Study).

Google's organic results are also subject to constant tweaking by Google in their endless quest to provide users with the best, most helpful, and most relevant results possible, while at the same time working to stop or at least minimize tactics by the thousands of webmasters aiming to "beat the algorithm" or "game the system." The next section will reveal the specific three-step process Google uses to find, scan, and determine where Web pages rank in organic results.

Small business, specifically *local business,* SEO should be a core element of your online reach program, so much so that we've devoted Chapter 7 to best practices in small business search engine optimization.

4. Google+ Local and Maps Results

According to Quora.com, at least 40 percent of Google searches are for local businesses and resources (http://www.quora.com/What-percentage-of-all-search-is-local). This is a huge opportunity for you and also a major driver of Google's resources and focus.

Beginning in 2008, Google has been placing increasing value on, and giving page-one real estate to, local businesses. Having gone through several name changes (Google Maps, Google+ Local, Google Places), face-lifts, and product iterations, Google's local business product has risen to prominent position in the search engine market, sparking a great deal of heated debate and anti-trust lawsuits from other local business directories and websites along the way.

As shown in Figure 9, the results of most searches for local businesses include several prominently displayed businesses, usually listed along with their respective positions on a map. Google uses the location of the "searcher" to provide relevant results. Usually, users no longer have to include location-related keywords when searching for local businesses—a search for "Dentists" or "Restaurants" will oftentimes produce local results without the need to include a city or other location-based text in the query.

KEY CONCEPT: Mobile Use Is on the Rise

Mobile devices represent the fastest growing segment of online searches. Experts predict that by 2015, half of the searches for local businesses will be done from mobile devices (smartphone, tablet, or GPS). The growing demand and opportunity have made mobile search a critical part of every local business online strategy. We will cover mobile marketing in the next chapter.

5. Blended Search

The last element of content found on a Google search results page is referred to as "blended," or, "universal" search. While the default search results often include elements from all media types—news, images, videos, blogs, and products—Google also lists these categories on the left sidebar/margin, allowing users to select the specific type of media they're seeking. For example, if you prefer to watch a video covering how to fix a kitchen sink, you would perform a search as normal, followed by clicking on "videos" to filter results to your liking.

The recent explosion in rich media has caused Google to develop powerful methods of categorizing and displaying content across all available formats. This is of great value to users as well. Because of this explosion, Google has recently purchased many brand leads for each major category of media: Picasa (images), YouTube (video),[4] and Blogger (blogs).

Categories of Blended Search

▶ Images
▶ Videos
▶ News
▶ Blog Listings
▶ Books
▶ PDFs
▶ Local / GEO
▶ Traditional Text Link Results aka Web Search
▶ Product Search
▶ Catalog Search
▶ Movies
▶ Music
▶ Maps
▶ Health
▶ Celebrity
▶ Job Search
▶ Recipes
▶ Financial/Stock Search
▶ People Search
▶ Comparison Search

Each category of blended search represents a powerful way to reach your target customers! How powerful would it be if a target client of yours were to Google your relevant keywords ("Business Accountant in Denver") and was met with the following:

---

[4] Everyone knows Google dominates the search engine market, with 70 percent market share, but can you guess who occupies the number-two spot? The second largest search engine in the world is, in fact, YouTube (http://articles.businessinsider.com/2010-11-02/entertainment/29985901_1_web-video-jawed-karim-video-views). YouTube gets over 660 million searches each month—eclipsing Bing! and Yahoo by an increasing margin. This means that your business must utilize video to reach and engage potential clients online.

▶ Your website in the organic results

▶ A YouTube video of you explaining business accounting

▶ An image of you at your most recent networking event

▶ Your Google Places listing showing up on a map

▶ A paid AdWords listing from your firm, offering a free consultation

How much trust would such first-page domination generate? How much more likely would searchers be to click to your website, contact you, and become your best new clients? Using multiple media formats to reach your clients will be a critical part of your online reach strategy.

HOW GOOGLE DECIDES WHO'S ON TOP

The goal of this section is to uncover the simple three-step process that Google uses to find and rank the immense universe of Web pages floating around cyberspace. Much of the process through which Google "finds," "reads," and ranks Web pages is fairly straightforward and commonsensical.

Google Bit Off More Than It Could Chew—The Entire Internet!

According to Netcraft, there are around 644,275,754 active websites on the Internet—and billions of individual Web pages, as most sites contain several pages. And this number is growing by 5 percent each month (http://news.netcraft.com/archives/2012/03/05/march-2012-web-server-survey.html).

Even more impressive is how effective Google is at what they do. Google has the self-appointed role of finding, scanning, and ranking this expanding universe of sites and delivering the intended result within fractions of a second.

Think about it: The next time you follow a whim to jump on your laptop and search for "the flight speed of a European swallow," Google's engine will somehow "decide" which of the billion or so Web pages are likely the most helpful for you, and display them in order of relevance within milliseconds.

To support their goal of producing better results more quickly, Google frequently changes their search algorithms, sometimes wiping out thousands of websites, companies, and even industries in the process. Although this may leave most of us small business owners with a feeling of helplessness at the whim of this elusive information-eating organism, the core process has changed very little—Google uses a simple, three-step process to produce those lightning-quick search results:

▶ **Crawling:** Google spiders—also known as Googlebots—scour the Web, following all the links on every page, and the links on those, and so on.

▶ **Indexing:** These spiders scan the text of each Web page they find, determining the subject matter of the content.

▶ **Ranking:** Google determines the order in which Web pages containing similar content are listed in search results, evaluating them based on trust, relevance, and authority.

Let's dig just a little bit more deeply into each of these three steps.

Crawling

Think of the Web as a series of individual documents (Web pages) linked together by strands, like a spider's web. Although you may often use the term "website," incorporating all the pages within, search engines see and scan each individual page on the Web independently. A website is simply a collection of related Web pages linked together using hyperlinks; without these links, the Internet would serve no purpose, denying us and search engines any way to find or rank information!

KEY CONCEPT: Understanding "Googlebots"

Google spiders, also known as "Googlebots," crawl the entire World Wide Web, scanning each Web page (i.e., billions of documents) and exploring its hyperlinks, storing this data in one of several indexes. This process continues until the search engine spider has found, "read," and indexed virtually every page on the Internet! Therefore, a great way for Google to find your site is for it to notice and explore links on other sites that point to yours.

Indexing

Once a Googlebot crawls a website, recording every page of the site, every word, image, and link, it then makes a copy of it, files it under the right category, and produces it within milliseconds on command! Google parses out and stores the code from these pages in massive data centers— Google's index—ensuring that data can be served up instantaneously. Google assigns a unique ID to each Web page, and even indexes the content of each page to identify precisely which terms it contains.

NOTE: Like Santa, Google Knows Whether You've Been Naughty or Nice. When you publish an article on your website, Google finds and scans it within days or even sooner, making note of who wrote it, how long (word count) and how original (unique) it is (an indicator of quality), what it's about, how many people "Like" it on Facebook and other social sites, and much more.

Ranking

This is where the rubber meets the road. Have you ever wondered why your site shows up on page three of Google for an important search term, while your competitor's enjoys the number-one spot, when both sites have roughly the same content?

Assuming your site has been found, crawled, and indexed, it's in the final step, Ranking, that the search engine battle is won or lost.

Upon receiving a search query, Google must first return only those results related to the query, and, second, rank these results in order of relevance and importance. This ranking process is known as a search engine algorithm. Each major search engine company maintains its own algorithm with the goal of producing the "best" (most useful and relevant) results.

Think of the ranking process as a filter: a search engine's mission in producing a search results page is to start with all the pages of data on the Web, then filter these pages through a series of screening steps, and, finally, narrow the list to what the search engine determines to be the "best" list of results.

Although complex in its entirety, Google's search engine ranking algorithm boils down to a few simple concepts that govern how they rank Web pages:

▶ **Relevance:** The first test a Web page must pass in getting ranking is relevance. For example, if someone searches for the term "vacations," Google's first task is to pull all Web pages that include this exact term, or "keyword." This is why On-Page SEO is the first step in an SEO campaign. Therefore, your ticket to even being considered in search results is relevant content!

▶ **Authority (also referred to as "Importance"):** Unlike relevance, authority is determined largely by backlinks, which are those links residing on other Web pages that point to yours. You may be familiar with the terms "Google Page Rank," or, "PR." Google's page rank system is a measure of authority related to a given search term. Authority—and, therefore, page rank—hinges upon links as a gauge of popularity. In simpler terms, Google's authority algorithm functions by treating the Internet like a massive voting system/popularity contest, treating each link to your site like a vote: if website A's subject matter is soccer and has 900 other soccer-related sites linking to it, and site B is also about soccer but has just 150 soccer-related links, then site A is judged to be the greater authority related to soccer and therefore ranks higher.

▶ **Trust:** The third phase of Google's ranking algorithm is trust, or, "Trust Rank." Trust is measured largely by how consistent and reliable a website is in providing accurate information to users, and this places a higher value on more established sites. Time, therefore, is a component of the trust algorithm, meaning websites that have been around longer get more trust points.

▶ **SPAM Filters:** One of the primary reasons that SE algorithms are always changing is due to the need to address "Black Hat SEO" practices, also called "search engine spamming." These are techniques deployed by site owners who try and game the system by gaining search engine traffic without increasing their rankings naturally, i.e., building authority with quality backlinks over time. Google is aggressive about such sites—excluding them from search results maintains quality and user satisfaction. There are several negative ranking factors that may have adverse effects on your search engine rankings without your knowing it. In Chapter 8, we'll show you how to keep out of hot water, focusing solely on ethical link-building methods.

KEY CONCEPT: **SEO Goes Beyond What's on Your Website**
One of the biggest mistakes small business owners make when it comes to SEO is focusing all of their energy on their website and not enough on getting high-quality links to their site from others. All other things being equal, usually the site with the most trusted backlinks will rank higher on Google.

In the next section, we'll dive more deeply into a simple-to-implement small business SEO plan.

CHAPTER CHECKLIST

✔ **Understand the Anatomy of Google Search Results**
- The search bar
- Paid search results: paid Google AdWords (PPC) ads
- Organic search results: natural results driven by SEO
- Google Maps and Local results (Google+ Local)
- Google blended search: includes all forms of online media

✔ **Understand the Three-Step Process Google Uses to Rank Web Pages**
- Crawl: Googlebots (Web spiders) scour the Web, following all the links on every page.
- Index: These spiders determine and store the subject matter (tops) of the content.
- Rank: Google determines the order in which Web pages containing similar content are listed in search results, evaluating them based on trust, relevance, and authority.

SEVEN

OPTIMIZE YOUR WEBSITE WITH SEO BASICS

"If you don't get noticed, you don't have anything. You just have to be noticed, but the art is in getting noticed naturally, without screaming or without tricks."

—*Leo Burnett*

If you've completed the steps outlined in the last few chapters and launched a basic WordPress site, you have already constructed the framework for a high-performance website. Congratulations!

Now what we need to do is systematically implement best practices related to each phase of the online marketing funnel: Reach, Engagement, and Conversion. This chapter is all about reach—using basics in small business SEO to ensure that your website shows up when and where your target customers are looking.

More so than most topics related to online marketing, SEO is one that's especially laced with fear, mystery, controversy, and misinformation. I'm willing to bet that, at some point, you have been exposed to, if not a victim of, bad SEO advice or services. This is due largely in part to two main factors:

▶ **Lack of a formal certification process or accreditation body:** If I told you I had a drill in my garage, would you readily let me perform a root canal on you, sitting on a milk crate, lodged in between the ping-pong table and workbench? Imagine having your business taxes done by a teenager who just pirated the latest copy of QuickBooks.

Like most folks, you likely place such important issues in the hands of licensed pros. But the world of SEO and marketing have no commonly recognized bodies that oversee and monitor the qualifications of its practitioners. Anyone can throw up a basic website and sell "SEO services." This leaves the average business owner in quite a quandary: you need help with your online visibility and marketing, but have no clear way to screen potential providers for quality and expertise.

▶ **Not knowing enough about SEO to ask the right questions:** This is yet another compelling reason we must all take ownership of our marketing, whether we do the work ourselves or not. This means paying attention to the metrics and knowing enough about your SEO strategy to gauge the performance of the contractors you may hire. Considering that most small business SEO firms charge from $400 to $3,000 per month, you'd better do all you can to ensure this investment can quickly produce a positive and measurable ROI.

Later in this chapter, we'll cover questions to ask SEO or marketing firms, and which certifications such entities should possess.

In the last chapter, you got the gist of how Google uses "trust," "relevance," and "authority" to rank Web pages. But how do these ranking favors apply *to your actual website*? To answer this, let's look at the major factors Google uses to assign rank to a Web page for a given keyword:

1. **The Structure, Age, and Performance of Your Website:** This includes the CMS your site is built on, the design and "user experience," performance (how long it takes for pages to load), and navigation. Google also evaluates your "internal linking structure"—how your pages link to each other, both from within your content itself and your site's navigation (menus).

2. **Domain Name and URL Structure:** It's no secret that Google rewards "exact-match domain names" in their ranking algorithm. All this means is that, when someone searches for "Boston Divorce Lawyer," for example, whoever owns the domain BostonDivorceLawyer.com will get a slight boost in search

results for this specific search query. Your URL structure—how the URL for each of your pages is configured—also plays a role. It's important to ensure that your URL structure uses keywords instead of coding language (www.travel.com/brazil would be much better than www.travel.com/locationID=5672_?11).

3. **Use of Keywords in the Right Places:** Employing your targeted search terms on your web pages is a critical factor in achieving top rankings (this is referred to as "on-page SEO"). There are several places you'll need to include keywords: in the titles of each page, the headings, the internal links, and in the content itself. In the next section, we'll delve into keyword research and lay out a simple method for boosting SEO.

4. **Quality of Your Content:** Google evaluates the quality of your content based on length, frequency (how often you add new content), and engagement (how long people read your content and how often they share/"Like" it using social sites). If I had to give one piece of advice to a typical small business owner, it would be: "Publish original content that addresses the main questions and concerns of your audience, often." We've devoted Section Four to creating a highly effective and easy-to-implement content strategy.

5. **Quality Score:** If you've done any PPC campaigns (specifically Google AdWords), you're probably familiar with the term "Quality Score." Quality Score is simply a set of factors Google uses to determine where paid ads rank and how much advertisers must pay for each click to their site. Google factors in bounce rate, social shares, page views, and over-optimization (deliberately using too many keywords within your site's content and meta data).

6. **Local Search Factors:** As I brought up in the last chapter, Google spends a great deal of time and resources on local ranking factors, ensuring that each search query is met with the most relevant results possible. It's critical that you optimize your website for local search, doing everything possible to help Google understand exactly where you're located and exactly what you do.

7. **Quality Backlinks from Trusted Sources:** Online marketing experts categorize search engine optimization into two categories: "On-Page SEO," referring to implementing SEO best practices within your site, and "Off-Page SEO," also called Link Building. Off-Page SEO involves obtaining high-quality links to your site from trusted relevant sources. All other things being equal, the site with the most backlinks wins. There are several great places from which to obtain backlinks, and very specific ways to format these links for best results (see Section Five: Reach—Increase Your Online Visibility).

8. **Social Factors:** One of the easiest ways for Google to screen out nondescript, "spammy" websites is to measure the level of social sharing your content garners. Also called "social signals," instances of social sharing (Likes, tweets, and follows) are a simple indicator of how valuable real people find your content. Of course, there are ways to manipulate this, too (hiring companies to generate disingenuous social shares), but at least Google is starting to place more value on social interaction, rewarding sites with the most social engagement.

9. **Reviews and Citations:** Just like in the pre-Internet era, few things today have higher value to small businesses than an endorsement or recommendation from a successful customer. Google has gotten pretty darn smart in their algorithm's ability to measure and reward small business who get reviews on trusted sites like Yelp, Google+ Local, and Merchant Circle.

If these nine factors have your head spinning, hang with me. Over the next few chapters, we'll reveal simple methods, tools, and checklists for you to easily implement SEO best practices.

RESOURCE: The Periodic Table of SEO Ranking Factors

Search Engine Land recently put together a "Periodic Table of SEO Ranking Factors," a great visual representation of factors related to small business SEO (http://searchengineland.com/seotable).

SEO IS ALL ABOUT KEYWORDS

Have you ever bought a car that you've had your heart set on for months, only to discover that suddenly, everywhere you look, you see people driving the same make and model? Your new cruising machine might as well be an iPhone or tribal tattoo—kind of cool to own until you realize everyone on your block has one. Obviously, the density of similar vehicles on the road didn't change—it was your perception that caused such an apparent shift. The same will hold true for keywords— you'll start looking at everything you do, publish, read, "Like," watch, tweet, share, and Digg differently.

Keywords are the core language of search engines, as each word in the title of your home page, blog post you write, Facebook profile you create, or YouTube video you upload is categorized based on the specific terms you use to describe them. This makes keyword research and deployment (geek-speak for "using them") immeasurably important for getting found by your target audience.

THE ONLINE BUYING FUNNEL

Before we start sifting and sorting long lists of potential search terms, it's important to understand how people search online, which partly depends on how far along they are in the decision-making or buying process, often referred to as the buying funnel.

There are three categories of searches that just about all Google queries fall into:

▶ **Informational Searches (about 80 percent):** As much as we'd all like to think that every potential customer of ours sits down in front of his computer with credit card in hand, ready to buy on the spot, the truth is that most searches on the Web are "informational" in nature, meaning that these queries are made by people earlier in the buying process, researching their options and seeking answers to their questions. An example of an informational search query would be: "Are plasmas better than LCD TVs?"

▶ **Transactional Searches (10-12 percent):** As the name implies, these searches refer to the user intending to take action by buying a product or hiring a local service provider. "Deals on plasmas in Chicago" represents a good transactional search.

▶ **Navigational Searches (5-8 percent):** These are the easy ones, when someone who already knows your brand or website, usually a loyal customer or visitor, types in your domain name to go directly to your site. Think eBay, Amazon, or Google.

It's easy to visualize these buying phases as a funnel: people start addressing a need they have identified by first researching the basics and gathering information, and then continually narrowing down their options, comparing specs and reading reviews. Finally, and only upon gaining enough information to feel comfortable, they use transactional queries to make their final decision. For best results in terms of reaching and engaging more of your target customers, it's important to focus on all three types of search queries.

Each phase of the online search funnel comes with its own set of keywords that you'll need to identify and target via your SEO and content writing. For example, if you sell "Coleman camping tents," you may want to target "best tent for families" within your informational strategy and "discount Coleman tents in Dallas" to capture transactional searches.

KEY CONCEPT: Education-Based Marketing Gives You a Jump on the Competition

Many small business owners are short-sighted when it comes to marketing, seeking immediate results and concentrating almost solely on finding their next customers (those searching with transactional queries). As much as I can relate to the need for "new business, pronto!" this hand-to-mouth thinking usually results in business owners missing the boat when it comes to content marketing. Focusing only on those customers who intend to "buy today" limits your potential to just 10 to 12 percent of the search traffic in your niche.

The better approach is to focus on the "informational queries," producing content that results in your website showing up when your target audience asks questions via search engines. This is the core of education-based marketing: educating your target customers by providing free, helpful information. Doing so helps to establish you as an authority and, in the process, to beat your competitors to the punch because you are able to reach and build trust (engagement) with your audience long before they ever get to your competitors.

In Chapter 10, we'll cover a simple process to help you identify a specific strategy for capturing informational search queries via helpful content.

KEY CONCEPT: Understanding the Long Tail of Search

Chris Anderson, Editor of *Wired* magazine and author of the book *The Long Tail*, coined the term "long tail" in his now-famous 2004 article (http://www.wired.com/wired/archive/12.10/tail.html). The core concept of the long tail as it applies to SEO is that, while most businesses focus on a few "short tail" keywords such as "Business Card Printing," or, "Tax Accountant," most of the searches on the Web resulting in traffic to your website come from "long tail" search queries, such as "What is the best type of paper for business cards?"

The following article by Matt Bailey describes the long tail quite well:

The principle of the Long Tail is the opposite of focusing on the top 10-20 keywords for marketing your website. The "top keyword" concept is reinforced by agencies that contract to gain rankings for 10-20 terms, maybe 30. However, when studying the referrals from the search engines and the traffic they generate, those that focus on the top 10-20 terms may be missing the majority of their market.

People tend to focus on the thousands of visitors that come to the site for the most popular terms. Most site managers are very happy to see the numbers increase for those specific terms, and even happier to see those terms consistently ranking well. Conventional thinking applies the 80-20 rule that the top terms provide 80 percent of the business, but in evaluating multiple sites, this has proved to be the opposite. An important marketing concept known as "The Long Tail" is used to describe the hundreds to thousands of keywords and key phrases that a website is found for, yet rarely noticed or exploited by owners of the website. (http://www.searchengineguide.com/matt-bailey/ keyword-strategies-the-long-tail.php)

B2B Long Tail SEO

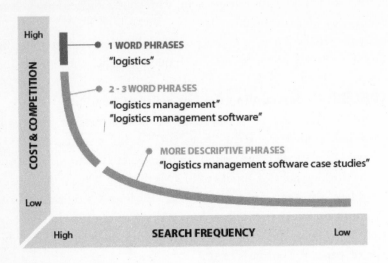

Figure 11: The Long Tail

Gaining a basic understanding of the Long Tail can go a long way in helping you generate much more website traffic than your competitors. While most small business marketers are focused on the ultra-competitive "short tail" keywords ("Dallas Business Lawyer"), well-informed marketers like yourself can scoop up hundreds or even thousands of visitors by writing content that targets long tail search terms ("What's the difference between an LLC and sole proprietorship?").

Throughout this chapter, we'll uncover an effective strategy for mapping out which specific topic and keywords you'll need to focus content on in order to generate qualified traffic from people in all phases of the buying funnel, using both long- and short-tailed search terms.

SEVEN SIMPLE STEPS TO SMALL BUSINESS SEO SUCCESS

Using your newfound knowledge of ranking, crawling, indexing, and optimizing, you can achieve great SEO results by implementing the following simple seven-step process:

STEP 1: FIND THE BEST KEYWORDS TO TARGET

The goal of doing keyword research is to ensure that every piece of content you publish online reaches the largest possible number of people within your target audience. This is accomplished by following a specific process that involves looking at both your competitors' sites and the behaviors of your target customers, as well as using a fair amount of common sense. Then, we will use a very simple and organized approach to "mapping out" the keywords you should be targeting, based on the products and/or services your business provides.

Just like your overall online marketing program, keyword research can be visualized as a funnel, with the top of the funnel representing a large laundry list of potential search terms, and the bottom being a very short list of search phrases that you should be using within your content and on your site. Following are the elements of this "Keyword Research Funnel":

1. **Create Your Huge Laundry List**
    At the top of the funnel, your goal is to generate a massive list of words and phrases, many of which you'll throw away. Much like a sculptor chipping away the inessentials until the perfect figure is revealed, we need a huge pile of words to begin.

    To start your keyword laundry list, open up an Excel or Google spreadsheet. You'll be using this as a tool to help you capture and manage keywords.

    Along the top columns of your spreadsheet, list the main category of business you provide, followed by the categories of products or services you provide. In the example list on the following page, I am using a printing shop to illustrate:

Category	Printing Shops keyword	Business Cards keyword
Keywords	printing services	business cards
	printing shop	best business cards
	printer services	free business cards
	screen printing services	templates for business cards
	digital printing services	business cards templates
	copy and printing services	how to design business cards
	copy printing services	business cards design
	cheap printing services	design business cards

Figure 12: A sample "Keyword Laundry List"

Now comes the fun part—creating the biggest possible list of potential keywords that you can muster for each of your products or services. Use any source you can think of, from brainstorming with your customers and employees, to conducting some top-secret spy work to analyzing which keywords your competitors are using. Use no filter and make no assumptions—there are no wrong answers.

Here are several great places to find potential keywords:

1. **A Simple Brain Dump:** Start with the type of business you own and add every possible keyword idea you, your friends, your co-workers, and associates think might make sense to target, and list them on a spreadsheet. Then add the actual names of the products and services you provide.

2. **Your Customers:** One of the most valuable exercises you can do is to list the most common questions you get from customers with respect to each of your main products or services. Almost without exception, every business owner can recite the three to five questions that their customers (and potential customers) most frequently ask.

3. **Competitors:** What better way to beat your competition than to find out which keywords are drawing traffic to their sites, then using the same ones for yours? You probably have the

names of the top five to ten competitors whose websites pop up every time your line of business is mentioned. Start with these websites, but also do a few Google searches for the main service you provide, including in your searches one or two main cities to which your business caters ("Dallas Divorce Lawyers," for example). Next, take your list of five to ten competitive websites and use SEM Rush (http://www.semrush.com/) and follow the prompts to find out which keywords are driving traffic to their sites. Add any of these search terms that apply to your business to your list.

▶ **Google's Keyword Tool** (https://adwords.google.com/o/KeywordTool): is a great FREE tool you can use to do keyword research and find additional keywords you might have missed. You can either type in a search query ("Chicago Pizza Shop") or a competitor's website and you will be presented with a great list of potential search terms you can use. Also displayed is the search volume (how many searches are being conducted each month) and competition (how many other websites are using or bidding on a given search term). What's really neat is that you can export your lists in Excel or text format by simply clicking on the "download" button. Add each of these potential keywords to your list.

Ubersuggest (http://ubersuggest.org) and Soovle (http://www.soovle.com) are great tools for helping you identify related keywords for any topic(s) you desire. Both of them work the same: you simply enter a search term, and receive instant reports of terms related to your query. While both tools are powered by "Google Suggest," Soovle returns results from several popular sites including Amazon.com, YouTube, Bing, and more.

▶ **Your Existing Website Traffic:** Assuming you already have a website, you probably have Google Analytics installed (if not, see the next section for instructions). One of the many powerful functions of Analytics is the "search queries" function, which provides specific details related to which search terms produced visits to your site. What better way to increase traffic than to use questions and topics from your audience that are already working!

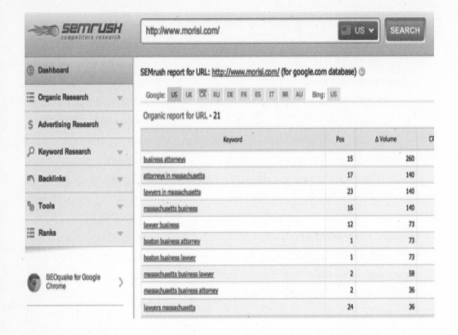

Figure 13: SEM Rush

KEY CONCEPT: **Don't Forget the Buying Funnel When Looking for Keywords.**

When looking for great keywords, it's important not to forget the "informational queries,"—the terms that your target customers are likely to be using in the beginning of their buying processes. When using the Google keyword tool, try typing in the questions you hear most often about your products or services. These informational queries will come in handy to use as topics for blog posts or videos when putting together your Content Road Map in Chapter 10.

2.   Remove Undesirable and Irrelevant Search Terms

Now you must refine your keyword list by excluding any keywords that don't apply to your business. For the most part, these irrelevant terms should be easy to spot (see following figure).

KEY CONCEPT: When It Comes to Keywords, Opposites Attract!
Don't over-eliminate during this refining process, as many of the keywords you assume to be irrelevant or undesirable could in fact be among your best sources of traffic and leads. For example, using our fictitious local printing shop, many folks might eliminate the term "printing wedding invitations online," as their business offers only local printing services. However, optimizing for competitive services or products that your business doesn't offer is one of the best ways to generate traffic from potential clients performing informational queries. Using the above example, our local printer could write a great blog post entitled "5 Reasons Why Using a Local Printer Is Better than Printing Wedding Invitations Online."

Virtually any adjective—cheap, free, low-cost, discount—can work. Even if you sell $5,000 sofas, you may influence and attain a few new customers by writing a blog post entitled, "Why Buying Cheap Sofas Costs More in the End."

Category	Printing Shops	Business Cards
	keyword	keyword
Keywords	printing services	business cards
	printing shop	best business cards
	printer services	business credit cards
	screen printing services	templates for business cards
	Canon printers	playing card shops
	copy and printing services	how to design business cards
	copy printing services	business cards design
	Ink jet cartridges	design business cards

Figure 14: Step 2 is about removing irrelevant keywords.

3. **Sort Your Keywords by Popularity Using Google's Free Keyword Tool**
Who doesn't want to be popular (aside from nearly every band coming out of Seattle in the '90s)? Within the realm of online marketing and,

more specifically, keyword research, popularity is defined as the number of searches conducted within a specific time frame (usually a month) for a given keyword. For example, with our friendly neighborhood printing company, it would be extremely beneficial to know that the search term "printing services" gets 165,000 "local" monthly searches while the term "printing shop" gets just 60,500. Measuring popularity is critical, as using the wrong keywords could result in much lower traffic!

The simplest way to measure and rank our targeted search terms by popularity is to use Google's Free Keyword Tool. All you need to do is "paste" your keywords from your Keyword Spreadsheet into the "Find Keywords" box and hit "Search," and you'll see how many searches, on average, are being conducted monthly for each of your terms.

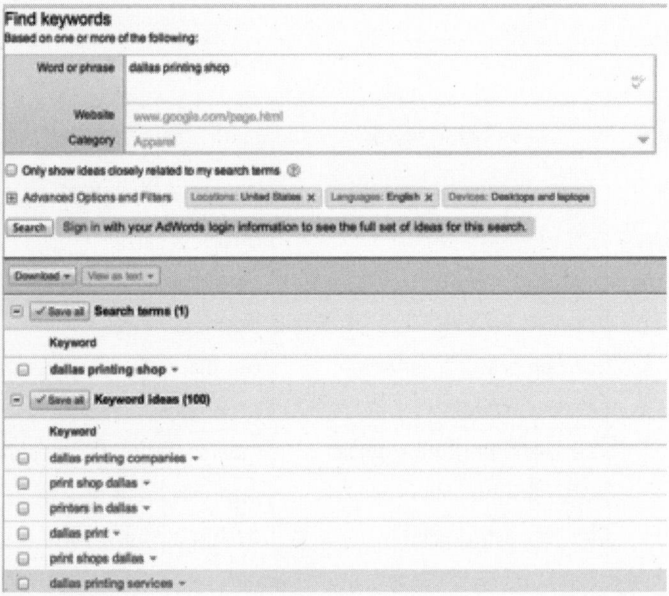

Figure 15: Using Google's Keyword Tool to measure keyword popularity

For each report you run (one separate report for each product or service category), all you need to do is download your list, complete with search volumes for each search term. To do this, just select "Download" in the space above your keyword list (Figure 16).

Figure 16: Using Google's Keyword Tool to download keyword reports

The last step is to add these search volume numbers back into your Keyword Spreadsheet. Remember to keep your keywords separated based on the primary products and service categories of your business (see following figure).

Category	Printing Shops keyword		Business Cards keyword	
Keywords	printing services	165,000	business cards	1,500,000
	printing shop	60,500	best business cards	33,100
	printer services	40,500	free business cards	165,000
	screen printing services	2,400	templates for business cards	110,000
	digital printing services	2,400	business cards templates	110,000
	copy and printing services	2,400	how to design business cards	74,000
	copy printing services	2,400	business cards design	74,000
	cheap printing services	1,900	design business cards	74,000

Figure 17: Step 3 allows you to rank your keywords by popularity.

KEY CONCEPT: Don't Worry Too Much about Variations of the Same Word

A common mistake small business owners (and their SEO experts) use is to "over-optimize" websites, creating a different page and content for each variation of a word. For example, an owner of a nail salon may create unique Web pages for "nail salon," "nail salons," "nail spa," "nail spas," "nail shop," "nail shops," etc. This outdated tactic is unnecessary, as Google is smart enough to associate related terms and synonyms automatically. Not only is this overkill, but doing so can get your site penalized by Google for "over-optimization."

Just as with virtually every other aspect of SEO and Google-friendly Web design, common sense rules. If you write high-quality content aimed at real human beings, you'll seldom have to worry about the technical details of each new algorithm change. In fact, you'll probably benefit because all Google is trying to do is create a better user experience by linking folks to high-quality content.

KEY CONCEPT: Why You Shouldn't Include Your City Name When Doing Keyword Research

Many people "localize" their keywords too early in the research process, by adding local-based keywords to their targeted keywords ("Denver printing services"). This is a mistake, as these long tail searches don't get enough volume to be measured and reported by Google. This doesn't mean that ranking number one on Google for "divorce lawyer in Branson, Mo" isn't a good thing, just that it would be below the radar.

If you include localized terms in your target keywords, you may be led to eliminate your most important keywords based on seeing "0 searches" in the keyword tool.

The best way to overcome this lack of available metrics is to assume that the most popular keywords in the country are also the most popular in your town. Outside of a few particular regional exceptions, like "DWI" vs. "DUI," or "soda" vs. "pop," this approach works extremely well. If "printing services" gets three times more results than "printing shop," it's probably most lucrative to optimize your website for "Dallas printing services."

In short, leave location-centered phrases out during the initial research process and add them in later during keyword deployment (discussed later).

4. Finalize Your Keyword Map

This step will result in a final, super-refined and relevant, traffic-generating list that will become the "map" that will guide you through setting up your website pages, blog posts, and even online listings and advertising. All you need to do is choose the best keywords and place them into two bins based on which end of the buying funnel they reflect: Informational or Transactional.

I recommend you practice a "less is more" approach, using the most popular and relevant search terms. You can always expand your list later to capture more "long tail" phrases down the road via blog posts and videos.

KEYWORD RESEARCH TOOLS AND RESOURCES:

► **SEOmoz Beginners Guide to Keyword Research** (http://www.seomoz.org/beginners-guide-to-seo/keyword-research): a quick and dirty course for the layperson.

► **Google's Keyword Tools** (https://adwords.google.com/o/KeywordTool)

► **SEM RUSH** (http://www.semrush.com/): provides useful information regarding any site on the Web, displaying metrics related to traffic, demographics, and both paid and organic keywords.

► **Market Samurai** (http://www.marketsamurai.com/): a very popular software application designed for fast keyword research, rank tracing, and more. I recommend watching their detailed video tutorials on keyword research.

► **Long Tail Pro** (http://www.longtailpro.com/): a new but extremely powerful software program that's especially useful for finding long tail keyword ides (for blog posts or videos).

Step 2: USE YOUR KEYWORDS IN THE RIGHT PLACES

It's time to take your ultra-refined Keyword Map and put it to use by "deploying" your keywords—placing your target keywords in all the proper places, both on your website and elsewhere.

WHERE TO USE YOUR TARGETED KEYWORDS: EVERYWHERE!

The following are some of the most popular and important places to use your keywords/targeted search phrases:

▶ Your domain name and URLs
▶ Titles of your Web pages and blog posts
▶ Headings of your Web pages
▶ Meta descriptions of your Web pages
▶ Content (articles, Web pages, blogs, etc.)
▶ Names and descriptions of photos and videos on your site
▶ Navigation on your website
▶ Internal links on your website
▶ Anchor text of inbound links
▶ Social media profile names
▶ Social media descriptions
▶ Paid online directory listings
▶ PPC (Google AdWords) ads
▶ In the "signature line" of your online forum profiles
▶ Comments you make on other blogs and community sites
▶ Guest blog posts you publish on others' sites
▶ Anywhere your business is listed (article directories, press release sites, social bookmarking sites, etc.)

If you recall from Chapter 6, gaining high-quality backlinks to your site is among the most important factors in your SEO success. Let's have another look at the list of where you'll need to place your target search terms, this time divided into On-Page and Off-Page SEO.

On-Page Keyword Deployment	Off-Page Keyword Deployment
• Your domain name and URLs • The titles of your Web pages and blog posts • The headings of your Web pages • Within the meta descriptions of your Web pages • Within your content (articles, Web pages, blogs, etc.) • The names and descriptions of photos and videos on your site • The navigation on your website • The internal links on your website	• In the anchor text of inbound links • On your social media profile names • In your social media descriptions • In paid online directory listings • In your PPC (Google AdWords) ads • In inbound links to your site (anchor text is key!) • In your signatures on forums you belong to • In comments you make on other blogs and forums • On guest blog posts you publish on others' sites • Anywhere your business is listed

Figure 18: Keywords should be used both on your site and wherever else your business is listed on the Web.

Quick Steps to Keyword Deployment

1. Use Keyword-Rich URLs

It's important that not only your root domain (website address) but also each Web page on your site includes the keywords you have deemed important to target. Many websites, especially those using older, outdated content-management systems or languages, may use "ugly URLs," presenting "un-friendly" URLs to render Web pages (e.g., http://www.OaklandBarberShop/page_ID=3635?.php). "SEO-friendly" URLs clearly reveal the topic of the page the URL belongs to (http://www/OaklandBarberShop.com/mens-hair-cut-pricing).

WordPress comes with friendly URLs right out of the box, as each Web page or blog post you publish uses "permalinks" to allow for URL configuration and customization. If you're managing your website yourself, simply check out YouTube for videos on how to do this.

2. Add your keywords to your page titles

Every Web page and blog post on your site has a page title. This title, also referred to as a "title tag," tells both Google and people browsing your site what each page is about.

These page titles appear in the top bar of your Internet browser and are also shown as the titles of your Web pages in the Search page results.

You can easily view this page by doing the following:

▶ On any Web page, right-click your mouse and select "View Source." Look at the top section, called the "head," and view the title tag (<title>). You can also see the title of any Web page using most popular Web browsers:

Figure 19: Viewing the title of a Web page

This is one of the most important ranking factors as well as being one where most small business websites fall short. Quite often, you will see "John Doe Law Firm," or, worse yet, "Home" used as a title tag. Unless you're trying to rank on Google for "Home," this is not good.

Here's a short list of best practices related to page titles:

▶ Each page title should be unique. Avoid "duplicate title tags," using the same terms on multiple Web pages across your site.

▶ Each page should focus on one main topic or keyword phrase. Avoid trying to "stuff" multiple keywords into your page titles, as this confuses search engines and visitors alike.

▶ Be sure to include "location-based" terms in your page titles. Now is the time to add to your Web pages the main city or town where you're located (see: "Localize Your SEO" in this chapter for more on local SEO).

▶ Keep each title tag to sixty-four characters or less. This ensures that your whole title will show up on search results pages.

▶ Place the most important keywords first in your page titles ("Bankruptcy Lawyer in Cleveland" is better than "John Doe Law Offices, Cleveland Bankruptcy Lawyer")

RESOURCE: Use the Yoast WordPress SEO Plugin to Make On-Page SEO Simple

If you're using WordPress or intend to do so, I recommend you use the Yoast WordPress SEO plugin (http://yoast.com/wordpress/), which allows you to configure and make changes to virtually all aspects of your SEO (page titles, meta descriptions, site maps, permalinks, and more) from a very simple, non-technical dashboard.

Once you download and activate this plugin, be sure to go through the "free tour" that pops up at activation.

3. **Add your keywords to the headings and content of your Web pages**

This should be one of the simpler concepts to grasp: you need to ensure that every piece of content you produce is focused on a single topic and contains your target keywords that are focused on that topic.

Although many SEO experts speak of complicated formulas for measuring "keyword density," all you need to do is write high-quality, original articles that are focused on a single topic (ideally 500 words or more), including your target keywords, frequently but naturally.

As with all aspects of SEO, focus on the users—the people who will actually be reading or interacting with your content.

Page Headings

Just like this book, a restaurant menu, and most other forms of written communication, Web pages make use of hierarchical headings to organize and make content more readable. These headings are created using html code, which you'll likely never see, as most of today's CMS systems like WordPress make use of WYSIWYG (What You See Is What You Get) text editors that make writing and publishing content as simple as using Microsoft Word.

Page headings range from most to least important, from "H1" down to "H6," and often reflect this in their font weight and size on most websites. All you need to do with regard to page headings is to include your search terms within your headers, but only if doing so is natural and serves the reader. You'll also want to refrain from using more than one H1 heading per page.

Photos and Videos Are Content, Too!

As you learned in Chapter 3, Google applies its search algorithms to virtually every form of content on the Internet. Photos and videos are no exception. Each time you publish a photo or video, it's important to use your target keywords when naming, describing, or tagging this media. For example, if you add a photo of your office to your home page, you'd be very well served to name the photo "Dallas Business Printing Services, Smith and Co.," instead of "Our office."

One small technical detail related to Web images is the use of "alt tags." "Alternative text" is text used to describe images whenever the image cannot be rendered, as would be the case with special screen readers for those who are visually disabled, for example. If you use a popular CMS system, you'll find it very easy to upload images and add or edit both the title and the alt attributes.

Content SEO Checklist

▶ Each piece of content (Web page, blog post, or video) should be focused on a single topic.

▶ Only use original content (written by you or someone you've hired) for publication on your website.

▶ Ensure that your content is at least 350 words in length (500-plus is preferred).

▶ Use keywords in your titles, page headings, descriptions, and tags.

Step 3: USE AN SEO-FRIENDLY WEBSITE STRUCTURE

The "structure," or how your Web pages are laid out, is an important element of SEO. Think of your website as an organizational chart or a filing cabinet, with each "block" or "file" representing a Web page or blog post on your site. The goal of an SEO-friendly site structure is to ensure that your content is very easy to find, both for Googlebots and for your users. This can be accomplished by doing four simple things:

1. **Use a "wide" website structure rather than a "deep" one.** Many Web designs make the mistake of creating "deep" website hierarchies, meaning the sites are structured in a linear, or deep, format, categorizing similar pages in neat rows and columns. While this may make sense for filing old tax returns, Web pages, especially the ones containing your site's most important content, should remain close to the surface, near the home page. This "wide" site structure (see the image to the right in the chart below) ensures that both search and real folks can easily see and access your content from the home page.

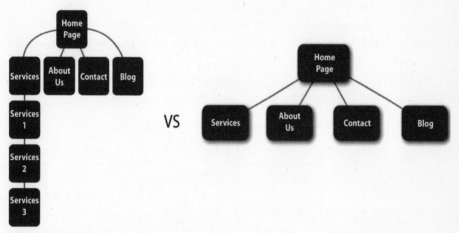

Figure 20: Deep vs. wide website structures

2. **Add target keywords to your site's navigation.** The navigation or "menu bar" of your site is the primary menu for your Web page, serving as the "at-a-glance" table of contents for your website. In addition to constructing your site in a "wide" format, be sure to include your target keywords to describe each of the services you provide. For example, instead of using the term "services" in your main menu, use a target keyword or phrase like "accounting services."

KEY CONCEPT: **Use Your Keyword Map to Lay Out Your Site Design**
The time and effort you've put into developing your keyword map is about to pay off: this map can serve as a ready-made template for laying out your website!

Each of the primary categories (of products and/or services) in your Keyword Map can be used as Web pages in your navigation. Each transactional keyword can then be used as a heading within these pages— for example, our famous printing shop, ACME, would use "Business Cards" as a page within the navigation menu. On this page, the page headings would be "Business Card Printers," "Cheap Business Cards," and "Fast Business Card Printing."

3.   **Add your keywords to your site's internal links.** One of the simplest and most effective ways to improve the structure of your site and increase user engagement is to employ a solid internal linking structure. A good rule of thumb is to ensure that a visitor to one of your Web pages can access any other page with just one or two clicks. Equally important is that each of these internal links uses keyword-rich anchor text.

		MAIN BUSINESS	PRIMARY SERVICES OR PRODUCT CATEGORIES
Main Navigation →	CATEGORY	PRINTING SHOP	BUSINESS CARDS
SEO Keywords →	Transactional Keywords	printers printing company business printing	business card printers cheap business cards fast business card printing
Content Pages →	Informational Keywords	how to hire a printer types of printing local vs. online printing	best types of business cards business card design ideas what to include on business cards

Figure 21: Using primary categories in your keyword map for Web page navigation

KEY CONCEPT: **The Importance of Anchor Text**
According to Wikipedia, "The anchor text, link label, link text, or link

title is the visible, clickable text in a hyperlink. The words contained in the anchor text can determine the ranking that the page will receive by search engines." Any time you click on a link leading you from one Web page to another (called a hyperlink, which can also be used in emails to link to Web pages), you'll probably notice that each of these links has its own text describing where the link should take you. Anchor text is simply the words used in a link to another site. If you click on a link that says "click here," "click here" would be anchor text. Any time other websites link to yours, it's ideal to use your targeted keywords in these links. For example, if your plumber brother agrees to link to your site, it would be much better to use the anchor text "Los Angeles Plumber," than, "Check out my brother's website." Using keywords in your anchor text, both within your website and on other sites linking to yours, helps tell people and search engines that your website is an authority on the topic these keywords describe.

4. **Ensure that your website is fast.** As previously mentioned, site speed is a factor in Google's ranking algorithm, so ensure that your site loads quickly and reliably. Aside from being "dinged" by Google, a sluggish website can also cost you money, as countless studies have proven that slow page load times cause users to abandon websites.

RESOURCE: Google's PageSpeed Insights
To check your site speed, use Google PageSpeed Insights (https://developers.google.com/speed/pagespeed/insights). Simply enter your URL and wait for a report to notify you of high-, medium-, and low-priority issues affecting page loading. If your website gets a PageSpeed score of 70/100 or higher, you are fine in the eyes of Google. If you're using a popular CMS, you usually have little to worry about, as these platforms factor speed into their designs.

Step 4: INSTALL GOOGLE ANALYTICS AND GOOGLE WEBMASTER TOOLS

Google Analytics (GA) is a "free service offered by Google that generates detailed statistics about the visitors to a website" (Wikipedia: http://en.wikipedia.org/wiki/Google_Analytics). Google Analytics is super-easy to install using three steps:

1. **If you haven't done so already, sign up for a free Google Account (https://accounts.google.com/NewAccount). You'll need a Gmail account for several aspects of your online marketing.**

2. **Sign up for Google Analytics (http://www.google.com/analytics/) and add your website to your new analytics account.**

3. **Paste the small "snippet" of code provided by Google Analytics into your website. If you need help, simply search YouTube for "How to Install Google Analytics." If you're using WordPress, there's a great plugin called Google Analytics for WordPress (http://wordpress.org/extend/plugins/google-analytics-for-wordpress/) that can help you install and manage Google Analytics.**

Once you've installed Google Analytics, you'll quickly be amazed by the plethora of information available: who's coming to your site, how they got there (from Google or another search engine, or another site on the Web), what pages they're visiting, how long they're sticking around, and, with a little customization, even which traffic sources are producing qualified leads!

In Chapter 9, we'll delve into the specific metrics that matter for keeping tabs on your marketing metrics. For now, it's important to get Analytics installed as soon as possible so you can begin collecting data for later analysis and tweaking.

Google Webmaster Tools is another great (and FREE) tool from Google that every website owner should use. It has tools that allow webmasters to:

▶ Submit and check a site map
▶ Check and set the crawl rate, and view statistics about how Googlebot accesses a particular site

▶ Generate and check a robots.txt file; also discover in robots.txt pages that are accidentally blocked

▶ List internal and external pages that link to a site

▶ See what keyword searches on Google led to a site being listed in the SERPs, and the click-through rates of such listings

▶ View statistics about how Google indexes a site, and whether or not it found any errors while indexing it

▶ Set a preferred domain (e.g., prefer example.com over www.example. com or vice versa), which determines how the site URL is displayed in SERPs

Installing Google Webmaster Tools is very simple and includes the same steps as installing Google Analytics; simply log in with your Google account and follow the simple steps provided here: (http://www.google. com/webmasters/)

RESOURCE: Using Webmaster Tools Like an SEO
http://youtu.be/tQQmq9X5lQw

Step 5: LOCALIZE YOUR SEO

Your small business is most likely a local business, serving customers within a defined geographic region. Often called "Local SEO," the art and science of maximizing online reach within a specific region has many nuances that make it its own category of search engine optimization.

While online retailers like Amazon.com or Zappos.com have their own challenges in improving search engine rankings and traffic, their efforts are often "global." For example, zappos.com ranks number-one on Google for "men's shoes." They aren't on the first page for "men's shoes Dallas," nor do they care to be.

▶ **Add your localized keywords to page titles and content.** If you haven't done so yet, add "location-focused" keywords to your Keyword Map.

▶ **Include your physical location on every page of your site.** One of the ways in which Google validates and assigns trust and authority to local businesses' sites is by checking for "citations" around the Web, trying to match the physical addresses on websites to business listings on trusted "local directories" like Yelp, Merchant Circle, and YellowPages. com. If your business is listed on local directories, Google will attempt to match up these listings with the address on your website to assign trust to your site. It's critical to be very consistent, as Google can and often does make mistakes upon encountering "address discrepancies." For example, if you use "STE 7" for your suite number on your online listings, be sure to do the same on your own site and elsewhere. Make it easy for Google to give your site the credit it deserves.

▶ **Include a Google map on your site.** Placing a map on your site is another win/win as it serves both masters of online marketing: search engines and visitors. Adding a map to your site is as simple as pasting a bit of code into the page(s) of your site: http://maps.google.com/ help/maps/getmaps/plot-one.html. I recommend you place the map in the footer of your site right below the address, or on your contact page if you're going for a sleeker or more minimalist effect.

▶ **Claim your local business listings.** These local directories are also great places to find new leads, as many of them boast high traffic numbers from consumers in search of local products and services. Although there are literally thousands of local directories out there, there are only a dozen or so you should begin with, including MerchantCircle. com, CitiSearch.com, Yelp.com, Manta.com. For a detailed list of local directories, see here: http://blog.hubspot.com/blog/tabid/6307/ bid/10322/The-Ultimate-List-50-Local-Business-Directories.aspx

▶ **Link to your Google+ Local page.** Google+ Local is Google's local business directory, which should tell you that you'll need a profile there. While we'll cover how to list your business online in Chapter 12, claiming or creating a Google+ profile for yourself and your business yields almost immediate improvement of online authority and search rankings, so you may want to go ahead and do it before getting to Chapter 12. To create your Google+ business page, go here: http://www.google.com/+/business/

You'll need to have a personal Google+ profile as well, which is easy as long as you have a Gmail account.

▶ **Get more reviews.** One of the factors Google takes into account when ranking local business websites is the number of organic reviews on trusted local business directories. If you don't have a reviews/reputation management plan in place, get one! At minimum, implement a process that requires you and your staff to ask for reviews on these sites. Reviews are a great form of "social proof" (covered in Chapter 6), greatly enhancing the trust that new website visitors gain in your brand.

RESOURCES: Local SEO Resources from around the Web

▶ **Watch Rand Fishkin's "Local SEO Checklist for New Sites"** (http://www.seomoz.org/blog/local-seo-checklist-for-new-sites-whiteboard-friday): This simple video covers the essential steps for applying best practices in local SEO to a new small business website.

▶ **David Mihm's Local Search Ranking Factors** (http://www.davidmihm.com/local-search-ranking-factors.shtml): This article goes into the subject a bit more deeply than you'll likely need, but at least browse it, as it lists local factors as determined by polling over thirty of the Web's top small business SEO experts—very useful information.

Step 6: OPTIMIZE FOR MOBILE SEARCH

According to Searchenginewatch.com (http://searchenginewatch.com/article/2120678/Mobile-Growth-Stats-Mobile-Web-Tips-to-Start-Marketing), "the U.S. now has more wireless customer connections than people. There are currently estimated to be 327.6 million active wireless customer connections in the U.S. The nation's population is estimated by the U.S. Census Bureau to be roughly 312 million. This means that today there are now more active broadband tablets, cell phones, and mobile devices than people in this country."

A quick glance around your household would likely reveal that we're not more plugged in, but actually more unplugged than ever. One in three

Internet sessions occur on a mobile device (smartphone or tablet), and searching for local products and services is the perfect resource for folks when they're on the go and in need of information.

The good news when it comes to "Mobile SEO" is that your small business can likely do without an elaborate strategy for mobile search. In fact, most small businesses will reap 95 percent of the mobile market potential by doing just two primary things:

▶ **Ensuring that your website uses a mobile theme or style sheet.** A quick glance at your website from your iPhone or iPad will quickly tell you whether or not you have a mobile-friendly theme. Most modern WordPress themes come equipped with mobile themes (or "style sheets"), but if not, you can usually ask your Web designer or marketing company to create one for around a hundred dollars. If you use a Genesis Theme by StudioPress.com, your site will be mobile-ready from day one.

▶ **Ensuring that your business is listed with local directories and GPS companies, and on local maps.** If you elect to use a provider of local listings services like Ubl.org or Yect.com, your business should be listed on mobile-focused services like OnStar, Mapquest, and Google+ Local (Google Maps). The best way to test your mobile-readiness is with your phone's map or GPS function, looking up your category of business and making certain your site shows up.

Step 7: PROCLAIM YOUR AUTHORSHIP

One of the most powerful and underutilized functions in small business SEO is Google Authorship. This is one of the ways in which Google has decided to help separate quality websites from "spammy" ones, by linking each site to an individual "Author"—the individual who publishes content on the website. Setting up Google Authorship simply requires that you link your Google+ profile to your website and vice versa.

Doing this provides two great benefits:

1. Your photo will show up along with your business in search results. This provides a distinct visual advantage and has been proven to yield higher click-through rates than text-only search results.

2. Your site can get a notable "bump" in online authority, as Google sees authorship as a positive ranking signal—you're putting an accountable and visible face with the name.

To set up Authorship for your site, go here: https://plus.google.com/authorship.

For more on Google Authorship, see Search Engine Land's "The Definitive Guide To Google Authorship Markup" here: http://searchengineland.com/the-definitive-guide-to-google-authorship-markup-123218

San Diego Criminal **Lawyer**, Criminal Defense **Attorney** in San ...
www.attorneylombardo.com/

by Domenic J. Lombardo - More by Domenic J. Lombardo
The **San Diego Law** Office of Domenic J. Lombardo is dedicated solely to the practice of defending criminal charges. Mr. Lombardo is a licensed criminal defe.

San Diego Source > San Diego County **Attorney** Directory
attorney.sddt.com/

The Daily Transcript / **San Diego** Source is **San Diego's** only information company reporting and providing hourly and daily business news, data and related ...

Lawyers Club of **San Diego**
www.lawyersclubsandiego.com/

Lawyers Club of **San Diego** • 701 B Street, Suite 224 • **San Diego**, California 92101 • Phone: 619-595-0650 Fax: 619-595-0657 ...

Figure 22: Google Authorship allows author photo and information to show in search results.

CHAPTER SUMMARY

While many business owners view search engine optimization as a complicated, technical process, any website owner can reap great benefits by implementing a few basic SEO strategies. At its core, small business SEO boils down to finding the best keywords to attract your audience and using them in the right places, including your URL's content and navigation. In this increasingly mobile world, every small business website must be optimized for smartphones, tablets, and whatever other gadgets loom on the horizon. By understanding the basic ways in which your target audience searches for local resources and information, and ensuring that your website and keyword strategy are aligned with long tail search queries, you will gain a significant advantage over your competitors.

CHAPTER CHECKLIST

✔ **Understand the Basics of Small Business SEO and the Keyword Buying Funnel**
✔ **Step 1: Identify the best keywords to use on your site**
   - Start with a your Huge Laundry List spreadsheet
   - Remove undesirable and irrelevant search terms
   - Measure popularity for each keyword
   - Finalize your Keyword Map with the best keywords for your business
✔ **Step 2: Use Your Keywords in the Right Places**
   - Use keyword-rich URLs
   - Add keywords to your page titles
   - Add keywords to the headings and content of your Web pages
✔ **Step 3: Use an SEO and People-Friendly Site Structure**
   - Use a wide rather than a deep site hierarchy
   - Use keywords in your navigation
   - Use keywords in internal site links
   - Ensure that your website is optimized for speed

✔ **Step 4: Install Google Analytics and Google Webmaster Tools**
✔ **Step 5: Localize Your SEO Campaigns**
  • Add localized keywords to page titles and content
  • Include your physical location on every page of your site
  • Include a Google map on your site
  • Claim your local business listings
  • Link to your Google+ Local page
  • Get more reviews
✔ **Step 6: Implement Mobile SEO Basics**
  • Ensure that your website is mobile-friendly
  • Get listed on GPS and maps sites

EIGHT

REACH YOUR AUDIENCE ACROSS THE WEB

"If you go looking for a friend, you're going to find they're very scarce. If you go out to be a friend, you'll find them everywhere."

—*Zig Ziglar*

Chapter 8 is all about spreading the word by listing your business in key places across the Web, especially places where your target audience hangs out, reaping the SEO benefits of strong backlinks in the process.

Until recently, many SEO strategies were focused on acquiring backlinks from other websites for search ranking purposes only, with little concern for reaching an actual audience. This misdirected approach caused business owners and SEO consultants to spend countless hours and dollars obtaining backlinks using sources and strategies that Google and other search engines no longer value, or, worse yet, penalize for poor link-building practices (such as "link networks," closed networks of websites that charge site owners for links on their sites).

Your approach to listing your business and building links should be driven by the primary goal of reaching your target audience and establishing real relationships with potential customers, influencers, and members of the media. If doing so results in SEO benefits via backlinks to your website, you should certainly do everything you can to maximize the benefit of these links.

In this chapter, we'll cover basic concepts in Google-friendly backlinking and how to create optimized business listings on the top business directories, social media and community sites, and other effective sources of online visibility.

THE FOUR PILLARS OF ONLINE REACH

While there are hundreds of individual channels through which to reach your target audience, it's helpful to view potential traffic sources in a simple structure I refer to as "The Four Pillars of Reach." Many small business owners find this to be a helpful way to view and measure online reach, as no matter which specific sources or campaigns your business uses to attract customers, they can only get to your website through one of these four pillars of online reach.

▶ **Organic Search Traffic:** visits instigated by organic search results pages
▶ **Paid Search Traffic:** visits resulting from paid search ads, using Google AdWords, Yahoo, or Bing (PPC) campaigns, both text and display ads
▶ **Referring Sites:** site traffic coming directly from another website containing a link to your site—can include online directory listings (free and paid), social media sites, and other categories covered in this chapter
▶ **Direct Traffic:** visits from the user typing in your website directly into their browser—can be the result of brand recognition from your target audience (when people familiar with you go directly to your website), email marketing (clicking on a link to your site from an email you've sent), or offline marketing campaigns, such as print advertising, direct mail, or events, where you direct your offline audience to your site using printed material with your URL on it

Most of the types of websites we'll cover in this chapter can help generate traffic for multiple pillars at once, creating a great synergetic effect. For example, your business profile on Yelp.com can result in referral traffic as a result of people seeing your listing and clicking through to your site, direct traffic through increased brand awareness, and organic search traffic as a result of the SEO-friendly backlink to your website helping your own site rank higher on Google.

Each traffic source must be measured and leveraged to its full potential. We'll cover tools and strategies for measuring your traffic sources in more detail.

SEO LINK-BUILDING BASICS

One of the most important yet least understood concepts related to search engine optimization is the need to obtain high-quality backlinks to your site. As you'll recall from Chapter 6, Google's three-step process for ranking pages (crawling, indexing, and ranking) depends heavily on the authority to determine which websites outrank others.

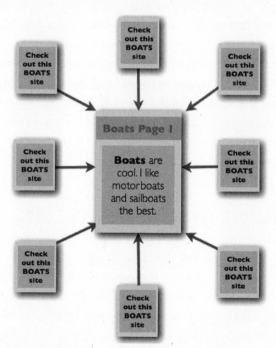

Figure 23: Obtaining backlinks to your site from trusted sources is still important for SEO.

For example, the reason Kayak.com maintains top billing in the organic search results for the keyword "travel" is because their site is seen as the "online authority" for travel-related topics. This authority comes largely in part from having so many other trusted websites link to them.

Therefore, if you want to be the online authority for your local niche, one of the best ways to do so is to ensure that other sites refer to you as such.

ALWAYS PUT HUMANS AHEAD OF SEARCH ENGINES

The best way to build high-quality backlinks is to consistently publish high-quality content that speaks to the interests and needs of your target audience, and market this content across several channels where your audience hangs out online. Many Google purists will tell you that any form of unnatural link building is a waste of time and you should just "let backlinks happen" naturally over time, meaning that if you produce great content, folks will eventually catch on and start mentioning it in their blogs and content, providing links from their sites to yours.

While I agree that you should never use robotic or "spammy" tactics to obtain backlinks, it would be foolish not to implement an online visibility strategy that takes backlinks into account. What's important is that you make decisions related to where to list your business online and obtain backlinks based on the goal of reaching your target audience first and reaping search engine or SEO benefits second.

NOT ALL LINKS ARE CREATED EQUAL

In the art and science of link building, quality rules: many sites have hundreds or even thousands of poor-quality, irrelevant links that are frequently "outranked" on Google by similar sites with a dozen or fewer high-quality links. It's important to spend your time focused on getting the highest quality links possible for your site.

The following criteria should be used to evaluate the potential value of a link to your site:

▶ **Relevance:** The website should be focused on a single topic that applies to:
  • Your community or location (such as a city directory or community news site)
  • Your business category (such as trade associations, or "vertical" directories like Lawyers.com or 1800Dentist.com)
▶ **Trust:** The website should have a higher page rank than yours, usually from being around longer with more relevant links itself.
▶ **Authority:** You should seek backlinks from established websites with high authority. This can (arguably) be measured by Google's Page Rank (http://www.prchecker.info/check_page_rank.php).

Although it may seem challenging to put these three criteria into practice, common sense applies: you want links from large, trusted websites that are focused on the same topic as yours.

BACKLINKS BEST PRACTICES

Now that you are familiar with the need for and potential sources of backlinks, here's a quick checklist of backlinking best practices that's sure to maximize your link-building efforts:

▶ **Never use software or spammy methods for backlinks.** Resist the temptation to engage with software applications, companies, and consultants offering cheap, quick-fix SEO and backlinking solutions. Use natural linking methods that are focused on your audience and treat the SEO benefits as secondary.
▶ **Diversify your anchor text.** One of the most prevalent, telltale signs of non-human backlinking is using identical, non-varied anchor text in your site's backlinks. For example, if 90 percent of the links to your site use the text "Boston Divorce Lawyer," you'll likely be punished by Google, as this is not a natural-looking pattern.
▶ **Deep links are better than shallow ones.** Another common mistake

in backlinking is to point all or most links to your home page. Most of your traffic, however, will land on your "deep," or inner, pages (blogs and content pages). It's critical to diversify your links throughout your site.

▶ **Obtain links from multiple sources.** Each of the top backlink sources covered in the last section should be used together as part of a healthy, varied backlinking system. Never place all or even most of your eggs in one basket—what works today may suddenly cease to work tomorrow.

RESOURCE: Use the Open Site Explorer from SEOmoz to Spy on Your Competitors

One of the fastest and most effective ways to outrank your competitors in organic search results is to find out exactly which backlinks are helping their sites rank for your target keywords and use this data to beat them at their own game: "out-link" them.

The Open Site Explorer (http://www.opensiteexplorer.org) is a tool that allows you to enter any URL on the web and obtain a list of their strongest backlinks. This tool is available at no charge for limited use (up to three searches per day), with a more powerful paid option available as well. Use it to track your links as well, setting a baseline before you set out to obtain strong backlinks and also re-running these reports frequently. If you use a consultant or external party to help build strong backlinks, ensure that they provide you with regular reports. Check these reports to ensure your new links are from relevant, authoritative sources, with keyword-rich, varied anchor text.

KEY CONCEPT: Avoid Black Hat Link-Building Penalties

Hundreds of marketing "experts" have spent millions of dollars of clients' money building "spammy" and robotic backlinks. These techniques, often referred to as "black hat SEO," are deployed with the goal of "fooling" Google, taking advantage of weaknesses in Google's ability to discern between natural and automated methods of link building. Google's recent "Panda" and "Penguin" algorithms, however, have targeted Web spam, poor backlink sources, and "over-optimization," so if you want to keep a clean slate with Google, base your link-building efforts around reaching your target audience and becoming an authority in your industry and community.

HOW TO GET THE MOST OUT OF YOUR WEB LISTINGS

Before you start clicking and begin registering your business all over cyberspace, lets make sure you get the biggest bang for your buck by covering a few best practices to use when listing your business online.

▶ **Apply the Funnel to Your Online Listings.** Regardless of the type of websites you list your business on—social media profiles, local business directories, or discussion forums—it's important to always keep in mind the trusted online marketing funnel:
  • **Reach:** using the right keywords in your business listings, descriptions, and anchor text
  • **Engagement:** Writing compelling copy that speaks to the needs of your audience, building trust and authority
  • **Conversion:** including an offer with a call to action, link, and phone number
▶ **Be Consistent.** Be sure to use the same screen name, photo or icon, and contact information across all of your online listings. This will not only help Google recognize and reward your involvement in online communities, but it will also reinforce your brand in the eyes of your audience.
▶ **Join the Discussion.** Don't treat your online presence as a one-time deal, creating a business profile and moving on. If you decide Facebook or online forums should be part of your strategy for increasing online reach, you have to be part of these communities, sharing valuable content, answering questions, and engaging in two-way communication. It's far better to pick two or three social media sites and really get engaged in them than to list your business on a dozen of them, never to return.

TOP TEN SOURCES FOR REACHING YOUR AUDIENCE

Here are the categories of sites that can be used to feed your pillars of online reach:

1. Friends and Family

One of the best and easiest ways to jumpstart your link-building efforts is to ask friends and family who have websites. I recommend you send out an email announcing your new site and ask them for a link. You can even call this a link-warming party (or not—depends on your sense of humor!).

2. Local Online Directories

As I covered briefly in the previous section, local directories are designed to help consumers find local products and services. You can set up each of these directory listings manually, or use a local listings service like Yext (http://www.yext.com) or UBL.org (https://www.ubl.org/). With local directory listings, it's critical that you're absolutely consistent with your business details.

TOP LOCAL BUSINESS DIRECTORIES:

- ▶ **Google+ Local** (http://www.google.com/+/learnmore/profile/)
- ▶ **Yahoo! Local** (http://local.yahoo.com)
- ▶ **Superpages** (http://www.superpages.com)
- ▶ **YellowBook** (http://www.yellowbook.com/)
- ▶ **Yellow Pages** (http://www.yellowpages.com)
- ▶ **Yelp** (http://www.yelp.com/)
- ▶ **Citysearch** (http://www.citysearch.com)
- ▶ **Merchant Circle** (http://www.merchantcircle.com)
- ▶ **Topix** (http://www.topix.com)
- ▶ **Insider Pages** (http://www.insiderpages.com)

RESOURCE: Local Directory Lists and Services
- ▶ Yext Power Listings: (http://www.yext.com/) allows you to create a

local business listing, syndicate it to the most trusted local directories, and monitor the results through a dashboard.

▶ Universal Business Listings (https://www.ubl.org/) is a similar site that allows you to create a single listing and syndicate it to all the top local business sites. In addition, UBL lists your business with several mobile and maps sites like OnStar, MapQuest, and more.

3. Local Community and Media Websites

A local authority site is simply an online hub whose content is centered around a specific community, such as a local newspaper website, Chamber of Commerce, local trade association, news station, community bulletin board, or an advertising site serving that specific community. A great strategy to get links from local authority sites is to volunteer to be a guest blogger, writing a valuable article for these sites or doing an interview related to your area of expertise. Press coverage is also a great opportunity to increase your local SEO authority. If you get a mention in the press, be sure to write a blog post or a press release (discussed in Chapter 10). Contact the media entity and ask for rights to publish and link to the articles or videos about your business. Finally, ensure that the media sites link back to yours.

4. Social Media Sites

Many business owners fall into the trap of getting involved in too many social media sites but not spending the time to understand or gain benefits from any one of them as a lead generation channel. Here's a quick list of surefire steps you can take for immediate social media traction:

▶ Claim your business name on social media sites ASAP!
▶ Use a professional and consistent logo on all profiles.
▶ Use your target keywords in profile descriptions.
▶ Focus on one or two sites that you can commit yourself to managing regularly.
▶ Join groups within your niche and interact with people, asking and answering questions.

▶ DO NOT SELL on these sites. Position your community as a resource, but refrain from spamming users with sales messages!

▶ Post links to valuable information. This helps users see you as an authority.

▶ Every time you publish a blog, video, or other content, post these articles on social sites.

▶ Include social media icons (Facebook "Like" buttons, for example) in all communications: website, emails, and newsletters/offline communications.

▶ Include a contact form on your Facebook business page.

▶ Experiment with paid Facebook ads. This will help you become familiar with the power of online demographic targeting.

TOP SOCIAL MEDIA SITES

First, claim your business name, starting an account on the "big four" social media sites—Facebook, Google+, LinkedIn, and Twitter. The first three allow you to create business pages. Be sure and include a link back to your website!

KEY CONCEPT: Build Your Audience Now to Set the Stage for Content Marketing

One of the most important activities you can engage in is increasing your count of fans and followers on social media sites. When you get to the last chapter of this book and launch your STAND OUT content marketing strategy, you'll be glad you did. Each piece of content you publish will be "syndicated" to your audience across several channels including social media, multimedia sites, and even to your own email list. The bigger your fan/follower base, the more reach your content will have. Pay attention to who follows your competitors on Facebook and Twitter and make friends with them. If you do the groundwork in this chapter, your content strategy will almost certainly increase your traffic and leads exponentially!

SOCIAL MEDIA RESOURCES

▶ **Knowem.com** (http://knowem.com/), helps you "search for and secure your brand name on over 575 social media sites."

▶ **Get 10,000 Fans** (http://get10000fans.com) is a great source for Facebook training and customized Facebook fan pages.

▶ **LKR Social Media** (http://lkrsocialmedia.com) is an authority on small business social media, offering great social media-focused content and resources.

▶ **LinkedInfluence** (http://linkedinfluence.com) is a very effective training course on using LinkedIn to grow your business.

5. Industry Websites

A great way to gain more authority within your niche is having other, more authoritative sites within your niche link to yours. Virtually every business category imaginable has at least a handful of associations, publications, or online directories focused on it. Getting your business listed on these sites may involve purchasing advertising, offering to write an article (which gets you attribution in the form of a link to your site), or simply contacting the site owners with a polite request.

6. Niche Blogs and Forums

Close cousins to industry directories and authority sites, these websites are centered on single, or small, closely related groups of, specific topics. Blogs and forums usually have tight-knit communities whose members spend significant time and effort discussing and sharing ideas focused on their passions or professions.

These sites are great platforms for interacting with other members of your community, keeping abreast of industry changes, tools, and best practices, and even meeting potential partners or clients. Industry blogs from other markets are also great sources for new ideas to blog about.

Blogs and forums are also great sources for relevant links to your website. Most forums and blogs allow visitors to register, creating a profile that includes their name and some personal information, including website URL and email address. There are two simple rules of engagement on these sites:

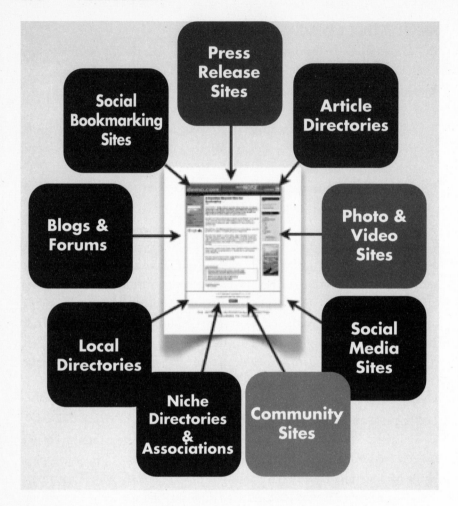

Figure 24: An effective visibility strategy should include listing your business on several categories of websites.

1. When adding your website, use your keywords in the anchor text instead of your web address URL alone ("Dallas Shoe Store" instead of "www.SmithsFootwear.com").
2. Never leave comments on blogs or forums for the sake of backlinks or SEO alone. This will only risk you getting

banned from these sites and potentially de-indexed from Google. Add value, always!

RESOURCE: Technorati Blog Directory

▶ **Technorati** (http://technorati.com/) is a search engine that's focused on blogs, with over 100 million blogs listed and counting. If you're having trouble finding industry blogs, use Technorati to find popular blogs related to your topic and business niche.

KEY CONCEPT: Use Guest Blogging to Increase Your Audience

A key step in understanding the "lay of the land" when it comes to your online niche is creating a list of highly trafficked, influential blogs. Create a list of the top five blogs that your audience already reads. You're probably already familiar with a few of them, but if not, do a Google search for "[your niche] blog" and check Technorati (above). Once you have a short list of power blogs in your industry, contact these bloggers and reach out to them via a short, personalized email, offering to write a guest blog or article for their site (this is called a "guest post"). Many bloggers will take you up on your offer, assuming you can produce an original, high-quality article that your/their audience will find useful. Guest posting can benefit both parties, providing a source of quality content for the site owner and additional traffic and exposure for the guest writer.

7. Social Bookmarking Sites

According to Wikipedia, "A social bookmarking service is a centralized online service which enables users to add, annotate, edit, and share bookmarks of Web documents."[5]

If you've ever saved a "bookmark" in your Web browser to allow for quick access, you're familiar with the concept. Social bookmarking simply applies this same process to the Web, allowing people to tag notable Web pages and share these bookmarks with others. The best way to use social bookmarking sites is to first join these communities, making friends and getting the lay of the land,

---

5 http://en.wikipedia.org/wiki/Social_bookmarking

then sharing helpful or interesting content with the community once you're familiar with these sites. Each time you publish a new piece of content, be sure to post links to the content on a few top bookmarking sites.

Social bookmarking sites can be a real driver of website traffic. Sites like Digg and Reddit that use popularity/voting systems can be great vehicles for getting your content viewed by hundreds or even thousands of new visitors. In Chapter 10, we'll cover a process for automatically syndicating your content to social bookmarking sites. For now, just be sure to list your business using the best practices outlined on the previous pages.

TOP SOCIAL BOOKMARKING SITES

- ▶ Digg (http://www.digg.com)
- ▶ Stumbleupon (http://www.stumbleupon.com)
- ▶ Delicious (http://www.delicious.com)
- ▶ Reddit (http://www.reddit.com)
- ▶ Pinterest (http://pinterest.com)
- ▶ Fark (http://www.fark.com)

8. Photo and Video Sharing Sites

Multimedia sharing sites like YouTube, Vimeo, Picasa, and Flickr may seem more appropriate for checking out the latest shots of kittens grappling, but a deeper look will reveal several powerful applications for small business owners. Creating a YouTube channel for your business can spark a whole new channel for online visibility, traffic, and leads, not to mention backlinks. Register your business on one or two of these sites:

TOP PHOTO AND VIDEO SITES

- ▶ YouTube (http://youtube.com)
- ▶ Vimeo (https://vimeo.com)

▶ Daily Motion (http://www.dailymotion.com)

▶ Metacafe (http://www.metacafe.com)

▶ Instagram (instagram.com)

▶ Flickr (http://www.flickr.com)

▶ Picasa (http://picasa.google.com)

9. Article Directories

Once again, Wikipedia says it best (http://en.wikipedia.org/wiki/Article_directory):

"An article directory is a website with collections of articles written about different subjects. Sometimes article directories are referred to as content farms, which are websites created to produce mass content."

In a nutshell, article directories are sites that allow outside authors to publish content. For example, if you were a family lawyer trying to generate traffic and links to your site, you could sign up for a reputable article directory like eHow, write an original article called "5 Tips For a Divorce-Free Marriage," and publish it on the directory.

TOP ARTICLE DIRECTORIES

Article directories have undergone a fair amount of scrutiny lately in terms of their "link value." Google has even gone so far as to de-index several low-quality directories out there, due mainly to their liberal rules related to duplicate and poor content.

However, if you take the time to write a truly helpful, quality article and publish it on one of the following higher quality article directories, you'll enjoy notable "link juice":

▶ eHow.com

▶ Squidoo.com

▶ EzineArticles.com

► HubPages.com
► Examiner.com

10. Press Release Sites

The purpose of a press release, or news release, is to announce something new or noteworthy related to your business—like an innovative product or service—with the goal of getting your release "picked up" and published by media outlets, thereby gaining traffic to your site and obtaining backlinks to your site.

When used properly, press releases can be very effective. It's important to use them sparingly, though—only when you have a truly interesting or newsworthy story to tell. I also recommend using a paid service like http://prweb.com since, as with many things, you get what you pay for.

Although press releases may not be a core element of your SEO and backlinking strategy, they can be extremely effective. I recommend you try at least one or two tastefully executed releases when the need arises.

Top Press Release Sites

► PrWeb (PRWeb.com)
► PR Newswire (http://www.prnewswire.com)
► PR.com (http://www.pr.com)
► BusinessWire (http://www.businesswire.com)

PRESS RELEASE RESOURCES:

► **Mashable's list of "20+ Free Press Release Sites"** (http://mashable.com/2007/10/20/press-releases/)
► **Great Article: How to Use the Modern Press Release** (http://www.copyblogger.com/how-to-use-the-modern-press-release/)

▶ **Article: How to Write a Press Release That Gets Attention:** (http://www.problogger.net/archives/2010/12/12/how-to-write-a-press-release-that-gets-attention/)

▶ **Video: PrWEB in Plain English: (**http://www.youtube.com/watch?v=1YB74txAaTc)

WHAT ABOUT PAID ONLINE ADVERTISING?

While these paid sources can be great sources of qualified traffic and leads, hold off on paid campaigns until your online marketing funnel is clearly defined and measured. I have seen too many businesses spend hundreds and sometimes thousands of dollars on AdWords campaigns, directories, and other paid campaigns that resulted in a very poor ROI due to improper campaign setup, traffic driven to poorly converting Web pages, and lack of measurement of results.

Once you implement your complete STAND OUT Online Marketing Strategy, you should most certainly invest in pay-per-click (PPC) and other forms of paid advertising, particularly Google AdWords. But for now, spend your time and money on creating and marketing great content. Once you have a solid foundation in place—a website with specific landing pages, helpful blog and/or video content, and Analytics to track your results—you'll see much greater results (and spend less money) with paid traffic sources, as you'll be plugging additional traffic sources into a funnel that's already working.

CHAPTER SUMMARY

It's important to emphasize that no single ranking strategy can produce number-one results—you must implement all of the strategies for consistent long-term results. While getting and staying in Google's "good graces" may seem like a complicated and perhaps daunting undertaking, it only takes a little knowledge and a bit of common sense.

As part of their never-ending quest to produce the best possible experience for its 1 billion monthly users, Google frequently changes its search ranking algorithm. These changes seldom yield adverse affects on high-quality websites that produce high-quality, original content often and obtain backlinks from trusted, ethical sources.

A critical step down the path from content consumer to content publisher is getting your business listed in each of the categories of websites covered in this chapter. Doing so will lay the foundation for content marketing strategy and allow you to start building an audience of qualified fans and followers.

CHAPTER CHECKLIST

✔ **Understand the 4 Pillars of Online Reach**
- Organic search traffic
- Paid search traffic
- Referring sites
- Direct traffic

✔ **Apply Backlinking Best Practices for SEO Benefits**
- Avoid automated link-building tactics
- Diversify your anchor text
- Build "deep links" to all pages to your site
- Obtain links from multiple sources

✔ **Get the Most Out of Your Online Listings**
- Apply the funnel to your listings
- Be consistent with your branding
- Join the discussion

✔ **List Your Business in the Right Places**
- Friends and family
- Local online directories
- Local community and media websites
- Social media sites
- Niche and industry sites

- Blogs and forums
- Social bookmarking sites
  ◊ Photo and video sharing sites
  ◊ Article directories
  ◊ Press release sites

NINE

MEASURE YOUR ONLINE MARKETING FUNNEL

"That which is measured improves. That which is measured and reported improves exponentially."

—*Karl Pearson, Pearson's Law*

When applied to small business online marketing, the quote above represents one of the most important, powerful, and business- and life-changing concepts you're likely to encounter.

Recall Marketing Metrics from the 5M's of Marketing in Chapter 1. Measurement and, more specifically, managing and making decisions based on actual, quantitative feedback (metrics) is what separates the successful from the unsuccessful. By nature, small business owners face immense challenges in finding the time and money to spend on business growth in the form of marketing and advertising. These constraints create a very slim margin for error, as most small business owners can't afford to make too many mistakes.

Given this razor-thin margin for error, you'd think that most small business owners would be masters of metrics, paying close attention to which sources are resulting in qualified leads by measuring both prospects and conversions at every step of the online marketing funnel. However, this is seldom the case, as illustrated by the masses of small business owners I've interacted with. In fact, most of the time, the opposite is true: most business owners practice "spray and pray" marketing, spending money on multiple marketing and advertising sources, and making spending decisions based on feelings.

BENEFITS OF MEASURING YOUR ONLINE MARKETING

Getting serious about metrics-driven marketing can benefit your bottom line in several ways:

▶ **Trimming the fat:** Without metrics, you have no idea if you're spending too much or too little on any traffic or lead source. Imagine what would happen if you could confidently either kill or improve your non-performing marketing channels and maintain those which have proven themselves to be real winners.

▶ **Continual improvement:** What if, through studying your website traffic patterns, you realized that one of your pay-per-click (PPC) ads was producing double the traffic or leads? Or if a call to action on one of your Web pages generated three times the conversion rate as other offers? What would happen if you tested this winning offer on all your Web pages?

▶ **Focusing your energy:** Using metrics to measure which content your visitors are finding most engaging can help you better focus all your messaging and resources toward areas that are sure to have the highest impact on your audience.

Small tweaks add up to huge profits. Recall from Chapter 7 that, all things being equal, if all you did was increase your conversion rate from 1 percent to 2 percent, you'd have twice as many leads and clients to show for it. That could add up to double the revenue! Metrics are the key to improvement.

TAKE THE FIVE-MINUTE MARKETING METRICS COMPETENCY TEST

To help set a baseline of knowledge and determine the health of your metrics-based marketing mindset, take a moment to answer the following questions without looking up the answers:

1. Where does your site rank on Google for your targeted search terms?
2. How many unique visitors does your website get each day?
3. What percentage of your visitors convert into leads (either Web or phone leads)?
4. How much are you paying to acquire a new lead?
5. What is the average value of a new lead?
6. What percentage of leads convert into sales?
7. What is the value of a new customer to your business?
8. What is the lifetime value of a customer?
9. What is the ROI for each of your sources of leads?

If you're like most small business owners, you probably have a very good sense of answers to questions 4 and 7, as the flow of leads and customers is one thing that keeps most of us up at night. But you must be able to answer all nine, or at least have the answers to them within easy reach. This is true for all kinds of businesses, in all markets, period.

By the end of this chapter, you'll have the tools and metrics in place to track all of your marketing, saving and making a ton more money.

TRACKING TOOLS USED IN THIS CHAPTER

This chapter sets up a plan that will streamline the setup and management of your marketing program, making tracking your marketing simple, fast, and affordable. We'll use the same three-step online marketing funnel to do so, tracking specific metrics for our Reach, Engagement, and Conversion. We will also implement a basic "overarching tool" to help track the ROI on all of your marketing, both offline and online.

In order to do this, we'll be using three types of tools:

1. **A Search Engine Rankings Tool:** Since organic traffic will always be a big source of new visitors and leads on your website, it's important to measure how you're ranking for your target search terms. In order to accomplish this, you can use a basic,

free tool, or a more robust, paid tool. Both will be covered in the next section.

2. **A Tool to Measure Web Analytics:** While I recommend the industry standard, Google Analytics, there are several other great tools out there. What's important is that you have a tool that provides immediate insight into your visitors' behavior in arriving at and interacting with your website.

3. **A Basic Excel Spreadsheet:** We'll use a spreadsheet to create a customized "Marketing Dashboard" for your business. There are dozens of robust, expensive applications, but to begin with, we'll use a simpler, more modest tool.

THE SIMPLE WAY TO MEASURE YOUR ONLINE MARKETING FUNNEL

Let's look now at a few key metrics related to each of these stages and how to measure them properly.

The Online Marketing Funnel

Goals		Measures
Increase visibility and traffic from your target audience	**REACH**	Search engine rankings, impressions, website traffic
Encourage audience to consume your content and view you as a trusted authority	ENGAGEMENT	Time on site, bounce rate, social shares, page views
Generate qualified leads, subscribers, and customers	CONVERSION	Leads (phone and Web forms), opt-ins

Figure 25: The online marketing funnel as related to metrics

Step 1: MEASURE YOUR ORGANIC SEARCH RANKINGS

An extremely important measurement to monitor is where your website ranks organically on Google SERPs (Search Engine Results Pages) for your target search terms, ideally in comparison to your main competitors. Specifically, you need to know how exactly your Web pages rank for each of these search terms. As you can imagine, you'll see much more website traffic if you rank number one for "Boston Furniture Store" rather than number nine. By tracking your rankings, you'll be able to pinpoint which search terms need "SEO love" in the form of website changes or additional backlinks.

HOW TO MEASURE SEARCH RANKINGS

- ▶ **Google Webmaster Tools** (see Chapter 5 for installation instructions) automatically tracks which search terms are showing up on search results pages, along with the number of impressions (how many times your keywords were displayed), click-through rates, and even changes in rankings. The downside of using Webmaster Tools is that you can't add your own search terms, meaning you only get information related to search terms that you're already ranking for, and additionally you can't compare your rankings with those of your competitors.
- ▶ **SEOmoz Rank Tracker** (http://www.seomoz.org/rank-tracker) is a paid tool offering many robust features. According to the website, the tool "retrieves search engine rankings for pages and keywords and stores them for easy comparison later. PRO members can also track selected rankings over time and can even sign up for email alerts to be notified about changes."
- ▶ **Bright Local** (http://brightlocal.com/) is the tool my company uses and recommends to small businesses. This tool's search rankings reports (see Figure 26) are very simple to use, while still providing powerful data. What I really like about Bright Local is that it shows where your site ranks both presently and historically, allowing you to monitor which keywords are moving up and down in the rankings.

san diego criminal defense attorney |◇×	✦ 2
san diego criminal defense lawyer |◇×	✦ 2
san diego criminal lawyer |◇×	⬇ 5
attorney criminal law san diego |◇×	⬇ 4
best criminal defense lawyer in san diego |◇×	⬇ 3
best criminal lawyer in san diego |◇×	✦ 4
	✦ 39
best criminal lawyer san diego |◇×	⬇ 4
criminal attorney san diego |◇×	⬇ 3
criminal lawyers san diego |◇×	⬇ 5
drug lawyers san diego |◇×	✦ 8
arrest warrant san diego |◇×	⬇ 5
	⬇ 6
attorneys san diego |◇×	✦ 5
best criminal attorney san diego |◇×	⬇ 4
best criminal defense attorney in san diego |◇×	● 3

Figure 26: An example of Bright Local's search rankings reports

RAVEN TOOLS RESOURCES

Raven SEO Tools Setup Guide: http://media.raventools.com/documents/SEO-Setup-Guide-062411.pdf

http://www.youtube.com/watch?v=PwB48KXAdc4&feature=share&list=PL46B1044D9B72299F

Setting up Raven Tools is a snap: simply authorize Raven to sync with your Google Analytics account and enter your keywords from your Keyword Map and your top competitors, and you're off to the races.

▶ **Measure Benchmarks:** Obviously the benchmark for search engine rankings is that you want your targeted search terms to rank within the top three organic placements. This is easier said than done, but again, by setting a baseline, you've actually taken an important step that few small business owners take. Measuring where your targeted keywords are ranking in comparison to those of your competitors will start you down the path of continual improvement.

▶ **Best Practices:**
- Include both local and non-local versions of your keywords (i.e., track both "dallas hvac repair" and "hvac repair").
- Measure what's already working: Don't miss the keywords that are already driving traffic to your website. From Raven Tools or Google Analytics, simple go to Analytics > Google Analytics Keywords and you'll see the top search terms that are already bringing visitors to your website. Oftentimes a few SEO tweaks (writing new content or sprucing up existing pages) can bring a keyword that's already working several steps up in the rankings!
- Add all new content to your SERP tracker: If you make a new video called "5 Ways to Extend the Life of Your Air Conditioner," add the search term(s) you are targeting with this new video to your SERP tracker (e.g., "extend air-conditioning life").
- Tag your keywords in order to know what's working: Raven Tools and other rank tracking tools allow you to "tag" each search term. Using the above example, you could tag your new search term, "air conditioning life," with the tag, "Videos." If you do this consistently, you will gain great insight into which traffic channels are driving visitors to your site.

Step 2: MEASURE YOUR ONLINE WEBSITE TRAFFIC

Google Analytics Overview

As the business and website owner, you need to log in to Google Analytics and understand how to find and decipher the basic metrics related to the three stages of your online marketing funnel. Don't wait for a monthly report from a highly paid consultant (who probably did little more by way of reporting than set up automatically emailed reports from Analytics in the first place). By then, it's too late. You need real-time access and insight into what's happening with your website and online marketing.

What Kinds of Data Are Available in Analytics

Google Analytics reveals some incredible data that's extremely useful for improving your website and online marketing right out of the gate:

▶ Who's coming to your website
▶ Where they are located
▶ What type of device they were on (PC or mobile)
▶ Which websites lead them to yours
▶ What search terms they used to get to your site from Google
▶ How long they stayed on your site
▶ Which pages (blogs, articles) are the most popular
▶ How many Web pages they visited and which ones
▶ Which pages they exited your site from
▶ How many visitors were new vs. how many returning

And with just a small amount of customization, Google Analytics can become an ultra-powerful, turnkey management tool, providing a complete view of conversions from both free and paid marketing sources. Here are just some of the data points available with just a few small tweaks:

▶ Conversion rate: the percentage of visitors that become leads
▶ Phone tracking: which search terms and content resulted in phone calls
▶ CPC tracking: which ads and keywords in your AdWords campaigns are generating leads

Keep It Simple

You can already imagine how access to this much data can help inform your Web design, content, and marketing strategies, but it's important to keep it simple and stay focused on a few core metrics that you most need to effectively measure your online marketing funnel. Once you have this "metrics foundation" in place, feel free to "take the blue pill" and dive into the wormhole of analytics.

Measuring Your Website Traffic

Once you've established a system for monitoring your search engine rankings, we'll use Google Analytics to measure key metrics for each stage of the online marketing funnel, starting with one of the most important "Reach" metrics: traffic.

KEY CONCEPT: Understanding Common Analytics Terms

Many people get confused by the multiple traffic-related terms floating around cyberspace. Let's clear this up before we move on:

▶ **Browser Cookie:** "A cookie, also known as an HTTP cookie, Web cookie, or browser cookie, is usually a small piece of data sent from a website and stored in a user's Web browser while a user is browsing a website. When the user browses the same website in the future, the data stored in the cookie can be retrieved by the website to notify the website of the user's previous activity. . . . This can include clicking particular buttons, logging in, or a record of which pages were visited by the user even months or years ago," (Wikipedia: http://en.wikipedia.org/wiki/HTTP_cookie).

▶ **Website Visit:** When someone or something (like a Googlebot) visits a website. Each time you visit a website for the first time, that site places a "cookie" on your browser. This is how Google can distinguish between new and returning visitors. Even if you visit fifteen pages on a website during the same browsing session, this still counts as one visit.

▶ **Unique Visitor:** A unique user or person visiting a site. For example, if you visited the same website four times, Google Analytics would record this as "1 unique visitor and 4 visits." This is why the number of visits is usually higher than unique visitors (see Figure 27).

▶ **Page Views:** The total number of pages visited within your website within a given time frame. This number can be divided by the number of visits to give you the pages per visit (Figure 27). Obviously the higher number, the better, as more page views per visit indicates greater user engagement.

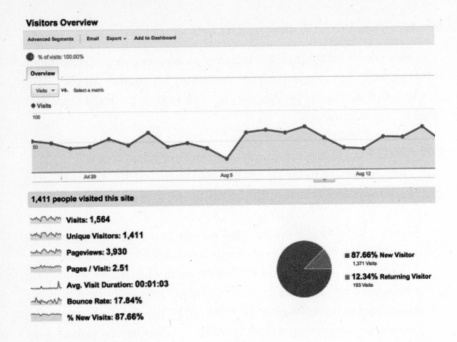

Figure 27: Google Analytics displays valuable metrics within hours of installing the application.

▶ **Benchmarks:** The prime traffic number is Unique Visitors (also referred to as "uniques"). The benchmark for monthly unique visitors is simple: measure the current number and increase it. For most local, small business sites, 400 to 4,000 unique visitors per month is within the typical range. Unique Visitors will be the litmus test for the "Reach" phase of the funnel, as most of your promotional efforts (SEO, paid advertising, and offline marketing) are designed to drive people to your website, where most of your conversions happen. Conversions happen in other locations where the business places a call to action. These "offsite" activities must be tracked and scrutinized against the online marketing funnel as well.

▶ **Best Practices:** The important thing is knowing where your visitors are coming from, as this is the only way to move the needle on traffic. Once you've set a baseline for site traffic, it's important to dig a bit more deeply and find out why your traffic is increasing or decreasing, as well as who is visiting your website and for how long and how they got there in the first place. The following Google Analytics reports work together to provide a clear picture of your current traffic and opportunities for improvement.

Demographics: where (what country and city) your visitors are coming from. This is simple to access from your Analytics Dashboard (Audience > Demographics > Location). Paying attention to where your visitors are located helps to ensure that your content and SEO strategies are targeting the right market. This report can come in handy in helping you segment your market from country right down to city level (or even further with some light customization).

▶ **Benchmarks:** Naturally, you want most of your traffic to come from your target market(s). If your business utilizes a hybrid approach, both selling products online and serving a local market, you have a unique Analytics model that's outside the scope of this book.

▶ **Best Practices:** It's important to monitor where your visitors are coming from and, more importantly why. If you run radio, print, or other media campaigns targeting specific regions, it's critical to measure the reach resulting from your investments. It's also critical to ensure that your SEO and content writing efforts are hitting their mark, i.e., reaching the right visitors. For instance, many local business website owners write great content but fail to "localize" it, resulting in an unfortunate lack of targeted traffic.

Traffic Sources: Not to be confused with "referring sites" (the specific websites that lead visitors to yours), traffic sources are made up of the four pillars of traffic as described in Chapter 8: search, referral, direct, and paid traffic. It's important to pay attention to where your traffic's coming from, not only to help pinpoint untapped sources for greater Reach, but also to identify underperforming sources.

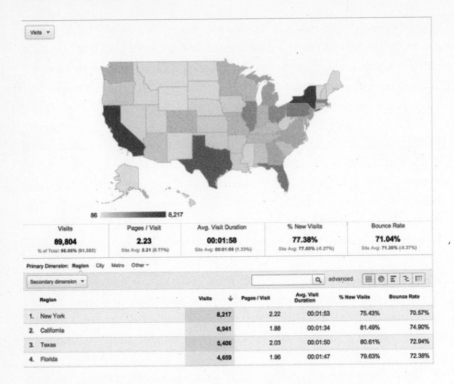

Figure 28: The Demographics Location report is a great way to measure targeted traffic.

▶ **Benchmarks:** There is no standard ratio for traffic sources, as your ideal mix should be based on what works for your business and your unique reach strategy. For example, a local retailer of decorative beads and craft supplies may be able to drive a ton of paid traffic (Google AdWords) to its site, based on the less-competitive, lower cost of keywords, while a "mesothelioma lawyer" may use an SEO-heavy traffic strategy based on the unfeasible high cost of paid traffic. Yet another approach may be a B2B cloud software company who relies on referral traffic from sales channels and partner sites. As you become more adept at Analytics and metrics-based marketing, you'll certainly find your ideal mix.

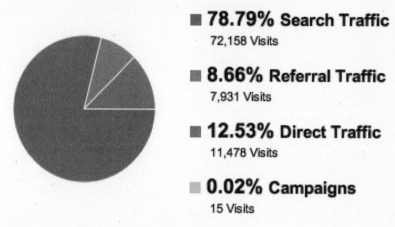

91,582 people visited this site

78.79% Search Traffic
72,158 Visits

8.66% Referral Traffic
7,931 Visits

12.53% Direct Traffic
11,478 Visits

0.02% Campaigns
15 Visits

Figure 29: Traffic sources in Google Analytics

▶ **Best Practices:** The best way to manage your site's traffic sources is to measure, test, and improve all available channels of online Reach and traffic. Diversification is also a good insurance policy—you should be generating traffic from other websites, search engines, and paid sources. The key is that you test which traffic actually converts (covered in the next section).

Organic Search Traffic: This report shows a ranked list of keywords, typed into Google and other search engines that brought visitors to your site. Reviewing this keyword list not only reveals opportunities for new content, but also helps ensure you're getting targeted traffic— visits from your target customers. For example, if you run a sporting goods store, but are getting a significant amount of traffic from the term "football tickets," you can't expect high conversion rates from your site.

Organic search traffic reports can also reveal insights into the rest of your marketing funnel as well. This report reveals helpful metrics relating to user Engagement including Pages/Visit, Average Visit Duration, and Bounce Rate (Figure 30).

	Keyword	Visits	Pages/Visit	Avg. Visit Duration	% New Visits	Bounce Rates
1.	(not provided)	117	1.41	00:02:29	85.47%	71.79%
2.	(not set)	85	1.65	00:00:51	78.82%	72.94%
3.	lawyer ratings directory	16	1.25	00:04:20	93.75%	43.75%
4.	law firm seo	11	1.64	00:02:41	45.45%	54.55%
5.	aaron fletcher seo	5	2.40	00:09:23	80.00%	20.00%
6.	lawyer facebook cover	5	1.00	00:00:00	100.00%	100.00%
7.	law facebook covers	4	1.00	00:00:00	100.00%	100.00%

Figure 30: The Organic Search Traffic reveals more than just online Reach.

▶ **Benchmarks:** The important benchmark for organic search traffic is growth. If you have a new and relatively small site, you should focus on aggressive growth from organic traffic. This will occur mainly by writing quality content catered to your target audience.

▶ **Best Practices:** The best way to increase organic traffic is to ensure you're publishing new content often and that this content targets the right search terms while speaking to the needs of your audience. In most cases, lack of organic traffic can be attributed to failing to utilize SEO basics. It's important to look at your "Search Overview" report (Figure 32) and be sure that the search queries responsible for most of your traffic are targeted toward your business.

An additional way to increase your organic traffic is to look at what's already working and improve it. Simply view your Search Overview report and look for high-search-volume and well-targeted keywords that are already generating hits to your site and write more content to increase your online reach for these keywords.

Referring Sites: Using the scenario in the image above, viewing a "referring sites" Analytics report would itemize the specific websites that resulted in 138 referring visits.

Keeping track of referring sites provides insightful feedback into which REACH campaigns are working on drawing more eyeballs to your site. For example, if you suddenly notice a spike in traffic from a forum you belong to or a local community media site, you'd better be investigating the cause of this and doing what you can to turn the spike into a geyser of traffic! This information can also help you determine where to place your time and money in building traffic.

▶ **Benchmarks:** Most healthy sites draw from 15 to 30 percent referral traffic. Again, the ideal ratio depends on your model.
▶ **Best Practices:** As previously mentioned, it's critical to know where your quality traffic is coming from. You may find that you get a great number of high-quality visits from paid sources like online directories, or from reviews sites like Yelp or Merchant Circle. What's important is that you find new sources for referring traffic and measure their effectiveness, all the way through conversion!

Social Referrals: This is a subset of "referring sites," but one that warrants its own focus and measurement. Syndicating your content across multiple social and content sites will be a key component in your content marketing strategy. As such, it will become increasingly important to pay attention to how well your social media channels drive traffic to your site.

The Social Sources report (Social > Sources) is a great starting point for measuring your Reach attributed to your off-page interactions.

▶ **Benchmarks:** This is strongly dependent on your business' content marketing strategy (we'll cover this soon enough). The takeaway is that you should monitor your social reach.
▶ **Best Practices:** The two most important activities any small business should be doing when it comes to social media sites are:
  • Increasing your following on social sites
  • Publishing and sharing helpful content on these sites that drives visitors to your own site.

OTHER MEASURES OF ONLINE REACH

As the definition of Reach describes, you can measure any vehicle or source of visibility for your business. These include impressions (for display and PPC advertising), circulation or audience for print, radio or television, and many more. You now have a solid understanding and the ability to start tracking these fundamental metrics easily and properly. This foundation will provide you with the platform you need to move forward, adding metrics to your heart's content.

Step 3: MEASURE USER ENGAGEMENT

Engagement is simply measured by how well your content resonates with your audience as they interact with it. With the exception of social media engagement (Sharing, "Liking" and "Following"), most Engagement Metrics can be measured using Google Analytics. In fact, many of the most useful metrics are prominently displayed as soon as you log in to GA, right on your dashboard.

Returning Visits: Few actions show more engagement than when someone arrives at your website and finds it useful enough to come back again.

As Figure 31 illustrates, you can see what percentage of users are new in comparison to the percentage returning, right from your Google Analytics dashboard. However, if you'd like to dig a bit more deeply and learn just how many times and how recently your visitors have come by, you can access the "Frequency & Recency" report (Standard Reporting > Audience > Behavior > Frequency & Recency).

- ▶ **Benchmarks:** There is no solid baseline for return visits, as these metrics vary widely for each type of business and marketing strategy. For example, a retail business may place a great deal of emphasis on creating and measuring repeat business, driving existing customers back to their website with offers, coupons, or seasonal content, while a business with a model that serves clients just once, such as a divorce lawyer, may place more value on new client acquisition. What's important is that you set goals for repeat visitors and measure against them.
- ▶ **Best Practices:** The core secret to getting more repeat visits to your site is to ensure that their first visit was useful enough to leave a great impression. You can create this scenario by publishing great content. The next step is to stay in contact with your visitors, maintaining a solid relationship via email, social media, or even offline methods like direct mail and telephone (see Chapter 13 for getting

started with nurture campaigns). There are several reasons to trigger communication with your audience: announcing a new blog post on your site, communicating a sale or special promotion, or sharing content from others that you think your visitors will find useful.

Frequency & Recency

Advanced Segments	Email	Export ▾	Add to Dashboard	Shortcut BETA

% of visits: 100.00%

Distribution

Count of Visits   Days Since Last Visit

Visits

2,002

% of Total: 100.00% (2,002)

Count of Visits	Visits	Pageviews	Percentage of total ■ Visits ■ Pageviews	
1	1,499	2,779	74.88% 75.54%	
2	197	339	9.84% 9.21%	
3	78	181	3.90% 4.92%	
4	56	102	2.80% 2.77%	
5	37	64	1.85% 1.74%	
6	25	35	1.25% 0.95%	
7	17	18	0.85% 0.49%	
8	13	31	0.65% 0.84%	
9-14	35	60	1.75% 1.63%	
15-25	17	28	0.85% 0.76%	
26-50	20	30	1.00% 0.82%	
201+	8	12	0.40% 0.33%	

Figure 31: The Frequency & Recency report provides useful engagement metrics.

Time on Site: Displayed as "Avg. Visit Duration" on your GA dashboard, this is a simple measure of how long the average visitor stays on your site. Measuring your site's average visit duration is simple—the summarized numbers are right on the main screen (Figure 27). As with all metrics, you can dig as deeply as you'd like, comparing visitor duration for organic vs. paid, articles vs. videos, and so on. For now, get into the practice of increasing the amount of time folks are staying on your site. Remember, every second amounts to an increased chance of a visitor becoming your next customer.

▶ **Benchmarks:** Most experts would agree that an average of two minutes or more on your site is a good start. If your site averages one minute or less, this should be a red flag that you're either not reaching the right traffic or your site design and content need a major makeover.

▶ **Best Practices:** The best ways to increase time spent on your site is to make sure that your content is well written and focused on the needs of your target audience. Another useful tool is online video. The best way to keep a visitor engaged on your site for five or ten minutes is putting up a helpful five or ten-minute video.

Pages per Visit: Also displayed in your GA Dashboard is the "Pages/ Visit" metric. Optimizing your website and content to increase this number is a surefire path to increased user engagement and the leads or opt-ins that'll surely follow. Once you've gotten over the hurdle of getting visitors to stay on your site and consume your content, the next step is to get them to consume more than one page of it. You don't want otherwise engaged website visitors to leave your website early, only because they were unaware of other helpful content you've made available.

▶ **Benchmarks:** Anything greater than two is a great number to shoot for. This might seem low, but remember this is an average. If you find a way to increase pages per visit to five, ten, or more, do so by all means.

▶ **Best Practices:** Increasing pages per visit usually comes down to a solid navigation and site structure that makes it easy for your visitors to access other content related to what they're currently reading or watching. Most CMS platforms use "categories" to help organize articles and content. Another great way to increase page views is to include a "similar articles" or "next steps" section at the end of all your content pages.

Bounce Rate: This often ill-defined term describes the percentage of visitors to a website who leave that site without visiting additional pages. Many people believe that a bounce is defined by how long a visitor stays on your site, but this is not the case. If I Google, "How to know if my home has termites," and land on your article titled as such, hitting my back button after spending ten minutes reading the article is still a bounce! In most cases, bounces are a sign that someone has arrived on the wrong website, at least in their mind.

Your site's bounce rate is shown in your GA dashboard. As with other core metrics, you can measure bounce rates against all other reporting criteria. Want to know what percentage of Facebook users come to your site and bounce compared to those from Twitter? There's a report for that. Start with the overall metrics and get more granular over time.

▶ **Benchmarks:** Much like Returning Visits, this metric varies greatly depending on your business niche. For most local business websites, I recommend starting with a benchmark of 50 percent and working from there, but the following schedule may assist you in setting a more specific goal:

Google Analytics Benchmark Averages for Bounce Rate (http://www.blastam.com/blog/index.php/2012/02/what-is-bounce-rate/)
- 40-60 percent content websites
- 30-50 percent lead generation sites
- 70-98 percent blogs
- 20-40 percent retail sites
- 10-30 percent service sites
- 70-90 percent landing pages

▶ **Best Practices:** A higher than normal bounce rate can be caused by any number of issues we've already discussed, including poor design, navigation, or usability. A significant number of bounces are due to untargeted traffic, some degree of which is, to an extent, unavoidable.

It's important to monitor which search queries result in high bounce rates. To do this, go to your "Search Overview" report (Traffic Sources > Search > Overview) and you'll see a column that displays bounce rates for each inbound search term (Figure 15).

You can do the same for your Content. Go to your "Pages" report (Content > Pages) to see which pages on your site are producing the greatest and fewest bounces.

Figure 32: GA allows you to see which search queries and content resulted in high bounce rates.

OTHER MEASURES OF USER ENGAGEMENT

To get a complete picture of user engagement, you'll have to go outside Google and your website. Any place where users interact with your content is a place to measure engagement. Any time someone watches a YouTube video you created, or reads a guest blog post or comment you left on a LinkedIn discussion group, they are engaging with your content. Although you'll likely want to start tracking this "offsite" engagement, it's important to establish a solid foundation and get the basics down first.

Besides, most truly engaged folks will end up on your website anyway, at which point you'll catch them in your "referring sites" reports.

One significant on-site measure of user engagement is social sharing. Each time someone "shares," "Likes" or "re-tweets" a piece of content from your site is a major "double-win," as your content has now been made available to that person's social network and is also measured by Google as a sign of quality and authority.

Step 4: MEASURE CONVERSIONS

All the care you've taken in selecting your target market, refining your writing skills, and streamlining your Web design should culminate in the bottom of the funnel. Conversions are the tip of your marketing spear, the final exam to clearly gauge the effectiveness of all your marketing efforts. In the real world of small business marketing, there are only two grades handed out: A's and F's.

Of the three phases of the online marketing funnel, conversions are the most straightforward and the simplest to track, because all roads lead to the bottom. For each visitor, viewer, and audience member who enters your funnel, there are only two possible outcomes: they either A) take action or B) fall off along the way.

Conversion tracking is very easy to set up, so not doing so is a marketing tragedy, as you've already gone 90 percent of the way in measuring your funnel. We must close the loop and learn how to discern which search terms, traffic sources, and content on our site are generating valuable leads. You can't afford not to measure the ROI of your marketing expenses.

The good news is that setting up Google Analytics to track conversions is a fairly straightforward process. After implementing a few slight customizations, tools, and tricks, you'll have a complete online funnel tracking system in place.

GOOGLE ANALYTICS GOALS

Analytics Goals are defined as the measurement of a desired user behavior. The best way to understand the concept of Goals is to think of e-commerce sites using goals to track shopping cart sales. Online merchants are masters at tracking visitors' behavior effectively with Goals through each step of the "buying funnel"—from selecting products to registering, to the shopping cart, and finally, checking out. A conversion is synonymous with a "goal completion." Goals are perfectly designed to use for small business lead tracking as well. Each time a visitor fills out a web form can be counted as a goal and measured in Google Analytics.

Using Goals to Track Web Leads and Opt-ins

Goals are nothing more than page views. For example, if you want to track conversions, you can set up the following systems for response each time a lead form gets filled out on your site:

1. **Create a "Thank you page" that will be sent to users after they complete your form. This will be used to track goal completions.**
2. **Configure your lead form to place users on this thank you page. Nearly any Web form provider you use will allow you to set this up (see Chapter 7 for more information).**
3. **From your main Analytics menu, go to "Conversions > Goals."**
4. **Name your goal in the "Goal Name" field. Be descriptive, as you will likely use several types of conversion goals (downloading a white paper, opting in to a mailing list, etc.). Next, ensure "Active" is selected, select "URL Destination" as the Goal Type, paste your "thank you" URL into the space provided (see following figure), and save your new goal using the "save" button on the bottom of the screen.**

Your goals will now appear in your analytics reports, allowing you to quickly measure and improve upon your website's conversion rate from Web forms (page 185).

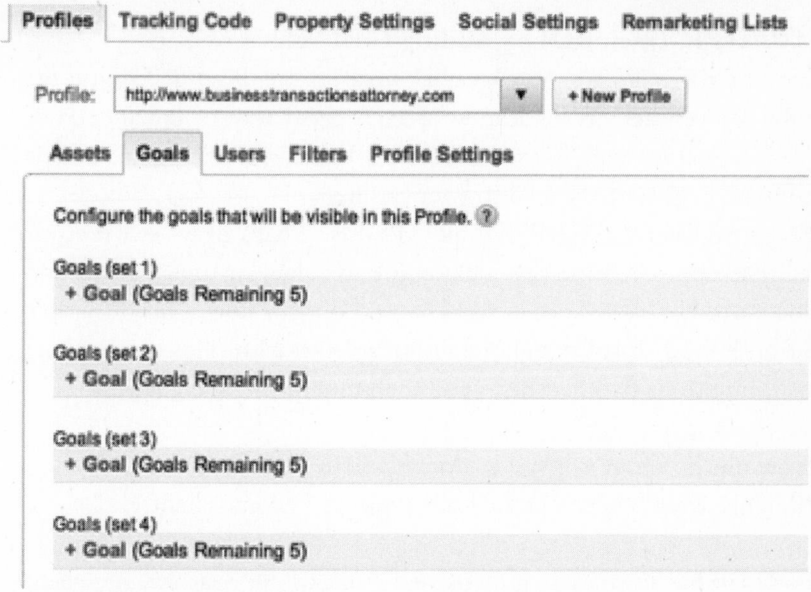

Profiles   Tracking Code   Property Settings   Social Settings   Remarketing Lists

Profile: http://www.businesstransactionsattorney.com   ▼   + New Profile

Assets   **Goals**   Users   Filters   Profile Settings

Configure the goals that will be visible in this Profile. ⑦

Goals (set 1)
+ Goal (Goals Remaining 5)

Goals (set 2)
+ Goal (Goals Remaining 5)

Goals (set 3)
+ Goal (Goals Remaining 5)

Goals (set 4)
+ Goal (Goals Remaining 5)

Figure 33: Using goals to track conversions in Google Analytics

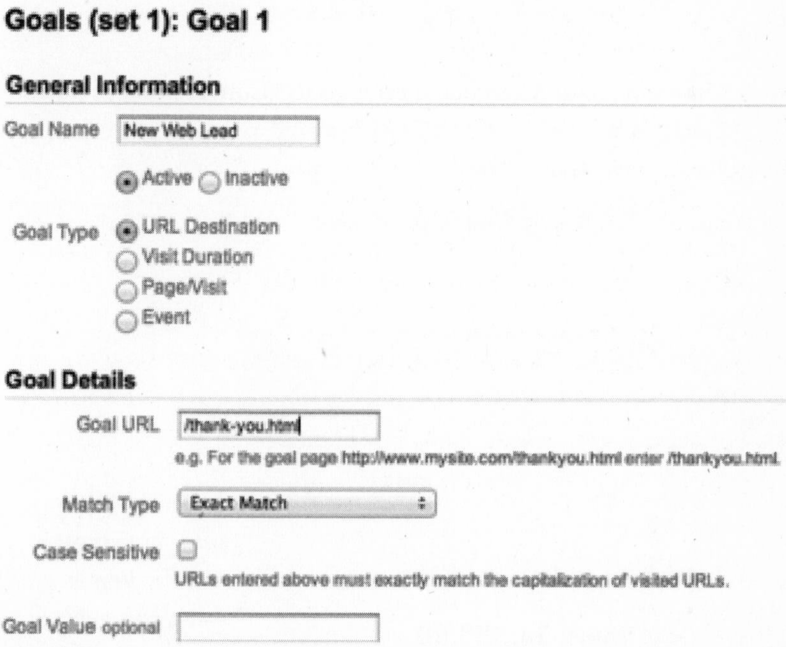

Goals (set 1): Goal 1

General Information

Goal Name   New Web Lead

◉ Active ○ Inactive

Goal Type   ◉ URL Destination
            ○ Visit Duration
            ○ Page/Visit
            ○ Event

Goal Details

Goal URL   /thank-you.html
e.g. For the goal page http://www.mysite.com/thankyou.html enter /thankyou.html.

Match Type   Exact Match   ⬍

Case Sensitive   ☐
URLs entered above must exactly match the capitalization of visited URLs.

Goal Value optional

Figure 34: Naming your goals in GA

KEY CONCEPT: Track ROI by Adding Goal Values

One of the main reasons we track conversions is to determine the ROI for a given activity or lead source. A great way to enhance your conversion goal tracking is to add a "Goal Value" for each goal. This is the estimated value of the lead to your business.

Not sure what the value of a new lead is? That's okay—we'll cover overall marketing ROI metrics including lead value, customer value, and lifetime customer value later in this chapter. But for now, a bit of simple math can reveal a close enough goal value to start with. This can be done by answering these two questions and then multiplying the answers:

▶ How much is your average customer worth (estimated)?
▶ Roughly, what percentage of leads typically become clients?

For example, if you run a menswear store where your average client spends $200 per visit, and you close around 10 percent (0.1) of your inbound Web leads, your estimated average lead (and goal) value would be $20.

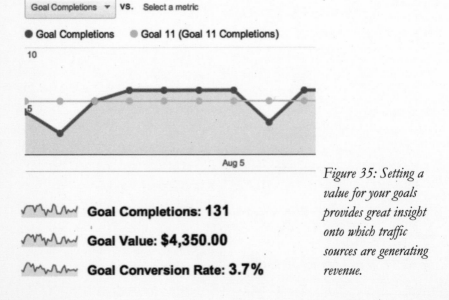

Figure 35: Setting a value for your goals provides great insight onto which traffic sources are generating revenue.

In addition to red-hot leads from customers ready to buy now, there are other important visitor actions that should be implemented and tracked as conversions. For example, if your business model hinges on repeat sales, you would benefit greatly from implementing a nurture program, a system that allows you to build a list of subscribers and follow up with them via email, sending offers, gifts, or valuable content to them over time. (See Appendix A for more on lead nurturing and lead management.)

Setting up conversion tracking for opt-ins or subscribers works the same as doing so for lead forms: simply designate a "thank you page" to use as a goal completion. Remember to assign a value to your goal. The value of a new subscriber on your nurture list is lower than that of a hot sales lead, but it is nonetheless significant.

To get a rough idea of your average subscriber value, simply figure out the total sales value of your list and divide by the number of subscribers. For example, if you send out emails each month to a list of 1,000 subscribers, resulting in $10,000 in sales, your average subscriber value is $10. Knowing your average subscriber value is extremely helpful in determining how much to spend on acquiring new subscribers.

PHONE TRACKING IN ANALYTICS

For those willing to go the extra mile in tracking lead generation, great spoils await in phone tracking. Imagine the efficiency and cost savings that could result from knowing where each inbound opportunity came from, and how many calls were generated.

Smart businesses have been using trackable phone numbers since long before the Internet. Doing so requires little more than a few unique phone numbers that you could assign to different marketing promotions. Each dedicated number forwards to your business number, recording a call in the process. If you place a dedicated phone number on "Postcard A" and a different one on "Postcard B," you can measure which promotion garners the better response.

Nowadays, call tracking has gone a step further with the integration of call metrics into Google Analytics.

How Analytics Call Tracking Works

There are two main approaches to Analytics call tracking:

▶ **Dedicated phone numbers:** This is the same old-school method previously mentioned, using dedicated phone numbers or extensions to measure sources for inbound leads. The main benefit of this approach is simplicity—all you need to do is place your dedicated phone numbers on your ads and landing pages and let your call tracking reports reveal which lead sources produce the best ROI. The drawback is that you have to place your numbers on these promotions and on your Web pages separately, which can get clunky and takes time. This method also provides limited levels of detail, such as which keywords or specific PPC ads are leading to phone calls.

▶ **Dynamic phone call tracking:** This is the method I recommend. Dynamic phone call tracking involves little more than pasting a small piece of JavaScript (code) onto your website (similar to setting up Google Analytics) wherever your phone number would normally appear. What happens next is extremely powerful: each visitor on your site will be presented with a different "dynamic" phone number. Each phone call is tracked in amazing detail right down to the source, campaign, or keyword.

RESOURCE: Google's List of Recommended Call Tracking Providers http://www.google.com/analytics/apps/results?category=Phone-Call-Tracking

I recommend you start tracking your calls immediately. Doing so will truly close the loop on your marketing, giving you a distinct advantage over many of your competitors in that your marketing dollars can stretch much farther than theirs.

ANALYTICS RESOURCES FROM AROUND THE WEB:

▶ **Occam's Razor** (http://www.kaushik.net/avinash/) is a wonderful blog by Avinash Kaushik, Author of *Web Analytics 2.0*. Avinash is known for publishing very detailed, yet easy-to-understand, articles related to every aspect of metrics-based marketing and Google Analytics.

▶ **Google's Analytics Blog** (http://analytics.blogspot.com/) is another comprehensive resource for understanding and using Google Analytics, with the additional benefit of the accuracy that comes with getting information "straight from the horse's mouth."

Step 5: USE A SIMPLE DASHBOARD TO TRACK YOUR MARKETING ROI

The final step in becoming a lean, mean small business marketing metrics machine is creating your "Marketing Metrics Dashboard." This will serve as a tool to organize, track, and learn from your marketing. Each month, you'll sit down, grab a cup of coffee, and "crunch the numbers" by adding the required metrics to your Marketing Dashboard.

Measuring your numbers over time is an extremely important exercise, as doing so gives you a true "big picture" of how your metrics are trending over time. By keeping your fingers on the pulse of your metrics, you'll be sure to spot opportunities to exploit positive trends (such as a 200 percent increase in visits from referring sites), as well as squash potential problems (like a sudden drop in conversions, which would let you know your Web forms aren't working properly!).

I recommend you start by doing this yourself, at least in the beginning. This will give you a true understanding of your marketing metrics and how your strategy pans out in the form of new visitors, leads, and customers. Once you've mastered this, after six months or so you should outsource it off of your own desk, either by delegating it to someone else within your company or by using an online marketing software solution (listed at the end of this chapter).

To begin, we'll use a simple Excel spreadsheet or Google Doc and enter key metrics associated with your marketing funnel.

1. Enter Your Analytics Data

The first portion of your Marketing dashboard will consist of the metrics we covered in the last section. All you need to do is log in to GA and enter the data points outlined in Figure 36.

2012 - 2013			
ANALYTICS	September	October	November
Visits	542	739	1814
Uniques	357	537	1344
Pages/ visit	1.53	1.61	2.21
Duration	0:01:21	0:01:16	4:31:00
Bounce rate	76.75%	74.7%	71.28%
Behavior			
New visitor	64%	70%	72%
Returning visitor	36%	30%	23%
Traffic Sources			
Search	27%	18%	8%
Referral	50%	39%	47%
Direct	22%	42%	38%
Campaigns	1%	1%	5%
Performance			
Avg. page load time	12.61	10.01	18.55
Conversion rate	1.11%	0.95%	1.21%

Figure 36: The first section of your Marketing Dashboard should include your basic GA metrics.

After just a few months, you'll start noticing trends in each of these metrics. Some will be going up, some down, and others may stay flat. The important thing is that you're noticing and reacting to these changes.

There's one metric not found in Analytics that we'll need to complete this section of the Dashboard: new customers. This is simply the number of new customers you acquired during a given month, as a result of your online marketing efforts. This should be an easy number to come up with, as it's likely the main one on your mind.

2.   Add Your Sales and Profit Numbers

Once you've entered all your Google Analytics data into your Dashboard, it's time to go "old school"—roll up your sleeves and grab your calculator. Figuring out the ROI for your online marketing isn't complicated as long as you take it step by step and use a great tool like your Marketing Dashboard.

Open up your Marketing Dashboard and add the following metrics:

▶ **New sales:** the total gross sales amount (cash receipts) from your marketing efforts. This should not include revenue from existing clients or recurring revenue, just new, first-time sales.

▶ **Gross profit margin:** for most businesses this is a relatively fixed cost. If you have a recent financial statement or even a good educated guess, that's fine. It's better to put a number down and refine later.

▶ **Gross profit:** multiply your new sales by your gross profit margin. Set up a simple formula to do this automatically.

▶ **Acquisition costs:** the total amount spent on directly acquiring customers. This line item should consist of your PPC, SEO, paid advertising, and even content development expenses.

▶ **Net profit:** your true profit, calculated by subtracting your acquisition costs from your gross profit.

▶ **Average order value:** the new sales divided by the number of new customers.

▶ **Gross profit per order:** the total gross profit divided by the number of new customers. This number represents the remaining revenue after overhead costs have been deducted.

▶ **Cost per acquisition (CPA):** the cost of acquiring a new customer; also called acquisition cost. This number is calculated by dividing your total acquisition cost by the number of new customers.

▶ **Net profit per order:** computed by dividing the total net profit by the number of customers. If your business has a low repeat order frequency, this is a critical number to measure, as it tells you how well your marketing funnel is working. If you're paying a $200 CPA to get a customer but your profit per customer is $150, something is wrong. However, if your business hinges on repeat patronage, you should focus more on lifetime customer value.

▶ **Lifetime customer value (LCV):** the average profit for the entire customer relationship—the net profit per order multiplied by the total number of orders.

KEY CONCEPT: LCV Is the Marketing Concept of a Lifetime

Lifetime customer value might be the most important metric for you to master, as doing so has caused breakthroughs and exponential growth for thousands of business owners. The reason for this is simple. Most business owners are shortsighted, deciding how much to spend on acquiring a new visitor or lead based on the one-time order value of a customer. For instance, if a local clothing retailer with $300 net profit per order turned down a marketing campaign with a $300 cost per acquisition, he might be missing the boat big time! At a glance, it may seem foolish to spend all your profits getting a new customer, but the key is lifetime value. This same retailer might learn, after doing some light math, that her average customer comes into her store twice per year, for three years. This information changes everything, as it indicates that this same average customer has a lifetime value of $1800! Now, would you spend $300 to acquire a customer for a profit of $1500? This is why you must determine and base your acquisition costs on the lifetime value of a customer. In fact, some business models even involve losing money on customer acquisition. Think of your cable or cell phone company—they'll gladly give you free equipment at a loss, because they're smartly focused on lifetime customer value (LCV). Of course, viewing your customers' potential over the long haul will cause you to focus much more of your attention on influencing their lifetime value. Most shortsighted marketers don't use nurture or customer loyalty campaigns very well if at all (see Appendix A). Now that you're measuring LCV, however, you'll naturally want to improve it. Think about which irresistible offers you might be able to use in your business to gain new customers or subscribers.

▶ **Cost per lead (CPL):** the expense required to generate a lead. This is your total acquisition cost divided by the number of leads. This metric tells you how much you're paying for each new lead in your pipeline and how much you should be paying for leads.[6]

▶ **Lead value:** the total profit value of the average lead. Lead value is your total ROI divided by the number of leads. Although many

---

6 To learn more about the difference betweek CPL and CPA, see this Wikipedia article: http://en.wikipedia.org/wiki/Cost_per_action.

companies measure lead value based on the one-time value of a client, this is shortsighted, as you will find many more available channels for acquiring leads based on the higher and more accurate LCV.

▶ **Cost per visitor (CPV):** the expense required to get a visitor to a website, calculated by dividing your total acquisition cost by the number of visitors to your site. This metric keeps your CPV much lower than your visitor value. For example, if you're paying $2.00 to acquire a visitor to your site, but your visitor value is $1.50, you'll have a tough time making a profit.

▶ **Visitor value:** the total profit value of a single website visitor. Visitor value is determined by dividing your total ROI by the number of unique visitors for the same period.

▶ **Return-on-investment (ROI):** the total net profit over the lifetime of a customer or customers. ROI is calculated by multiplying the LCV by the number of customers. I can't stress enough how important it is to maintain a long-term view of your marketing. With the example in Figure 37 below, this business would have made a net profit of only $1,000, but the real ROI is $6,000.

CONVERSIONS		
Lead forms	23	21
Phone calls	43	49
Total leads	66	70
Conversion rate	4.22%	3.89%
New customers	10	7
Lead conversion rate	15%	10%
SALES INFO		
New sales	$15,000	$11,000
Gross profit margin	20%	20%
Gross profit	$3000	$2200
Total acquisition cost	$2000	$1500
Net profit	$1000	$700
CUSTOMER INFO		
Average order value	$1500	$1,571
Gross profit/ order	$300	$314
Cost per acquisition (CPA)	$200	$214
Net profit/ order	$100	$100
Lifetime customer value (LCV)	$600	$600
ROI		
Cost per lead (CPL)	$30	$21
Lead value	$91	$60
Cost per visitor	$1.42	$0.92
Visitor value	$4.25	$2.59
Total ROI	$6,000	$4,200

Figure 37: Once you've added sales and ROI metrics, your Marketing Dashboard will be complete.

While these metrics may seem tedious at first, be sure and track them consistently. You will be amazed by how well these numbers start working together to help steer your decisions and help you take your business to the next level.

NEXT STEPS AND ADDITIONAL RESOURCES

Once you've gotten comfortable using the Marketing Dashboard, you can really start to home in on the sources of your visitors, leads, and customers and compare them based on quality and ROI. For example, you may find that you can pay half as much to get traffic from Facebook than from LinkedIn, only to find that Facebook converts at such a low rate it's actually more expensive in the long run.

The golden rule is that not all traffic is created equal. This is why measurement is critical.

The simplest way to measure your sources of traffic and leads separately is to use the same Marketing Dashboard we've been working with, but with a few tweaks:

▶ Create a new tab on your spreadsheet for each month and list your marketing campaigns as columns.
▶ Add a field called "Impressions" above visits to indicate the target audience size for your campaigns. In the case of advertising, use circulation. With direct mail, this would be the size of your mailing list, and with Google AdWords or other PPC campaigns, it would be the impressions.
▶ To measure traffic from offline marketing sources (direct mail, print ads, etc.), use a separate landing page. For example, on a postcard, use www.YourSite.com/SummerSpecial instead of your home page. You can do the same with dedicated phone numbers.

The end goal is that every person your business comes into contact with is tracked through every stage of the funnel. While this takes some elbow grease and determination to set up, the payoffs are measurably huge.

MARKETING METRICS AND LEAD TRACKING RESOURCES:

▶ **Hubspot** (http://www.hubspot.com/) provides an all-in-one online marketing platform that integrates analytics, social media, landing pages, and more. While HubSpot may be a good fit for some small to medium (b2b) business owners, I would only recommend using their services in conjunction with your own WordPress or other CMS website and never any third-party paid CMS system.

▶ **Reach Local** (http://www.reachlocal.com/) is a very popular full-service online advertising company that specializes in small business advertising, lead generation, and tracking. Their services may be a bit pricey for the average small business, but they have a great reputation and are a very stable company.

Site: http://YourWebSite.com	MARCH 2013		
	Google Adwords	**Direct Mail**	**Yellow Pages**
REACH			
Impressions	1564	1,799	21000
Visits	55	40	700
Ctr	3.52%	2.22%	3.33%
CONVERSIONS			
Lead forms	20	18	170
Phone calls	9	9	400
Total leads	29	27	570
Conversion rate	1.85%	1.50%	2.71%
New customers	5	3	17
Lead conversion rate	17%	11%	3%
SALES INFO			
New sales	$15,000	$11,000	$11,000
Gross profit margin	20%	20%	20%
Gross profit	$3000	$2200	$2200
Total acquisition cost	$2000	2000	2000
Net profit	$1000	$200	$200
CUSTOMER INFO			
Average order value	$3000	$3,667	$647
Gross profit/ order	$600	$733	$129
Cost per acquisition (CPA)	$400	$667	$118
Net profit/ order	$200	$67	$12
Lifetime customer value (LCV)	$1200	$400	$71
ROI			
Cost per lead (CPL)	$69	$74	$4
Lead value	$207	$44	$2
Cost per visitor	$36.36	$50.00	$2.86
Visitor value	$109.09	$30.00	$1.71
Total ROI	$6,000	$1,200	$1,200

Figure 38: With a few small tweaks, you can use your Marketing Dashboard to break out specific traffic sources.

CHAPTER SUMMARY

Using simple tools like Google Analytics, Google Webmaster Tools, Bright Local SEO Tools, and an Excel spreadsheet, even the least tech-savvy business owner can gain tremendous insights into key metrics associated with each phase of the online marketing funnel. This real-time data can provide significant competitive advantages and cost savings all by itself. By keeping your finger on the pulse of your marketing you can not only find new opportunities for growth, but also quickly pinpoint sticking points or unprofitable sources. Great advantages await you if you're focused enough to implement "closed loop" Web lead and phone tracking and hold every traffic source accountable all the way through ROI. What's important is that you get into the metrics mindset and start tracking what you can. Don't worry if you can't measure every aspect of your marketing right away—get started now and the increase in leads and sales will help keep you on the path to metrics masterdom.

CHAPTER CHECKLIST

✔ **Step 1: Measure Your Search Engine Rankings**
  - Choose the right tool: Raven Tools, Google Webmaster Tools, or manual tracking

✔ **Step 2: Measure Your Website Traffic**
  - Unique visitors
  - Demographics
  - Traffic sources
  - Organic search traffic
  - Referring sites
  - Social Referrals

✔ **Step 3: Measure Your User Engagement**
  - Returning visits
  - Time on site
  - Pages per visit

- Bounce rate
- Pages (content)

✔ **Step 4: Measure Your Conversions**
- Use Google Analytics Goals to track Web leads and opt-ins
- Track inbound phone calls

✔ **Step 5: Use a Marketing Dashboard to Track ROI**
- Use an Excel or Google spreadsheet
- Add your key Analytics metrics each month
- Add your business numbers: Sales, Profit, and ROI
- Track each marketing campaign separately

PART FOUR

THE STAND OUT
CONTENT STRATEGY

TEN

OUTPUBLISH YOUR COMPETITION WITH A CONTENT MARKETING PLAN

"Think like a publisher, not a marketer."

—*David Meerman Scott*

Where does content development fall on your list of marketing priorities? How often do you blog or add content to your website? Do you have a strategy for figuring out what to write about or how to use content to reach more potential customers?

Your answers to these questions are probably typical of the average small business owner. After reading these next few chapters, your answers will likely change dramatically, and change your business for the better in the process.

Content is King. Think of all the preparatory work we've done thus far as planning and foundation-laying for a long-lasting, ultra-effective website and online business (the castle). But it's your content that will rule supreme. And, as with any other king, the quality of your conduct (with your content) will ultimately determine the fate of your reign (your online business). In fact, no single activity you undertake with the goal of reaching and engaging your target audience can produce nearly as many results as the frequent development and publication of high-quality original content.

THE CASE FOR CONTENT: EDUCATION-BASED MARKETING

Many small business owners are stuck in the pre-information age mode of marketing: gearing all their marketing time and money towards "finding the next client, now!" While we might admire this strategy in its focus on the right priorities, this method actually needs to be retired, and fast! This "interruption-based" approach is the most expensive and least effective way to build a business.

"You no longer need to spend tons of money interrupting your potential customers. Instead you need to create remarkable content, optimize that content, publish the content, market the content, and measure what is working and what is not working. A savvy inbound marketer is half traditional marketer and half content creation factory."

—*Dharmesh Shaw and Brian Halligan, Authors of* Inbound Marketing

As salient as this quote from Halligan and Shaw may be, education-based marketing is not, in fact, a new concept. For decades smart marketers have been using educational materials in the form of free consumer guides and pamphlets containing valuable educational materials.

However, content *is* the new currency of the online economy. You can change your Web design in five minutes with the click of a mouse, but two years of high-quality, audience-attracting blog articles can be irreplaceable.

Why Education-Based Marketing Works

Education-based marketing works for the same reason that buying someone you hope to get to know better a drink before you ask for a sleepover date does: before anyone trusts you, they have to like you. And before they like you, they have to know you. This golden, three-step map for building relationships has proven effective more often than any other:

1. **Know**
2. **Like**
3. **Trust**

The core of education-based marketing is giving your prospects access to highly valuable and helpful information targeted at fulfilling their needs, while asking for nothing in return (or very little, in the case of an opt-in form for an e-book or download). This "low-pressure" approach starts the relationship with your prospects. They will now know and like you for providing them with great educational content. And, as they read your content, becoming engaged with you, seeing you as the expert in your field, they'll grow to trust you.

BENEFITS OF CONTENT MARKETING

There are several powerful benefits of content marketing:

► **You get there earlier.** As you should recall from Chapter 5, the majority of online searches are informational. By targeting and producing content geared towards these "top of the funnel" searches, you'll enjoy early-bird privileges through the opportunity to establish a relationship before your competitors reach the prospect.

► **Content can make you the authority in your niche.** If, over the next year or two, you prolifically add blog articles to your website, describing virtually every aspect of your business and industry, people will notice you as the expert in your field.

► **Google loves content.** I'll say it again: Google loves and requires great content. This means detailed, original articles that people are sharing and linking to. Another huge benefit of content marketing is traffic. Every blog or video you post acts as a long-term traffic magnet, adding visitors to your website.

► **You get to hang with the big publishers.** When I was a kid, every family in America watched *The Waltons* or *Little House on the Prairie* every Sunday night. Did we do this because the shows were that great, or because there were only two TV stations? I'll let you make the call, but the point is a significant one: In today's highly fragmented digital environment, people no longer have to choose from two flavors of media. This "de-centralization" of media is making it increasingly easier for anyone with a blog and something interesting to say to reach an audience.

▶ **It filters out deadbeat leads.** When done properly, content marketing is a great method for increasing your conversion and closing rates, while eliminating time-wasting, unqualified leads. People who consume your content gain a better understanding of their options and have many of their questions answered before you hear from them. They also gather insight into how your company works and what you have to offer. When these folks do contact you, the chances of them converting into clients go through the roof!

FORMS OF CONTENT

There are several popular and effective types of content, any or all of which are worth exploring and utilizing, depending on the type of business you're in and the needs of your audience. The following are the most popular and most useful for small businesses:

▶ **Blogs:** Derived from the 1990s term "weblogs," which were used to describe "keeping a journal (or log) on the Web," a blog is simply an organized platform for publishing content focused on a specific topic. Some blogs are formal and corporate, while others are used as casual platforms for personal commentary. Your blog should be the primary publishing medium and center of your STAND OUT content strategy.

▶ **E-books and Whitepapers:** Each of these is a longer-form piece focused on a simple topic. E-books are the preferred of the two formats, as they make great "lead magnets" by representing education-based marketing at its best: Give your audience highly valuable content in exchange for permission to follow up with them (via capturing their basic information on a Web form). E-books are highly "shareable" as well and are one of the most underused media by small business owners. This is largely because creating e-books seems complicated or intimidating, but these are both myths that we'll dispel in Chapter 9. An e-book can also make a great direct mail or POS (point of sale) piece. Whitepapers are technical reports that, despite their popularity, I don't recommend using due to their low level of effectiveness.

▶ **Video:** Video provides the ultimate medium for all three phases of the online marketing funnel. One phrase I use often is, "If a picture is worth a thousand words, a video is worth a thousand customers." The creation of online video is now accessible to every small business owner, as it's become extremely simple and inexpensive—what ten years ago would have cost $5,000 and a film crew can now be done in twenty minutes with a $200 camera. Chapter 10 will reveal how to start adding video to your content marketing strategy.

▶ **Podcasts and audio recordings:** Podcacts are extremely popular (iTunes alone boasts over 500 million users), are easy to make, and offer a brand-new content marketing channel for small business owners willing to put forth the time and effort.

▶ **Infographics:** Infographics are "graphic visual representations of information, data or knowledge" (Wikipedia: http://en.wikipedia.org/wiki/Infographics). Many infographics have become viral, creating immense exposure for and awareness of their authors. For an example, see "Dog Owners vs. Cat Owners," here: http://editorial.designtaxi.com/news-dogvscat1207/1.png

▶ **Webinars:** Although not typically thought of as content, webinars are nothing more than content presented to an online audience. Webinars are a great tool for leveraging "repurposed content"—taking your existing content and extending its reach by presenting it in a different form (covered later in this chapter).

THE STAND OUT CONTENT MARKETING STRATEGY

In Chapters 11 and 12, we'll dig into the mechanics and "how to's" of writing and producing great blog articles, e-books, videos, podcasts, and webinars. But first, it's important to put into place an overall strategy for ensuring that your content accomplishes its goal of reaching and engaging your target audience. We'll call this your STAND OUT Content Marketing Strategy.

Here's what the typical small business content marketing process looks like:

1. **Write an article.**
2. **Post it on your website.**
3. **Wait for loads of traffic.**
4. **Get frustrated at the lack of traffic.**
5. **Conclude that blogging must not work and stop blogging forever.**

If this looks even remotely like your blogging process, you're about to experience a business-changing revelation.

A key insight into effective content marketing is that writing is a relatively small part of the process. It's the "before" and "after" steps that make or break your content strategy. Needless to say, your content must be of great value to your audience or none of this matters. Without doing the right research before you produce content, and properly promoting your content afterward, even your best cornerstone pieces may fall on deaf ears . . . and blind eyes.

SEVEN STEPS TO BECOMING A CONTENT MOGUL

First, it's important to consider the big picture—how your content will be used for maximum impact with your target audience. Understanding and implementing the following seven-step STAND OUT Content Strategy will be key in taking your website and online brand from obscurity to domination within your target market.

Step 1: CREATE A CONTENT ROAD MAP

The first step in the STAND OUT Content Strategy is Mapping. It's critical to ensure that the content you're about to produce is part of a "bigger plan." In this case, the bigger plan is a "Content Road Map," a tool used for planning out your content and ensuring that it will provide the most "bang for your buck" in terms of reach and engagement. Your

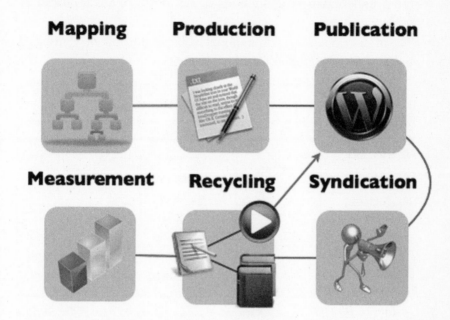

Figure 39: The Seven-Step STAND OUT Content Strategy

Content Road Map will serve as a template for managing the development of content, thereby converting your targeted "informational keywords" into traffic-producing, trust-building articles.

The good news is, you've already done most of the work.

If you recall from Chapter 5, we spent some time creating a "Keyword Map" and learned that "informational search queries" make up most of the searches online. Catching your audience in the research phase is the core of your content marketing strategy. Thus, producing lots of question-answering, traffic-generating content will provide you with a clear advantage over your online competition.

You'll also remember that we discussed how your keyword map is used to implement keywords on your website:

▶ Each of the main categories of products and services your business offers should be the main, "top-level" pages of your site.
▶ The transactional keywords should be used within your Web pages

(titles, body and meta descriptions, as well as anchor text for backlinks to your site)

▶ The informational keywords should make up the bulk of your blogs, FAQs, videos, and other forms of content.

		MAIN BUSINESS	PRIMARY SERVICES OR PRODUCT CATEGORIES
Main Navigation →	CATEGORY	PRINTING SHOP	BUSINESS CARDS
SEO Keywords →	Transactional Keywords	printers printing company business printing	business card printers cheap business cards fast business card printing
Content Pages →	Informational Keywords	how to hire a printer types of printing local vs. online printing	best types of business cards business card design ideas what to include on business cards

Figure 40: Use the Informational Keywords from your Keyword Map (Chapter 5) to create a great Content Road Map.

Now all you need to do is transform each of your targeted informational keywords into a human-friendly blog post, video, or other form of content.

How to Create Your Content Road Map

1. **Open your Keyword Map spreadsheet and open a new tab.**
2. **On this tab, create the following columns (see Figure 21):**
   ▶ Category: represents the main product or service category the article will address
   ▶ Content format: used to specify which form your new content will be (blog, video, infographic, e-book, etc.)
   ▶ Target search phrase: should be one of the "informational keywords" from your keyword map (Figure 40)
   ▶ Keywords to use: lists the top keywords related to the product or service category from your keyword map

- ▶ Title: where you'll convert your target search phrase into a human-friendly, attention-grabbing headline
- ▶ Publish date: indicates the date your content was (or will be) published on your website

Repeat this process until each of your target search phrases are listed in this format. Once you've written and published each new article, list the publication date on your spreadsheet.

KEY CONCEPT: Use an Editorial Calendar to Plan Your Content

Most, if not all, large media companies and content providers use some form of editorial calendar religiously. An editorial calendar is a planner used for scheduling the future publication of content. Block out specific times each day or week to plan, write, and publish content. Since you're busy, unless you schedule the development of content it will likely not happen. Just saying you'll "write two to three blogs per week" isn't enough—you have to create and commit yourself to an editorial calendar to help you stay on track and organized. To create a basic editorial calendar, use your Content Road Map to schedule the development and publication of content. If you're using WordPress, there's a great plugin called "Editor Calendar"(http://wordpress. org/extend/plugins/editorial-calendar/) that allows you to schedule your blog posts and other forms of content ahead of time and helps you manage the content marketing process.

Your Content Road Map and editorial calendar serve as the core content marketing tools for your business. Using this system to plan your content publishing will also "keep you honest," providing a record of how often you're publishing new content on your site (and nudging you when you're not doing so).

Figure 41: The WordPress Editorial Calendar plugin is a highly recommended FREE tool.

Step 2: PRODUCE GREAT CONTENT

In case you're new to the world of writing, blogging, and content creation, let's first establish what "great content" is, and then lay out a clear plan for how to write and produce it.

WHAT IS GREAT CONTENT?

Great content is any form of content that accomplishes the following three fundamental goals:

▶ Reaches a specific target audience.
▶ STANDs OUT and engages readers through its focus on their questions and needs, as well as its structure and format.
▶ Moves readers toward some desired action, such as subscribing to your newsletter or contacting you.

If these three goals of great content remind you of the online marketing funnel, that's because your content must be optimized for all three phases in order to be effective. To this end, every piece of content you develop should pass an "online marketing funnel checklist" which we'll cover later in this section.

THE FOUR STAND OUT RULES OF QUALITY CONTENT

Over the next two chapters, we'll cover best practices specifically for creating blogs and videos. This section covers a few powerful, over-arching "rules of quality" that apply to all forms of content. Each piece of content you produce should follow every one of these STAND OUT Rules of Quality Content:

▶ **Do Not Outsource Content Creation.** Much of the last decade has seen a preponderance of companies and SEO agencies publishing second- or third-rate content for the sole purpose of getting more SEO traffic. This is a fool's errand, as not only has Google caught on to such tactics, but what good is traffic that brings folks to your website only for them to consume poor content that falls flat on engagement and conversion? Your content should be used as a platform for building relationships with your target audience. Only you can build those relationships, so only you should produce the content.

There are no shortcuts when it comes to producing quality content. Of course, if you have an employee or business partner who truly knows and can represent your business, it's fine to share the content development workload.

▶ **Publish Original Content.** This means that you should never reword or restate the same old common articles floating around the Web related to your topic. It's important to add to the conversation, striving to be a thought leader and an authority in your niche. This doesn't mean you have to re-invent the way people clean their teeth or buy produce. Adding to the conversation is simply taking a common topic or question and injecting it with your personal style, technique, or experience in handling it. Even if you write a "curated" blog post (covered below), it's critical to include your personal impression, reaction, or recommendation regarding the subject matter.

▶ **Publish Content Often.** Remember that every blog post and video you create will act as a permanent "traffic magnet," adding to your website's traffic and conversions. If you can publish one new blog post per week at first, that's fine. This volume will actually place you in the top 10 percent of small business content producers. However, I challenge you to do one post per day. You don't have to sit down and write a full 500- to 700-word article from scratch. There are several ways to produce quality content without starting from a blank page, including quick video blogs, content curation, expert interviews, and more. See the next section, "Sources and Ideas For Your Content."

▶ **Check Your Work.** It's important not to confuse casual with sloppy. Each piece of content you produce should be proofread, ideally by a third party, for basic spelling and grammar errors before hitting the presses. A skilled proofreader can be found at Odesk.com or any other outsourcing site covered in Chapter 4. If this is outside your budget, at least have a skilled second pair of eyes look over your content before it goes live.

No matter what forms your content takes, following the STAND OUT Rules of Quality Content will keep you on the straight and narrow path to becoming an authority in your niche. Producing high-quality, relevant content that reaches, engages, and builds relationships with your target audience is the core of any successful content marketing strategy.

If producing great content seems easier said than done, Chapters 10 and 11, the STAND OUT Content Strategy section of the book, are devoted solely to the content creation process. Together, these three chapters (10 and 11 and this one) will provide all the information you need to launch a super-effective STAND OUT Content Strategy.

KEY CONCEPT: How to Go from 0 to 7200 Monthly Website Visitors
One of the steadfast rules of content marketing is that larger websites get more traffic than smaller ones. The following example illustrates the

snowball effect in traffic and business growth than can occur as a result of frequently publishing quality content.

Let's say, after becoming familiar with and getting into the habit of publishing content, you agree to publish just four new blog posts per month (one each week) on your site. Let's assume that each new article you publish generates just one visitor per day to your website (thirty per month). Just publishing four new articles each month, each one averaging one visit per day, you will have generated 120 new visits to your site each month (4 articles x 30 visits per article = 120).

Blogs per month	Monthly Traffic	Articles after 1 Year	Monthly traffic
1	30	12	360
4	120	48	1440
20	600	240	7200

Figure 42: Monthly traffic chart

If you maintained this pace of just four new articles each month for one year, the numbers start to look pretty darn good: You'd have forty-eight new articles and around 1440 new visits each month! Pretty powerful results for the low investment of just one new article per week.

Let's look at one final, over-the-top scenario. What would happen if you published twenty new pieces of content each month for one year? Using the conservative traffic projections above (one new visitor per article, per day), you would have 240 new articles and around 7200 new visits each month!

At any volume, the content your produce can become one of your greatest assets in building an online business. So what are you waiting for? Let's get blogging!

Step 3: PUBLISH YOUR CONTENT

Before you upload your new article or video to your website, it's critical to ensure your content is optimized for each phase of the Online Marketing Funnel.

CONTENT OPTIMIZATION CHECKLIST

REACH:

▶ Is the article focused on a single topic (target search term from your Content Road Map)?
▶ Is the article original?
▶ Is the article 500 words or more?
▶ Does the article include keywords in the right places?
  • Title
  • URL
  • Headings (H1, H2, etc.)
  • Body
  • Meta description
  • Internal links
  • WordPress-specific content tasks (categories, tags, and permalink)

ENGAGEMENT:

▶ Is the copy focused on the reader's needs and questions?
▶ Does the copy follow the six-step sales letter format?
  • Grab readers with an attention-grabbing headline
  • State the problem
  • Make your promise
  • Present the solution
  • Build social proof and authority
  • Call to action with offer
▶ Is the article readable?
  • Short paragraphs
  • Clear headings
  • Bulleted and numbered lists
  • Engaging images or supporting graphics
▶ Is the article shareable?
  • Include social sharing icons
  • Allow reader comments

CONVERSION:

▶ Is there a clear call to action and offer?

▶ Is there a lead or opt-in form visible from the content?

▶ Is there a large, clearly visible phone number on the page?

KEY CONCEPT: **Track Your Content Publishing Process**

In order to stay on track and ensure you're not missing any critical steps along the way, expand your Content Road Map by including the major steps of the content marketing process. Documenting this process for each new blog post or video you create will make managing your content strategy much simpler. For example, you can add simple check boxes for each of the three phases of the Content Optimization Checklist. As we move through the content marketing process, I'll add more tasks to the Content Road Map.

By following steps 1–3, you've come a long way toward reaching content marketing status: you've implemented a very organized system for planning, producing, and publishing high-quality, targeted content. Most of your competitors will have no such system in place, making your Content Road Map itself a tool of competitive advantage.

However, the next three steps, which are all about the marketing part of the content marketing process, will launch your online visibility into the stratosphere!

Step 4: SYNDICATE YOUR CONTENT

"Syndication: to publish simultaneously, or supply for simultaneous publication, in a number of newspapers or other periodicals in different places" (http://dictionary.reference.com/browse/syndicate). Within this traditional definition of syndication lies one of the most powerful nuggets of your content strategy: the act of taking a single piece of content and syndicating it across multiple channels on the Web.

WHY AND HOW CONTENT SYNDICATION WORKS

Content syndication is where the "marketing" in content marketing comes in. A true game-changer for your business, content syndication boils down to being active instead of passive in your efforts to help get your content in front of your audience. Instead of posting a new blog post on your site, then sitting back waiting for it to be found, content syndication is all about actively reaching your audience across the Web and letting them know about your great new content! Think of content syndication as any other form of advertising: the goal is to get your message in front of as many targeted eyeballs as you can.

Remember, most people within your target market aren't hanging out on your website. They're on social media sites, industry sites, online forums, and discussion groups. Each time you publish content you think they'll find interesting, you need to announce it on these channels, such as "Hey—I just wrote a great article on 3 great gluten-free meals your kids will love. Check it out here."

Blogging Without Syndication

Figure 43: Most bloggers write a post and wait for results that will likely never come.

The time you've spent setting up profiles on social media, bookmarking, and other similar tasks is about to pay off. Each of these hubs is about to become a "broadcasting channel" for your business, reaching both existing and new members of your target audience and exposing them to your content.

As Figure 44 illustrates, syndicating content across multiple channels can turbo-charge your visibility and traffic through exposure to a much larger audience.

KEY CONCEPT: The Viral Snowball Effect of Social Media Sharing

As effective as content syndication can be at getting your content in front of more people, there's an even more dramatic upside that can occur through social sharing.

Say you publish a new post on your Facebook Business Page, announcing a new article on your blog. Not only will this post have the potential to get in front of the 1,000 fans who follow your business, but your blog has the potential to reach all of your followers' friends as well! Each time a person "Likes" or "Shares" a link on Facebook, an update gets posted on that user's page. This update can expose your content to tens or even hundreds of thousands of new eyeballs via this sub-viral effect.

Blogging and Syntication!

Figure 44: Content syndication gets your content in front of more eyeballs, more quickly!

The way syndication works is simple:

▶ Produce a piece of quality content (we'll use a blog post as an example).

▶ Publish this new article on your website (of course, only after you've mapped and optimized the content!).

▶ Spread the word, posting links to your new content across the Web, leveraging every available channel for reaching your target audience (see below).

SEO BENEFITS OF CONTENT SYNDICATION

There are two notable "byproduct" benefits of content syndication:

1. **Google "loves" social engagement.** As previously discussed, Google rewards social sharing in their ranking algorithms. What better way to judge the popularity and authority of a website than by the "thumbs ups" received via social shares?

2. **Google rewards quality backlinks.** Any time a trusted authority links to your site, they pass on a portion of their trust and authority to you. Syndicating your quality content to multiple online channels greatly increases the chance of having it first get noticed and then get linked to.

A LIST OF POTENTIAL CONTENT SYNDICATION CHANNELS

For each form of content you produce, there's an ever-growing ecosystem of highly trafficked sites ripe and ready to help your content reach its target audience.

In the next section, we'll discuss powerful and little-known methods for "re-purposing" your content, making it available in multiple formats. This will create even more opportunities for content syndication using the categories of sites listed:

▶ **Social media sites:** These should be the core pillars of your content syndication strategy. Facebook, LinkedIn, Twitter, and Google+ are all highly trafficked resources for reaching more folks, regardless of the type of content. Every time you add content, make it a mandatory practice to publish notifications on social media sites.

▶ **Your email list:** If your business has any potential for repeat patronage, you need to build a subscriber list, pronto. One of the most loyal, best traffic sources will be email traffic, or visits resulting from an email you sent to your subscriber list. Each time you publish content, be sure and send a "broadcast" email to your list announcing this new content with a link to it. Of all the available channels for content syndication, your list of prospects and clients are likely to be the most loyal and engaged.

▶ **Article and content sites:** Most trusted article and content sites (like Ezinearticles.com) allow you to publish original content on their sites, as long as it's original and exists only on your site. If you choose to publish your content on article directories, be sure to place it on your site first and let it get indexed with Google first. This way, Google will recognize your site as the original author and reserve authorship credit for your site only.

▶ **Press release sites:** As long as your content is related to something truly newsworthy, such as a new product, service, or business offering, press releases are a great way to gain quality exposure from potential customers and search engines alike.

▶ **Video sites:** Each time you create video, it's important that you not stop at YouTube. Just as with articles and written content, there are multiple channels for posting videos. At the very minimum, you should syndicate your content to Vimeo, YouTube, Daily Motion, and MetaCafe. And don't forget your social media sites as well, all of which allow you to post video.

▶ **Photo and graphics sites:** If your content contains graphics or is graphics-based, don't forget to syndicate it to the top graphics sites such as Flickr, Picasa, and Pinterest. Depending on your niche, photos may play a greater or lesser role in your content strategy. While a restaurant or home remodeler might benefit greatly from a photo-heavy content plan, a tax accounting firm or funeral parlor may see more traction from other forms of content.

▶ **Podcasting sites:** All it takes to create a high-enough quality podcast is stripping the audio content from your videos or webinars and uploading them to your blog.

While technology will continually morph content into new delivery systems, the essence of a successful content syndication strategy has and will remain the same: to present your content to your target audience in the most compelling format, wherever they hang out online.

Although it might seem like a daunting task to create blogs, videos, infographics, and whatever else is surely coming down the pike, I have a trick up my sleeve—one that will soon be up your sleeve, as well: Content Recycling.

RESOURCES: Save Tons of Time Using Automated Syndication Tools

As effective as content syndication can be to your business, you may feel a bit overwhelmed by the amount of work required to post your content to dozens of places on the Web, each one requiring you to log in, set up an account, and update with each new blog post you write. It sounds like syndicating the content will take longer that creating it in the first place! Not to worry—you won't have to spend hours posting and reposting the same content all across the Web. Luckily, this content syndication monotony has been solved through several syndication tools, two of which you'll find extremely useful.

▶ **OnlyWire** (http://onlywire.com): According to its website, OnlyWire "is a Social Media Engine™ that auto-submits your content and status posts to Social Media Networks such as Facebook, Twitter, LinkedIn and WordPress with speed and simplicity. OnlyWire provides a History of all your Submissions, Analytics of your traffic and a Messenger tool to monitor and respond to all the comments from your posts." At the time of this writing, OnlyWire's service allows customers to post updates on more than forty-six social networks. This is a huge savings in time and harnessing of syndication opportunities.

I can't say enough about how useful this tool is. You just log in, create a new update, add a brief description of and link to your new content, and voila! Your submission goes to dozens of social media sites in minutes. Better yet, OnlyWire has a WordPress plugin that makes syndication even easier—you can set OnlyWire to automatically syndicate each new page or blog post you publish on your site.

▶ **OneLoad** (http://www.oneload.com): OneLoad is a great site for easily managing and syndicating video content. The process is very similar to uploading a video to YouTube, with one clear difference: When you hit "send," your video gets posted in several places (those which you specify) simultaneously. Destination sites include the top video and social media sites.

Figure 45: OneLoad helps you manage and syndicate video content.

Step 5: RECYCLE YOUR CONTENT

This strategy we're about to cover is one of those "lightbulb" moments that can drastically change the path of your small business.

Step 5 is all about the art of "content recycling": taking a single piece of high-quality content and transforming it into multiple forms of media. Let's say you authored a great article (blog post) that really resonates with your readers, increasing your online reach and traffic in the process. Why not take the content from the article and make it into a quick video, and syndicate the video to all the top video and social media sites? Instead of stopping there, why not also take that video and use the audio portion for a podcast? How about using that article outline for a webinar? Better yet, why not take a handful of related blog posts and combine them into an e-book, and use the e-book as a free giveaway for anyone who opts in to your mailing list?

Content recycling is one of the simplest yet most powerful strategies in your STAND OUT content marketing arsenal. Simple because you've already done the hard part—creating the content in the first place; powerful because content recycling allows you to exponentially multiply the reach of your content with little more than a bit of tweaking and formatting.

Remember, your target audience may prefer to look for and consume content in different formats. While many folks would likely seek answers to their questions through a simple Google search, an increasing number of Internet users are searching on video, social media, and other types of sites as well. Content recycling helps you cover your bases and be everywhere your customers may be looking.

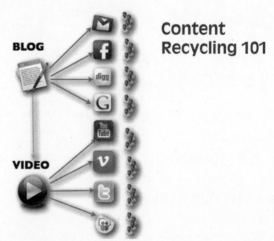

Figure 46: Publishing your content in multiple formats is a powerful way to increase your reach.

How to Recycle Your Content

Regardless of the original form of your content, it can likely be re-formatted and syndicated across the Web, each time reaching and engaging more potential customers. The key is to get into the mindset of asking yourself, "What other forms could this be published in?" and to create a content recycling checklist to keep you on track:

1. **Choose which format to start with. Using your Content Road Map, pick a topic and decide whether the content would be best presented on your website as an article, video, or infographic.**
2. **Next, follow your content marketing process by creating your content, publishing it on your site, and syndicating it.**
3. **Finally, decide which other formats your content should take and repeat step 2 with each additional format.**

Say you decide to create a video entitled, "5 Ideas for Beautiful Yet Inexpensive Wedding Invitations," where you show off invitation styles you recommend and tips for saving money in creating them. After publishing your new "video blog," kick into content marketing overdrive by doing the following:

▶ Syndicate your new video on the top video and social media sites.
▶ Upload your video to Slideshare as a presentation.
▶ Create a transcription of your video.
▶ Publish this transcription as an article accompanying the video on your site.
▶ Syndicate the article to article directories, social media, or bookmarking sites.
▶ Create a simple "infographic" of the content and publish it on Pinterest.

Won't Google or People View My Recycled Content as Duplicate?

Duplicate content can actually be a good thing, as long as it's original and not published in the same form multiple times on your or other sites. If your content is good, people will appreciate the steps you've made in making it more convenient to access and understand. Besides, seeing your content and brand repeatedly in multiple places online will only help strengthen the connection between you and your audience.

Once you get the hang of it, content recycling can help give you a significant advantage over your competition. While they continue to publish blog posts or maybe even the occasional video, you'll be churning out content like a mini *New York Times,* getting four to five times the traction from each piece you create.

Step 6: MEASURE THE IMPACT OF YOUR CONTENT

All the dedication, research, planning, writing/filming, posting, and publishing converge into one place: measurable results. As much fun as all your hard work might be, it must be quantified. You must measure how well your content does at reaching, engaging, and converting your target audience.

By measuring the impact of your content using Google Analytics, you'll gain key insights into opportunities for even greater gains in visibility and traffic. You'll also be able to spot and address sticking points and get to the bottom of non-performing articles and videos.

In Chapter 8, we covered the basic principles of using Analytics to measure your funnel, along with several key metrics associated with your content marketing. Now that you've gained a deeper understanding of the role your content plays in attracting and engaging your target audience, we'll want to revisit a few of the key metrics you should be using to keep your finger on the pulse of your content marketing.

Once you get into the habit of producing and syndicating your content on a regular basis, it's important to get answers to the following content marketing-related questions:

Figure 47: Your "Content" report in Analytics is a key tool for measuring which content is generating the most traffic and conversions.

▶ **Which forms of content are working the best?** If you create an article and video focused on the same content and the video on your site generates twice the traffic and twice the time spent on your site per visitor, you should obviously create more videos covering similar topics.

▶ **Which syndication channels are generating the most traffic?** If you shoot a new article out to your top four social media sites (let's say Facebook, Twitter, LinkedIn, and Google+), it's important to pay attention to which of these sources generates the most traffic back to your content. Of course, you have to factor in the size of your audience: if you have 100 Twitter followers and 10,000 Facebook fans, you should expect more traffic from Facebook. Use a percentage of your audience as a gauge.

▶ **What content is resonating with my audience?** By looking at your "Content" report in Google Analytics, you can sort by "Avg. Time on Page" to see which articles are the most sticky. If certain blog posts or videos are keeping visitors engaged for five to ten minutes, while others have them headed for the door in thirty seconds, you'll have some obvious clues into which direction to take your content marketing plan.

▶ **Have my social shares increased?** If you see some of your content is getting tons of "shares," either on your website or on social media sites, take note of this and aim to replicate this positive behavior.

▶ **What are the best opportunities for content recycling?** One of the key principles of content marketing is to do more of what's working! To get extra mileage from your content, simply look at which articles are most successful in generating traffic to your site and recycle these. Take your top five traffic-generating articles and create videos, webinars, and infographics, or even put them together into an e-book. What works in one medium is likely to work as well, or even better, in others.

▶ **Is my content generating targeted traffic?** You might find that certain content generates a ton of visits but a high bounce rate and low visit duration. For example, if you publish an article focused on "best business card designs" that attracts visitors looking for "best business credit cards," you'll be able to pinpoint non-targeted traffic through the high bounce rates. This will prompt you to change your article(s) to be better focused on your target search terms and audience.

KEY CONCEPT: Be Sure to Track Your Content in Search Results

In Chapter 8, we covered tools for tracking your target keywords on search results pages. It's important to point out that each new piece of content you add should be tracked using your SERP tracking tool.

Doing so will keep you focused on creating highly targeted content, while also ensuring that you're measuring how well each piece does in Google rankings. Each time you publish a new article, be sure to add that article's target keywords to your SERP tracking tool. For example, if you write an article titled, "5 Simple Low-Calorie Cupcake Recipes" that targets the keyword phrase "cupcake recipes," you should add "cupcake recipes" to your SERP tracking tool and monitor your rankings. If you find your new articles aren't getting enough traffic, it's important to know where your site's ranking.

Each of these metrics work together to give you a complete picture of how well your content is doing at hitting its mark in terms of reach, engagement, and conversion. By consistently producing high-quality, targeted content on multiple formats and syndicating it to multiple locations across the Web, you'll be well on your way to attaining an insurmountable advantage over your competition.

LEARN MORE: Great Content Marketing Resources

▶ **"I Love Marketing"** (http://ILoveMarketing.com) is a great podcast show hosted by two extremely successful small business marketing experts: Dean Jackson and Joe Polish. These guys really understand education-based marketing and give away tons of free content (practicing what they preach).

▶ *Optimize: How to Attract and Engage More Customers by Integrating SEO, Social Media, and Content Marketing* (http://optimizebook.com), by Lee Odden, is a wonderful new book that dives deeply into how every aspect of your content marketing program can be "optimized" to work together for better results.

▶ *Content Rules* (http://www.contentrulesbook.com) is another very well-written book by Ann Handley (founder of MarketingProfs.com) and C.C. Chapman, which digs deeply into the content marketing process. This book has tons of helpful tips, resources, and numerous case studies revealing how popular brands use content for increased visibility and user engagement.

▶ *Content Is Currency* (http://www.contentiscurrency.com) is another new book that does a fantastic job of covering the content marketing process in great detail. The author, Jon Weubben (also author of *Content Rich,* another great content and SEO book), is a very well-regarded expert in content marketing.

CHAPTER SUMMARY

Content truly is king in our new cyber economy. Today's consumers are smart, savvy shoppers, researching and evaluating their options before making even the simplest of buying decisions. This new content-driven marketplace creates a great opportunity for those business owners who get on board and produce high-quality, targeted content on a regular basis.

Your STAND OUT Content Marketing Strategy hinges on creating and distributing compelling content that positions you and your business as the trusted resource for your local niche. The business owner who answers the questions and concerns of his or her audience is the first to build a relationship, one that will often lead to new customers and growing market share.

CHAPTER CHECKLIST

✔ **Step 1: Create a Content Road Map**
- Convert your Keyword Map into usable titles for blog posts or videos
- Create an "Editorial Calendar" and schedule the development of content

✔ **Step 2: Produce Great Content**
- Avoid outsourcing whenever possible
- Publish original content
- Publish content often
- Proof your work

✔ **Step 3: Optimize and Publish Your Content**
- CONTENT REACH
  ◊ Is the article focused on a single topic (target search term from your Content Road Map)?
  ◊ Is the article original?

◊ Is the article 500 words or more?

◊ Does the article include keywords in the right places?

◊ Have you addressed WordPress-specific content tasks (categories, tags, and permalinks)?

- CONTENT ENGAGEMENT:

  ◊ Is the copy focused on the reader's needs and questions?

  ◊ Does the copy follow the six-step sales letter format?

  ◊ Is the article readable?

  ◊ Is the article shareable?

- CONTENT CONVERSION

  ◊ Is there a clear call to action and offer?

  ◊ Is there a lead or opt-in form visible from the content?

  ◊ Is there a large, clearly visible phone number on the page?

✔ **Step 4: Syndicate Your Content Across the Web**

- Social media sites

- Your email list

- Video sites

- Press release sites

- Photo and graphics sites

- Podcasting sites

- Any media-specific sites that may apply

- Use OnlyWire and OneLoad to automate content syndication

✔ **Step 5: Recycle Your Content**

- For each new piece of content you publish, identify other formats that would work:

  ◊ Articles

  ◊ Videos

  ◊ Podcasts

  ◊ Infographics

  ◊ E-books

- Syndicate your recycled content to all relevant channels

✔ **Step 6: Measure the Impact of Your Content**

- Which forms of content work best?

- Which syndication channels work best?

- Use your most popular existing content for recycling

- Track each new piece of content in your SERP tracker

ELEVEN

WRITE YOUR WAY TO THE TOP WITH BLOGGING BASICS

"Where the Internet is about availability of information, blogging is about making information creation available to anyone."

—*George Siemens*

Think of this chapter as a copywriting crash course designed to prepare you to start blogging. We'll cover setting up your blog, what to write about, how to structure your blog posts, and even best practices in copywriting to help ensure that your message engages your audience and compels them to take action. By the end of this chapter, you'll be ready to start creating great content.

BLOGS DEFINED

Nowadays, blogs have become robust business publishing tools, acting as the primary content delivery mechanism for most small- and medium-sized businesses. A blog is perfectly designed for small business content publishers, including those who aren't extremely technological, as getting started takes little more than deciding which of the popular blogging platforms to use and selecting a design template for your blog.

Most blog templates are pre-designed with best practices in website usability in place. By now, most people have grown accustomed to consuming content in blog format. Nearly all blog platforms work the same way, displaying an index of categorized articles in reverse chronological order.

SETTING UP YOUR BLOG

If you launched your website using WordPress, you're probably aware that WordPress themes come with a blog already in place. Since WordPress began as a blogging platform, your WordPress site was born to host your blogs and content with little or no customization.

If you're not using WordPress to power your website, you can still easily add a WordPress blog to your site. Please see the following resources for further details:

RESOURCES: WordPress Beginners

▶ WPBeginner (http://www.wpbeginner.com) is a great site for getting started with WordPress.

▶ Lynda (http://lynda.com) offers simple, how-to training videos covering virtually every category of software, from basic Microsoft Office to advanced coding and graphic design applications. I highly recommend their WordPress tutorials.

Step 1: SELECT A BLOGGING PLATFORM

The first step in setting up your blog is deciding which blogging platform to use. There are two primary types of blogging platforms and choosing the right one is critical:

▶ **Hosted blogging platforms:** Hosted blog platforms are self-hosted platforms that do everything for you. All you need to do is sign up, select a blog theme, and start blogging. Popular hosted blog platforms include:

- Wordpress.com
- Blogger.com
- Typepad.com

While hosted platforms might seem easy, I do not recommend using them because you surrender control of your blog to these third-party providers and lose most of the "link juice" (SEO authority) in the process. For example, if you set up a blog on wordpress.com (http://yourblog.wordpress.com), you'll be blogging and adding content to Wordpress.com instead of your own site.

▶ **Stand-alone platforms:** The other type of blogging platform is the stand-alone or "client hosted" platform. This means that you host your blog on your own domain, just like you would with any other self-hosted website. Launching a self-hosted blog requires installing WordPress on your own domain through your hosting provider. In the past, most new bloggers steered clear of self-hosted or stand-alone blogs due to increased cost and technical limitations. These days, however, you can get a self-hosted WordPress blog up and running in about ten minutes using a "one-click install" and hosting costs around $5 per month with most popular hosting providers. See Chapter 4 for details on one-click installs and WordPress hosting.

KEY CONCEPT: Understand the Difference Between Wordpress.com and Wordpress.org

Blogging novices often become confused by the term "WordPress" as applied to setting up and hosting blogs. It's important to point out that "wordpress.com" and "wordpress.org" are entirely different animals:

▶ Wordpress.com refers to the hosted blogging platform, where users add content to blogs hosted on wordpress.com.

▶ Wordpress.org lets you download open-source files to, and run WordPress on, your own domain.

▶ When looking at themes, plugins, or technical support for your WordPress site, be sure and use http://wordpress.org, as this site relates to your self-hosted website/blog.

Step 2: ORGANIZE YOUR CONTENT

Once you've launched your blog platform on your domain there's one more critical step required before you start writing and publishing content: setting up your blog categories.

One of the greatest advantages of using a blogging platform like WordPress is the power of "taxonomy," or organizing your content within defined topical categories. Wordpress uses "categories" and "tags" to organize blog posts and present them to readers.

Best Practices for Blog Categories and Tags

▶ Use as few categories as possible to classify your blog content. Remember that simple navigation always trumps complex.

▶ Ensure that each new article you publish gets assigned at least one category.

▶ Assign two to three relevant tags to each article you post.

▶ Try to use the same tags for multiple articles.

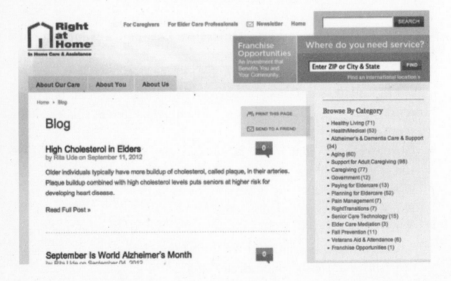

Figure 48: Right at Home uses clearly defined blog categories.

Figure 49: Tag Clouds allow users to find content related to common keywords (source: http://en.wikipedia.org/wiki/Tag_cloudhttp://wikipedia.com).

COPYWRITING CRASH COURSE: HOW TO WRITE ENGAGING CONTENT

Putting your thoughts on paper is a challenge that new bloggers often face. Expressing one's ideas through the written word is an art form unto itself, one that can take years to master. It goes without saying that many of us will never be acclaimed writers or experts in content development.

But we don't need to be. In fact, one of the greatest blunders new writers make is trying to emulate formal or professional prose when blogging about their businesses. This makes even the most patient writer bang her head against the wall, struggling with the awkwardness that comes from trying to write in the voice that a professional writer would.

The best way to develop super-engaging, high-converting content is to be yourself and write as if you were sitting across the table from one of your customers, having a casual conversation. In fact, this is the exact formula used by many of the most successful bloggers online: writing in a casual, informal, and personal tone. And it can work wonders for your content development as well. One of the best ways to STAND OUT is to personalize your content, making it your own through your unique style and perspective.

To write informally, all you need to do is relay information that you're already knowledgeable and passionate about in a style that comes naturally. To make things even easier, I'll give you a structure (blog template) in the next section.

To help you get started, here are a few valuable pointers on writing in a casual, conversational style:

▶ **It's not about you.** Every aspect of your articles should be solely focused on the needs of your target audience. They are looking or answers and information related to specific topics. These topics should dominate your content headlines, graphics, and body.

▶ **Be yourself.** Oscar Wilde once said, "Be yourself, everyone else is taken." This applies especially well to writing content. Let yourself off the hook and just write in a conversational tone. If you're sarcastic, be sarcastic. If you're serious and high-strung, write in that voice. When you let your personality shine through in your content, people will naturally pick up on it and feel much closer to you.

▶ **Write intimate copy.** One of the best copywriting strategies that works across all media is to focus on a single person. Avoid using terms such as "you readers" and "each of you." Instead, target each piece of content at a single person—the "avatar" or "user persona" that is your ideal customer.

▶ **Keep it light and informal.** If you've ever been to a website that's written in "corporate speak," you're well aware of how boring, useless, and almost offensive such uninspired drabness can be. If great content acts as an engagement magnet, corporate speak acts as customer repellent. Keep it casual and light while still informative.

KEY CONCEPT: Take Your Readers Down the Slippery Slide

The STAND OUT Blog Post Template consists of six sections, each designed with a single purpose in mind: to grab the reader's attention and get them to the next element. For example, the only goal of the headline is to get readers to read the introduction. And the goal of the introduction is to get readers to read the body. "Your readers should be so compelled to read your copy that they cannot stop reading until they read all of it as if sliding down a slippery slide" (Joe Sugarman, *The AdWeek Copywriting Handbook*).

Your audience will only take a ride down "the slippery slide" if your copy is focused on their questions and needs. This simple template serves as a boilerplate to help you structure your articles and ensure your slide transports your readers smoothly from headline to article and through your call to action.

THE STAND OUT BLOG POST TEMPLATE

Even after you've found your personal writing style or voice and figured out what to write about, you may still struggle with how to format the information you're trying to communicate. The best way to avoid falling victim to "blogger's block" is to give your creative juices a bit of a jumpstart in the form of a blog post template.

The Following STAND OUT Blog Post Template is a mash-up of several popular blog post structures (see "blogging resources" at the end of this chapter). This template represents a super-simple structure that can be used for just about any type of article. Use it to get started and, as you become more comfortable structuring your content, experiment with your own structures that work for you.

Six Elements of a Perfect Blog Post

Depending on the subject matter, you may choose to add or reformat specific sections of your articles, but every piece of content you publish should follow this structure:

1. Attention-Grabbing Headline

The headline is the core element in any form of advertising or copy. In fact, I've heard several copywriting experts say they spend 70-80 percent of their article creation time developing a great headline! This is for good reason: most Web surfers view Web pages and content in "scan mode," glancing over content for anything that stands out.

Your headline should grab your readers' attention and make them feel like skipping your article could be one of the worst decisions they've ever made! Each of the following headline formats is designed to hit certain well-known psychological triggers (such as curiosity, fear of loss, relevancy). These triggers work very well, as humans are often pre-programmed to react to certain stimuli on a subconscious level.

TEN HEADLINE FORMATS TO MAKE YOUR CONTENT STAND OUT:

1. **Use Humor ("Why SpongeBob Would Make a Great Accountant"):** People will always gravitate to content that makes them smile, even when researching something as non-comedic as the best grout to use with mosaic tile.

2. **Use Numbered Lists ("The 5 Best Electronics Gifts for Father's Day"):** Numbered lists are the linchpins of effective headline writing, used often in all formats, both offline and online. Numbered lists work well because they provide the reader with a sense of focus and curiosity.

3. **Personalize ("How to Tell If Your House Is Safe From Burglary"):** Relevance is a powerful tool used in all forms of copywriting. Making your headline personal (i.e., directly addressing the reader with words like "you" or "your") aids in grabbing the reader and making her think, "Hey, this is for me."

4. **Ask a Question ("Does Your Website Contain the 5 Secrets of Higher Conversion?"):** Asking a question can be useful in getting readers engaged through curiosity.

5. **Use Controversy ("10 Reasons Why Your _____ Is Killing You"):** Controversy will always turn heads, as it connects with sensitive and emotional parts of the brain. Any time you mention an issue in your headline that divides folks, it'll surely get attention. But be careful what you wish for—to avoid negative feedback, use controversy in a lighthearted manner.

6. **Leverage Mistakes ("The 8 Biggest _____ Mistakes and How to Avoid Them"):** No one likes to make mistakes, especially when researching a need, product, or service.

7. **Reveal Secrets ("4 Secret _____ Tips That Only the Pros Know"):** Secrets make us feel like we are being granted access to rare and highly valuable information. We can't help but try to find out what the "prize inside" is, especially when these secrets are relevant to our questions, needs, and interests.

8. **Use Similes and Metaphors ("Why Facebook Groups Are Like Your High School Prom"):** People are drawn to metaphors because we have a natural desire to connect something new with something familiar.

9. **Promise a Fantastic Result ("How to Save 70% on Your Next Grocery Bill"):** This example would work very well for an article covering home gardening or farming, for example. Results-focused headlines work so well because they focus on the "promise" or ultimate results and benefits of something, rather than on the features or tactics required to get there. Results-based copy works in all forms and sections of your content.

10. **Leverage Current Events and Pop Culture ("Top _____ Lessons from Dancing with the Stars"):** Using popular icons or events allows your content to piggyback off of popular issues that are already in the minds of your audience. Try to relate your copy to celebrities, news, or even gossip once in a while to help your articles STAND OUT.

KEY CONCEPT: Don't Forget SEO

Recall from the last chapter that your Content Road Map serves as your compass for creating content that's highly targeted towards your audience. Remember to include one or two of your target search terms in your title whenever possible. A good rule of thumb when it comes to balancing SEO with human interest in headlines is to think of your readers first, with a little SEO love thrown in for good measure.

For example, if you write an article targeting the search phrase "best wedding invitation designs," preserve the target search term in its exact form when devising a headline. Just add one or more of the ten headline formats on pages 238–9. You could use any of the following:

"The 5 Best Wedding Invitation Designs for Your Spring Wedding" (Use Numbered Lists);

"Are You Using the Best Wedding Invitation Design for Your Wedding?" (Ask a Question); or

"3 Secrets to Choosing the Best Wedding Invitation Design" (Reveal Secrets).

LEARN MORE: **How to Write Headlines That Work (copyblogger. com):** http://www.copyblogger.com/how-to-write-headlines-that-work/

2. The Introduction and Promise

After you've crafted the perfect, show-stopping headline, it's time to write the introduction. The introduction is an important element of your article, serving as a gateway between the attention-grabbing headline and the body section or "meat" of your article.

It's important to remember the "slippery slide" concept here, as the headline did its job of making your reader take notice of your article, but only long enough to read the introduction, where she will make an ultra-quick decision as to whether your article is worth the investment of time.

An effective introduction should connect with your reader by repeating the problem, issue, or question that brought him or her to your article, while creating some suspense and compelling him or her to read more.

A solid introduction is made up of three components:

1. **State the problem:** The problem is the main question, concern, or issue to your reader and the risks of not taking action and/or finding a solution.

    For example, for an article titled, "5 Simple Ways to Get a Raise at Work," the problems of the reader might include:

    ▶ Not making enough money
    ▶ Fear of asking for a raise

▶ Fear of asking for a raise and being rejected

No matter what your article is about, the purpose of its content will be to provide value or solve a problem for the reader.

2. **Point out the risks:** The risk is what happens to the reader if he or she does not read your article and gain the information needed to make a good decision or take the right action.

3. **Reveal the promise:** The promise is a very short, direct statement that explains what your article will cover. Think of the promise as a succinct description of the benefits your readers will gain from consuming your article.

Let's continue with our "5 Simple Ways to Get a Raise at Work" article topic and create a sample introduction, combining the problem statement and promise:

{PROBLEM:} "Asking for a raise at work can be a stressful experience. Many employees feel certain it's time for a promotion and/or raise but are unsure how to ask or perhaps even afraid of being denied their well-deserved increase in compensation. **{RISK:}** If you don't approach asking for your promotion the right way, you may end up spending months or longer being paid less than you're worth—or worse! **{PROMISE:}** In this article, we're about to reveal three surefire, time-tested methods for asking for a raise, increasing your odds of getting that promotion you deserve, and ensuring that your boss appreciates your value and sees you as an indispensable resource!"

3. The Body Section

The body is the meat of your article, outlining the simple steps, points, or resources that your reader tuned in for. For this section, dig right in and get going with the details of your blog post.

In the body, it's important to stay on point and present your topic clearly and concisely. One of the most popular body formats for many writers and bloggers is the bulleted or numbered list format. Depending on the type of content, this could be a list of points, techniques, steps (for "how to" articles), or arguments.

MAKE YOUR CONTENT HIGHLY READABLE

Before visitors start to read or consume your content, they'll likely give it a "what am I getting into" once-over, trying to gauge how easy it will be to read. If your visitors see long droning paragraphs (or the fact that your video is fifty minutes long), they'll likely bounce, searching for a more concise or more easily readable source of information. To make your content more readable, use small paragraphs, bulleted lists, and clearly defined headings. For video content, break up longer videos into smaller stand-alone segments of information. Think of each piece of content from an overall visual perspective. Does it seem long and droning, or concise, clearly organized, and "punchy"?

▶ **Short paragraphs:** Just about every person on the planet appreciates ease when it comes to reading content. There's no rule book that requires authors to write dense, text-heavy prose organized into ultra-long paragraphs. These days, most folks have grown to accept and appreciate less formal, more "conversational" formats, for both Web-based and printed content.

▶ **Clear headings:** Headings are powerful visual queues used to let your readers know how your content is organized. Most readers will "scan" your article before digging in, as a "second check" to make sure your content will meet their needs.

For short articles you may use very few headings (Title, Intro, Body, Summary, etc.) but for longer "epic" blog posts, you may very well find yourself using eight, ten, or even a dozen headings. All that matters is that you use headings to break up your content into logical separate "blocks" of information with clear, bold headings describing what's below each heading.

▶ **Bulleted and numbered lists:** Whether your article has three or twenty-three steps or points to be made, the structure is the same. Your bullet points could be arguments, specifications, steps in a process, lists of resources, or reviews. What's important is that you present your content in small, digestible chunks and use a clearly organized list.

Many writers find that thinking of their content in this simple framework helps them better organize their thoughts and write content more quickly. This format works great from a "user experience" standpoint as well, as most consumers of online content are familiar with this format and will likely appreciate the ease of use it provides.

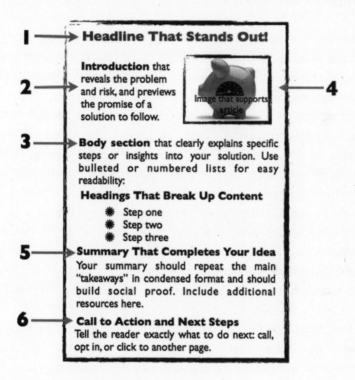

Figure 50: The STAND OUT Blog Post Template

4. The Supporting Graphic

The supporting graphic plays a critical role in reader engagement, providing a powerful visual that grabs your reader's attention while also revealing some clue as to what the article is about.

Countless studies have revealed the effectiveness of using photos and graphics in all forms of media. Use a photo or image in every blog post.

Best Practices for Using Images in Blogs

Many of the best practices for blog images share the same goal as other forms of content: to grab your reader's attention, add value, and keep them engaged. Here are a few of my top tips for ensuring that your blog images STAND OUT:

► **Consistency:** Make a decision to either use or not use images in your articles. Your readers will grow to expect constancy in the way your content is presented. I recommend including an image in every article.

► **Relevance:** One of the cornerstones of all things content-related, relevance plays an important role in the use of graphics in blogs. An article about "3 Delicious Gluten-Free Pizza Recipes" shouldn't have a picture of a gas pump. Don't treat your image as an afterthought, quickly adding whatever image you stumble upon. Be sure your image(s) are relevant to your copy.

► **Humor:** Just like headlines, your photos have a big job to do with a small amount of "real estate." Humor is on the short list of tools for grabbing your reader's attention. As long as you don't go overboard, a funny graphic or image will beat a dry stock photo any day.

► **Attention:** The use of bold colors, text, or graphics within your blog images can really help your article STAND OUT. We are all preconditioned to filter out advertising messages and bland content, making it more difficult to make an impact. However, certain images, like a stop sign, still demand our attention. Leverage attention-getting elements in your blog photos whenever possible.

► **People and Animals:** People and animals sell and grab attention like nobody's business. The younger the better—babies and kittens have been proven to garner more eyeballs than all the market research-driven fancy graphics combined.

► **Value:** If you're using a chart, graph, or other data containing graphics, it's important to add value right away. For example, an image labeled "New House Prices in Dallas" showing current median prices for several neighborhoods would stand on its own, providing readers with immediate value.

For a list of free stock photos sites, refer back to page 67.

5. The Summary

The summary section is a short but very important section. This is where you "bring it on home," leaving your reader with a succinct conclusion or takeaway from your article. This is also where you should use social proof, further establishing yourself as the expert in your niche, and also list additional resources that were not included in the body of your article.

It's important to use all three of these elements in your article summary and properly set up the article's call to action.

▶ **Sum up your content into a concise takeaway.** This is a simple one- to three-sentence summary of the article you've written. It should quickly remind the reader of the problem, risks, and solution.

▶ **Build social proof and authority.** Add one or two quick sentences about your particular expertise in the topic that your article is about. Nothing over the top, just a quick injection of social proof that reminds your readers that you and your business are the best at what you do.

▶ **List additional resources.** In many cases, your short blog article shouldn't be considered the comprehensive resource for the topic being covered. Therefore, the last element of the summary section is a place to list additional resources related to the article's topic. Doing this adds great value to your readers—value that they'll be sure to pick up on and reciprocate in the form of repeat visits, referrals, and patronage.

Let's create an example article summary by combining the aforementioned three elements:

{Takeaway}: "As stressful as asking for a raise can be, not doing so can result in worse consequences than asking and getting denied. When you consider how much is at stake, it's critical to follow a proven, three-step process to increase your odds of obtaining the promotion you deserve: Go above and beyond the call of duty, quantify your contribution, and present your offer with options. **{Social Proof}:** Over my fifteen years as a career consultant, I have helped hundreds of employees get well-deserved promotions and raises using these three powerful techniques.

{Additional Resources}: If you want to learn more about best practices in negotiating compensation, I recommend these great articles:

> Link to great article 1
> Link to great article 2
> Link to great article 3

6. Call to Action

Each time you develop a piece of content, it's important to keep the goal in mind. This keeps you focused on which topic and related keywords you should be using, as well as the desired action(s) you'd like your readers to take. Of course, all of your content should add value to, educate, and increase engagement from your target audience.

Many writers make the mistake of leaving a clear call to action out of their content. Even bloggers who do include a call to action at the end of their articles often miss the mark by not being clear or direct enough in communicating the desired action.

Your call to action needs to be clear, direct, and compelling. If you can include a special offer, even better. At first, using a strong call to action might feel uncomfortable, almost like handholding or overt salesmanship. However, if you believe in the value your business delivers to customers, you should be almost evangelical about ensuring your offers get seen and heard.

Types of Calls to Action For Blogs

▶ **Asking for feedback:** One the greatest benefits of blogging as a content publishing platform is its emphasis on two-way communication. Your WordPress website and blog allow user comments for every post. While your blog might initially seem like a ghost town, you'll soon start seeing comments, questions, and feedback on your articles. These comments are a great source for leads, information, and additional website traffic (each comment is user-generated content!). By asking a question at the end of your articles, you'll increase the number of interactive comments. Using our sample article, the author could include the following call to action: "Have you asked for a raise lately? Please tell us about your experience in the comments section below."

▶ **Phone calls:** Regardless of your type of business, few things work as well in building your business as phone calls from potential customers. At the end of your blog posts, simply state your offer and strong call to action: "For a complimentary consultation/appetizer/$20 coupon/room of carpet cleaning, call now: (800) 777-7777."

▶ **Lead or opt-in forms:** For some offers or types of business, phone numbers may not be the preferred contact method. If you're building a subscriber list, the end of a blog post is a great place to position a special offer and opt-in form. The same goes for lead generation forms. Lead conversion is about giving your readers several options for contacting you—options that are placed in prominent positions on your Web pages.

▶ **Social shares and Likes:** Given the amazing power of social media to increase your online visibility, and the increased emphasis Google is placing on "social signals" in their ranking algorithms, options for social shares and likes should not only be visible on all pages of content, but you also shouldn't be shy about directly asking for shares and Likes on your website.

KEY CONCEPT: How Many Calls to Action Is Too Many?

If you're new to content marketing and conversion, you'll be sensitive to "asking for the lead," concerned about appearing too pushy or "salesy" on your website. This fear of over-promotion almost always leads to under-promotion. Although you look at your website often, scrutinizing every element and noticing every opt-in form, phone number, and social media widget, your audience does not. They'll likely miss a great number of conversion and lead generation elements on your Web pages. This is why many of the top online marketers and large brands use multiple "conversion units" on every page. I recommend you use at least four conversion elements on each page of your site. The key is using different types to avoid over-promoting while still achieving a high conversion rate. For example, on one article page of your site, you could use the following conversion elements without pushing the envelope on usability:

▶ A phone number in the header
▶ An opt-in form in the sidebar
▶ A special offer (e-book or video) in the sidebar
▶ A call to action at then end of the article
▶ A social media sharing widget within your content
▶ A "leave a comment" section below the article

In this example above, there are six potential actions the visitor could take, all working together without detracting from the high-value content itself. The key is that you measure conversions, paying attention to which pages and offers convert the best and changing your Web page layouts accordingly.

Use this STAND OUT Blog Post Template to jumpstart your content development efforts and produce more high-quality articles more quickly. Don't view this template as "rudimentary"—this simple six-step approach to copywriting is used by some of the most popular sites and brands around. What matters most is that you publish something as soon as possible. As you start to earn your stripes in content development and blogging, you'll surely expand your palate of article formats and customize them to your liking.

TEN GREAT BLOG POST IDEAS

One of the fastest ways to jumpstart the content creation process is to use a proven framework or type of blog post and apply it to your business. Here are ten time-tested blog post formats that can easily be adapted to your industry or focus area:

1. **Other Blogs:** No matter how obscure your niche might be, it's highly probable that someone's already written about it. This is especially true if you operate a local business in a niche that's very common in other cities. One of the quickest paths to finding your voice and getting into the groove of blogging is to use the work of others for inspiration. If you want to create the leading organic gardening blog in Phoenix, you'll probably find similar sites in other cities to get ideas from.

    BLOGGING RESOURCE: Use Technorati and Google Blog Search to Find Similar Blogs
    Technorati is a great tool for finding content-rich blogs in your niche. Simply go to http://technorati.com and search for blogs within any topic area. After clicking on the search icon, you'll see a list of relevant results, along with their "Technorati Rank" (a ranking of all blogs on Technorati) and "Authority Score," which is Technorati's own method of measuring the relative authority of listed blogs.

2. **Content Curation:** Curation is simply collecting content related to your niche, summarizing it, and delivering it to your audience with your own twist. Content curation is a shortcut when compared with generating your own content from scratch. Nonetheless, your audience will greatly appreciate the work you've done in "filtering" and condensing information for them. Many of the Web's largest media sites, bloggers, and companies use content curation (also called aggregation) as their prime source of new content. When you think about it, most news companies don't write the news, they

Figure 51: Searching Technorati for "Wedding Planning" displays several great blogs to draw ideas from.

simply present the information with their own unique voice and perspective that resonates with their audience.

If you're a new blogger or content writer, use content curation as your starting point. You already have passion and expertise in your niche. Now all you need to do is stay abreast of industry trends and new content (using Google alerts, and your RSS reader—covered in Chapter 14) and report the "key takeaways" to your audience. Your readers will care less about the original source of the valuable content than they'll remember they got it from you.

3. **Customer Profiles:** There are few easier or more effective forms of content than real-life examples of customers using your products or services. This applies to any form of business, from pizza shops to podiatrists. Within your editorial calendar, be sure to add one or more case studies or customer profile articles. The simplest way to generate customer-focused content is to interview the customer(s) about their business/family, the challenges or needs they faced, and how your company met those

needs. Customer profile articles resonate on many psychological levels, establishing social proof, authority, and trust at the same time.

4. **Expert Interviews:** What better way to present highly valuable content focused on a topic your readers find important than to interview an expert? Regardless of your business niche, there are likely several categories of topics you could be writing about. Interviewing an expert allows you to "go deep" and examine nuances of your subject matter that you might not know. Most experts will gladly do interviews, as they love the additional exposure (be sure to include a link to experts' sites as a "thank you").

    There's no category of business where expert interviews wouldn't apply. For example, a pizza shop owner could interview a wine expert on the best wines to pair with Italian pies. A divorce lawyer could interview a relationship or family counselor, and a real estate agent could interview a home decorator or feng shui specialist. When you present valuable content from an expert, you share a bit of their expertise by proxy in the eyes of your audience.

5. **How To's:** Instructional content is the cornerstone of education-based content marketing. You can come up with five, ten, or even twenty "how to" questions that you commonly hear from customers. Simply add them to your Content Road Map and create your first great "step-by-step" blog today. Your audience will naturally reciprocate by sharing and recommending your content and, often, even frequenting your business.

6. **Top 10 Lists:** Seeing content presented in lists gives readers a sense of value and focus, piquing their curiosity in the process. A few months ago, I created a simple video, which I converted into a Slideshare Presentation entitled "Top 10 Small Business Web Design Mistakes (http://www.slideshare.net/FletchMonster/top-10-small-business-web-design-mistakes). This presentation made the front page of Slideshare, gaining over 3,100 views right off the bat. Had I titled the presentation "Several Web Design Mistakes," the impact would have been notably smaller.

7. **Leveraging Pop Culture:** We're all more aware of celebrities, reality stars, and media goings-on than we'd care to admit. Your audience will likely respond to content that relates your niche to pop culture and hot topics in the media. To paraphrase the great Frank Kern, "Great marketing is about entering the conversation that's already going on in the client's mind." Imagine the impact of articles titled "10 Affordable Ways to Dress Better Than Kim Kardashian," for a women's clothing retailer, or, "The Top 10 Celebrity Getaways You Can Afford," for a travel agent.

8. **Ratings and Reviews:** One of the by-products of becoming an authority in your niche is that your audience will value your opinion. Publishing ratings and reviews is one of the most effective ways to leverage your expertise and add value to your audience. All you need to do is consider which purchases your audience is likely to make and help them by providing insights into popular options. An auto mechanic can review tires, a barbershop shampoo, and a dog trainer flea meds. Make a list of the top "corollary" decisions made by your customers and create your first "2013 _____ Reviews" article.

9. **Company Info:** Giving your readers a glimpse into your company can go a long way toward converting visitors into buyers. Whether focused on the key ingredients of your products, unique processes, or even key members of your team, company-focused articles are a theme you should draw from. Start with a "Behind the Scenes" or "How We Make _____" article and go from there.

KEY CONCEPT: Babies and Kittens Aren't Just for Politicians Anymore

One of the best ways to engage, connect, and build trust with your audience is by incorporating your personal life into your content. This can include hobbies, interests, and even family, as long as you are comfortable with it.

At the end of the day, we're people: brothers, sisters, sons, daughters, mothers and fathers, and pet owners. For most of us, these roles play a larger role in our lives than our jobs do. Instead of limiting your content to the subject matter at hand, throw in some personal details, photos, or anecdotes. By establishing a connection on a personal level, your content will certainly STAND OUT from all your competitors' "business-only" websites and blogs.

10. **Industry News:** Gathering and reporting events and news related to your niche market is a great way to stay in contact with your readers. Close cousins to curated content, industry news posts require little more than staying abreast of and creating content covering newsworthy happenings that your audience finds interesting and useful (videos work great for this).

NEXT STEPS

Once you've written your first few blog articles, follow the STAND OUT content marketing plan covered in Chapter 10. You've done the hard part by creating your content, but don't forget to add the "marketing":

▶ **(Step 4) Syndicate your blog articles across the Web.**
▶ **(Step 5) Recycle your articles.**
▶ **Measure the impact of your content.**

CHAPTER SUMMARY

Once you've written a handful of blog posts, you'll find your own voice and never look back. The key is to just get started. One thing we producers of content have in common is that our first stuff usually stinks, at least in our own eyes. But without these first few "ducks," you'll never grow into the confident and prolific swan of a blogger you aim to be. The key to blogging is to write engaging content that addresses the questions and needs of your target audience. Your articles should be focused on them and written in a conversational and personal tone, allowing your engaging personality to shine through and establish a connection.

Recently I went surfing for the first time. I felt and looked like an injured turtle in a washing machine. But after hitting the waves just a few more times, I began to see that one day, I might actually stand up and ride a wave. The same goes for writing. Just as watching surfing videos on YouTube won't suddenly give me the skills to hang ten, reading all the copywriting books in the world can't replace a few hours of placing pen to paper (or fingers to keyboard) and bringing your message to life. Take action.

BLOGGING AND COPYWRITING RESOURCES

▶ **Copyblogger** (http://www.copyblogger.com) is the de facto resource for all things blogging, copywriting, and Internet marketing.

▶ **Problogger** (http://www.problogger.net) is chock-full of great resources spanning every aspect of blogging and online marketing.

▶ **17 Copy-And-Paste Blog Post Templates** (http://www.smartpassiveincome.com/blog-post-templates/)

CHAPTER CHECKLIST

✔ **Step 1: Choose a Blogging Platform**
  • Set up a self-hosted WordPress blog on your own domain
✔ **Step 2: Configure Your Blog Categories and Tags**
  • Your blog categories should match your main products and services
  • Use as few categories as possible
  • Ensure that each new article you publish gets assigned at least one category
  • Assign two to three relevant tags to each article you post
  • Use the same tags for multiple articles
  • Add a "tag cloud" to your blog to help visitors find related articles
✔ **Step 3: Understand Copywriting Basics**
  • Focus on your audience

- Be yourself
- Write intimate copy
- Keep it loose and informal

✔ **Step 4: Use the Six-Part STAND OUT Blog Post Template**
- Headline
- Introduction
- Body
- Supporting graphic
- Summary
- Call to action

✔ **Step 5: Experiment with Ten Popular Blog Themes**
- Other blogs
- Curated content
- Customer profiles (or case studies)
- Expert interviews
- How to's
- Top 10 lists
- Pop culture
- Ratings and reviews
- Company and product info
- Industry news

TWELVE

BE SEEN EVERYWHERE USING ONLINE VIDEOS

"Internet video is now 40 percent of consumer Internet traffic, and will reach 62 percent by the end of 2015, not including the amount of video exchanged through P2P file sharing. The sum of all forms of video (TV, video on demand [VoD], Internet, and P2P) will continue to be approximately 90 percent of global consumer traffic by 2015."

—*Cisco*[7]

Online video is exploding in popularity, while become extremely simple and inexpensive to create. These two factors make now the perfect time to start producing great content in video format.

Creating great-looking videos requires little more than a few hundred dollars of equipment and a few hours spent learning the ropes. In fact, you can make great videos without ever appearing on camera!

WHY VIDEO IS SO POWERFUL FOR SMALL BUSINESSES

Online video offers several unique benefits over other forms of content:

▶ **Great for Reach and SEO:** If you remember from Chapter 6, Google often produces "blended" search results, including video. While you may have a hard time reaching the top three in organic search results for very competitive search terms (keywords) using blog articles alone, you could

---

[7]http://www.cisco.com/en/US/prod/sanity/white_paper_c11-481360_test.html

very well achieve top billing using video, as that playing field is much less crowded. In addition, Google places great authority on YouTube content.

Videos also help your content STAND OUT on a page of text-based articles (see Figure 52). By nature, video thumbnails in search results have an advantage over text-only results in their ability to draw searchers' eyes.

And don't forget the power of YouTube itself. After you've created a few online videos, your YouTube Channel might act as its own pillar for traffic and lead generation.

Figure 52: Using "how to tie a tie" as an example search, the video results STAND OUT.

▶ **Increased Engagement:** Video content allows your audience to truly get to know you, building a stronger bond more quickly than they would by just reading an article. Countless studies have shown that adding video content to Web pages produces an immediate increase in time spent on a site. Videos are a great way to welcome each visitor to your home page or content and establish an immediate bond.

▶ **Time Savings:** Once you get over the learning curve while making your first or second video, you'll find that making videos takes less time than writing content! Think about how much easier it would be to jot down a few bullet points and make a quick video, compared to writing and editing a 700- to 1,000-word article.

▶ **Double or Triple the Bang for Your Buck:** Each video you create can be inexpensively transcribed into a text article (transcription) and the audio can be extracted for separate use as well. Remember, Content Recycling and Syndication are key components of your STAND OUT Content Marketing Strategy

APPLYING THE ONLINE FUNNEL TO VIDEOS

▶ **Reach:** Each video you create should use your target keywords in its title, description, and tags. Just like written articles, each video should be created from your Content Road Map and be focused on specific topics and keywords.

▶ **Engagement:** While video itself is generally more engaging than text alone, some videos are less engaging than others. Video engagement boils down to effective messaging and production value. Creating a highly engaging video requires all the same copywriting skills as a text article, with the added components of "production quality"—the sound, lighting, and composition elements specific to video.

▶ **Conversion:** As the most engaging content medium, video should also be held to the same standards as written content. Each video should have a specific call to action, not only within its messaging, but through the use of one or more great conversion tools that only video can offer, such as clickable offers, lead forms, and phone numbers.

CREATING EFFECTIVE, COMPELLING VIDEOS

Now that you see the benefits of adding online video to your content repertoire, let's dig right into producing your first awesome video blog post with my seven-step, foolproof process for creating and marketing high-quality online videos. Once you get started, you'll find this process to be much simpler and more fun than you might have thought. The skills you'll pick up by going through these steps will stay with you for the rest of your career.

Figure 53: This simple seven-step process will have you creating great online videos in a snap!

Step 1: SELECT THE RIGHT TOOLS

Many small business owners assume that getting set up with the tools and equipment required for making videos will cost thousands of dollars. But advancements in technology have granted us access to professional-level filming and editing tools at a fraction of this cost. In fact, you can acquire a complete "starter kit" with everything you need for less than $500. And you may even already have several of the required items.

Video Camera

The first item you'll need is a video camera. While you can create great videos without a camera (see "screen-capture videos" on page 273), I'm assuming that at least some of your video content will include you or another person in them, and for this you do need a camera.

WEBCAMS

If your videos will be less visual and more focused on you reporting on or delivering information in front of the camera, you may need to look no further than a high-quality HD webcam. In fact, many PCs and Macs have great cameras built in.

RESOURCE: The Logitech c920 Webcam

There are dozens of great webcams available for under $100, but I recommend the Logitech C920 Webcam (http://www.logitech.com/en-us/webcam-communications/webcams/hd-pro-webcam-c920), which costs around $90. This is truly a "plug and play" camera, and it's used by many video bloggers.

The key to using a webcam is to have great lighting and a simple, neutral background, which we'll cover in more detail in the next section.

There are a few notable limitations in using simple webcams, mainly that they require you to be sitting in front of your computer, and they limit the format of your videos to you talking to the camera without visual aids, such as a whiteboard or flip chart.

IPHONE

Many folks are surprised to learn that the iPhone can create high-quality videos. With its eight-megapixel iSight camera, the iPhone can record great video in HD (1080p) at up to thirty frames per second.

Check out these examples of short films made with the iPhone:

▶ http://youtu.be/La4JR-bYtns
▶ http://youtu.be/Z4UeametC-w

Most of us wouldn't expect to create high-quality videos with a mobile phone because most handheld-shot movies are "shaky," with poor lighting, composition, and audio. But when you use a tripod, microphone and neutral "backdrop," the iPhone's camera becomes a professional movie-making machine!

RESOURCE: Great Online Course for Making Online Video with the iPhone

iPhone Video Hero (http://ivideohero.com) is a great online course that costs $97. This video course demonstrates how to make video using the iPhone from start to finish, all in a very straightforward, step-by-step process.

Mini HD Cameras

Small, pocket-sized video cameras ("mini HDs") have become all the rage. Virtually every camera manufacturer makes some version of mini HD, ranging from $100 to $400, and they all do the same thing. I encourage you to read reviews and select a camera that fits your personal requirements, style, and budget. However, the pocket HD camera you choose must shoot in 1080p (refers to high definition screen resolution) and have an external microphone (mic) jack.

RESOURCE: The Kodak Zi8 Pocket Video Camera

The Kodak Zi8 Pocket Video Camera (http://www.amazon.com/Kodak-Zi8-Pocket-Video-Camera/dp/B002HOPUPC) shoots amazing high-quality video in HD, works very well with external microphones, and even has a built-in USB jack for easy movie uploading. The price ranges from $100 to $400, depending on whether you buy a new or used model. Although Kodak recently stopped making Zi8s, they are still easy to find online.

Figure 54: The Kodak Zi8 is a great inexpensive HD camera for video blogging.

DIGITAL SLR CAMERAS

If you're ready for network-quality, high-definition Web video, a DSLR camera is for you. DSLR stands for "Digital Single Lens Reflex," which means these cameras shoot digital images as opposed to film, and that the single lens "permits the photographer to view through the lens and hence see exactly what will be captured, contrary to viewfinder cameras where the image could be significantly different from what will be captured" (Wikipedia: http://en.wikipedia.org/wiki/Digital_single-lens_reflex_camera).

These cameras are top of the line for online video creation, costing from \$500 to \$2,000 or more. While DSLRs might take a bit longer to master based on the greater functionality, the payoff will be worth it because of the much higher quality results that can be achieved. The main differences between DSLR and Mini HD cameras are the available lens, lighting, and filtering settings. If you've ever seen a video where the subject is in focus while the background is "blurred," you can bet the video was shot with DSLR.

Based on the steep increase in price compared with the incremental increase in quality, I recommend you start with a much simpler and less expensive pocket HD camera and move up if and when your abilities and your profits from video content justify doing so.

RESOURCE: **The Canon 60D Is a Video Blogger's Dream Come True**
If you are leaning more toward "indie filmmaker" and less toward "complete video newbie," I recommend the Canon 60D (http://www.usa.canon.com/cusa/consumer/products/cameras/slr_cameras/eos_60d), a very powerful and extremely popular camera used by video bloggers everywhere. This camera costs around $1,000, depending on the configuration and where you buy it.

Microphone

One of the secrets of creating great Web video is audio. In fact, I would rather publish a fair quality video with great sound than a super-crispy HD video with poor sound quality.

Many Web videos are made without consideration for audio, using "built-in" microphones, resulting in audio that sounds distant, and is hard to hear and full of background noise. Creating excellent audio tracks, however, only requires one inexpensive tool: a lapel microphone. Lapel microphones are cheap, starting at $15, are dependable, and do a great job of capturing crisp, professional-sounding audio.

Of course, if you are using a webcam or creating a screen recording-based video, you can use a simple computer microphone.

RESOURCES: **High-Quality Microphones That Will Make You the Voice of Your Niche**
▶ **For video cameras:** Audio-Technica ATR-3350 Lavalier

Omnidirectional Condenser Microphone (http://www.amazon.com/Audio-Technica-ATR-3350-Omnidirectional-Condenser-Microphone/dp/B002HJ9PTO) is very inexpensive ($22), with an extra-long cord to accommodate any type of camera setup. I recommend you buy two to three, as they're cheap backups.

▶ **Computer audio:** If you're recording via a webcam or doing screen recordings, my favorite microphone is the Blue Snowball USB Microphone (http://www.amazon.com/Blue-Microphones-Snowball-Microphone-Textured/dp/B000EOPQ7E). At under $70, this is a very high-quality computer microphone that can capture voice and even musical instruments with very high range and clarity. It's important to note that the Blue Snowball uses a USB input so be sure your Mac or PC has one.

LIGHTING

Many new video makers make the mistake of placing too much focus on the camera and not enough on the composition of the video itself. With the right lighting, requiring as little as two strong lights positioned at forty-five degrees from the video subject, an iPhone or webcam-filmed video can look spectacular. By the same token, the best DLSR camera in existence would produce poor quality footage in the absence of decent lighting.

KEY CONCEPT: Use Three-Point Lighting for Better Looking Web Video

One of the quickest ways to dramatically increase the quality of your online video is to use the tried and true "three-point lighting system."

The following is a great overview of basic video lighting from mediacollege.com(http://www.mediacollege.com/lighting/three-point/).

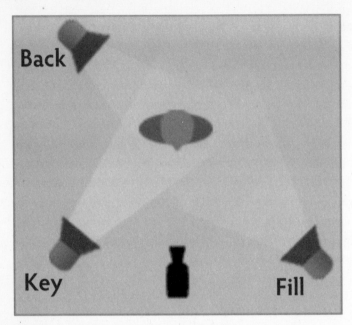

Figure 55: By following the three-point lighting system, your videos will STAND OUT in quality.

▶ **Key light:** This is the main light. It is usually the strongest and has the greatest influence on the look of the scene. It is placed to one side of the camera/subject so that this side is well lit and the other side has some shadow.

▶ **Fill light:** This is the secondary light and is placed on the opposite side of the key light. It is used to fill the shadows created by the key. The fill should usually be softer and less bright than the key, so to achieve this, move the light further away or use some natural sunlight if available. You might also want to set the fill light to more of a flood than the key.

▶ **Back light:** The back light is placed behind the subject and lights it from the rear. Rather than providing direct lighting, its purpose is to provide definition and subtle highlights around the subject's outlines. This helps separate the subject from the background and provide a three-dimensional look.

Here's a great YouTube video covering basic three-point lighting: http://www.youtube.com/watch?v=AcMX1RcNRYA

RESOURCE: The Cheap and Awesome Basic Video Lighting Kit

This basic lighting kit from Cowboy Studios (http://www.amazon. com/Cowboystudio-Photography-Portrait-Continuous-Umbrellas/dp/ B003WLY24O) is just $59 and includes everything you need to set up a great mini-video studio.

Editing Software

Once you start creating videos, you'll need video editing software to help you edit your videos. There are several simple-to-use and inexpensive solutions like ScreenFlow (Mac) and Camtasia Studio (PC) that can also be used to create videos without a camera. You've seen online videos of content being covered without a live human being on film, such as software demos, webinars, or online training sessions, and perhaps a voiceover recording of a PowerPoint presentation.

These "screen recording" videos are very popular and easy to create. We'll cover tips on creating screen recordings in this chapter, but for now, let's choose the right software application for the job:

▶ **For Macs:** ScreenFlow (http://www.telestream.net/screen-flow/) is a great software tool that I and many other online marketing and video content creators use. ScreenFlow is very easy to use for editing and creating screencast video with a few simple clicks of the mouse. At around $90, this is an extremely affordable application as well.

▶ **For PCs:** The video editing and creation program of choice is Camtasia Studio (http://www.techsmith.com/camtasia.html). This program works like ScreenFlow in that you can edit camera-produced movies and create screen capture movies as well. The price is similar, at $100. While Camtasia offers a Mac version of their software, I prefer ScreenFlow.

Optional Tools for Video Creation

Although you'll get far with the core tools needed for making online video, there are a few other great tools that you might find useful, depending on the type of video(s) you intend to create.

ONLINE PRESENTATION SOFTWARE

If you've ever had to endure a long, boring slideshow presentation, the word "PowerPoint" might send you into a boredom-induced coma. Most people use PowerPoint the wrong way, creating dozens of boring, unengaging slides and reading through them doing their best Ben Stein impression from beginning to end.

But using PowerPoint or Keynote to create awesome Web video is simple: create a quick presentation covering your topic of choice, including engaging graphics, photos, and text, and record yourself talking through the content using ScreenFlow or Camtasia.

▶ **Keynote** (http://www.apple.com/iwork/keynote/) is Apple's answer to PowerPoint. For $19.95, this software is a "must-have" for any Mac-based video creator. While Keynote shares many of the same functions and features with PowerPoint, the ease of use and ability to create stunning graphics and slides with little technical knowledge make this my software of choice.

▶ **PowerPoint** (http://office.microsoft.com/en-us/powerpoint/) is available for around $129 for Mac and PC and does a great job of facilitating the creation of slides used in screen recording-based video. You may already have PowerPoint installed on your machine, an added bonus if you're getting started with video on a tight budget.

BACKDROPS

If the location you intend to use for filming video doesn't provide a "neutral" background such as a white or gray wall, you might benefit from purchasing a cheap but effective portable backdrop.

RESOURCE: Fotodiox 5x7BW 5-Feet x 7-Feet Collapsible 2-in-1 Background Backdrop Panel

This cheap, lightweight, and effective panel (http://www.amazon.com/Fotodiox-5x7BW-Collapsible-Background-Backdrop/dp/B003Y2Q7QM) is perfect for those looking for a great way to improve composition for a very small cost ($49).

While this might seem like a lot of stuff to buy and learn to use, all you really need is a camera, a couple of lights, a lapel microphone, and editing software. Once you've gathered the required tools, it's time to start making your first video.

WHITEBOARD

While not typically thought of as a video-related tool, the whiteboard is among the most important tools in my video production arsenal. Many times, you'll want to draw while you talk, adding valuable visual content to your video. Instead of spending dozens of hours trying to add text and graphics in post-production, just use a whiteboard and draw yourself silly.

A whiteboard can also double as a nice clean backdrop. Purchase one large enough to cover the whole filming area of the camera, and avoid showing the borders or other distracting background elements (see figure below).

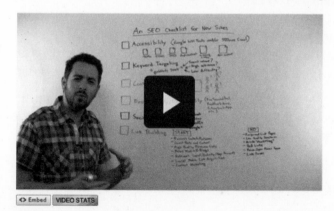

Figure 56: Rand Fishkin of SEOMoz.org uses a whiteboard to create great video content.

Step 2: OUTLINE YOUR CONTENT

Before you hit the "record" button and start revealing your best-kept business secrets to your audience, you need to know what to say. By creating a well-organized outline of your content, you'll find it much easier to discuss your topic on video, coming across much smoother and more polished than you will trying to "wing it" and talk through a topic without an outline.

All you need to do to create your video outline is use the six-part "STAND OUT Blog Post Template" from the last chapter:

▶ **Headline:** The title of your video (on your blog and YouTube)
▶ **Introduction:** States the problem to your audience
▶ **Body:** Lists your talking points in bullet format
▶ **Supporting graphic:** N/A unless you add graphics to your video later
▶ **Summary:** quick wrap-up that builds social proof and lists additional resources
▶ **Call to action:** Include your offer with the URL or phone number viewers should be directed to

Step 3: PRODUCE YOUR VIDEO

There are two ways to create a video: with a camera (live action) or without (screen recordings). First, let's cover the live action format. The following tips will help save time and ensure you're producing the highest quality videos possible:

LIVE-ACTION VIDEO BEST PRACTICES

Aside from lighting and ensuring you're using a neutral, solid background, there are a few more tips for ensuring your videos STAND OUT like no other:

▶ **Create good composition:** The rule of thirds: "a 'rule of thumb' or guideline which applies to the process of composing visual images such as paintings, photographs and designs.[1] The guideline proposes that an image should be imagined as divided into nine equal parts by two equally-spaced horizontal lines and two equally-spaced vertical lines, and that important compositional elements should be placed along these lines or their intersections.[2] Proponents of the technique claim that aligning a subject with these points creates more tension, energy and interest in the composition than simply centering the subject would," (http://en.wikipedia.org/wiki/Rule_of_thirds). This is a time-tested rule for the composition of subjects within a frame or photo that is used by painters, photographers, and filmmakers. The gist of the rule of thirds is that placing your subject within one third of the frame creates tension and contrast, making the image more interesting.

▶ **Choose clothing carefully:** Wear solid colors that contrast with the background and avoid busy stripes and graphics on your clothing.

▶ **Do a test run first:** Nothing is more frustrating than creating your online video masterpiece, only to download it to your computer and find out the microphone was off or that the camera shot cut off half of your head. Take the time to do a quick test run by filming ten to twenty seconds of video and then checking the lighting, composition, and audio.

Figure 57: Example of the "Rule of Thirds" from
http://www.clickphotodesignsblog.com

▶ **Record in 1080p or 720p:** Regardless of which camera you use, you should ensure that you are recording in one of these two HD formats. A good rule of thumb is to shoot the footage in the highest possible quality and then worry about size and compression later.

▶ **Keep it short:** When asked how long a video should be, I usually respond, "as long as the viewers stay engaged." Some videos might need to be eight to ten minutes in length in order to cover the topic properly. However, with rare exceptions, you should generally aim to create two- to five-minute videos. If you have a complex issue to cover, break the content into smaller chunks.

▶ **Remember pace, tone, and mood:** It's important to maintain a fast, fun pace and tone in your videos as opposed to droning, slow, and monotone. Remember, engagement is key and no one wants to be bored to death, no matter how valuable your subject matter is. Smile and convey a positive, high-energy tone and pace.

▶ **Get right to it:** A lot of video bloggers use lengthy "intros" with extended scenes of graphics and music. Don't do this—get right to the point. Use your content template and tell them what you'll cover, cover it, and close with a call to action.

▶ **Use the first take:** If you're a perfectionist like me, this will be a particularly hard pill to swallow. If you stop and re-record your videos every time you blink, stutter, or say "uh" between thoughts, you'll never actually launch a video. Use the first take, edit and publish your video, and move on to the next one. Believe it or not, your natural, comfortable speaking voice is more engaging and trustworthy than a "perfect," newscaster shtick. After all, when a customer walks into your place of business, you don't get a second take. Keep it real and conversational and pretend you're speaking to one person.

CREATING VIDEOS WITHOUT A CAMERA

Screen capture movies (or screen recordings) are very simple to create and are an effective alternative to "live-action" videos. If you're presenting or demoing a product such as a software, service, or website, screen recording videos might be your weapon of choice. They work great for sales and marketing videos as well.

Creating screen capture recording videos is a simple process:

▶ Open up your video editing/screen recording software.
▶ Click the "record" button and the software records your voice and screen actions.
▶ Talk through your on-screen demo or Keynote/PowerPoint presentation.
▶ Click "stop recording" when you're done.
▶ Now you're left with a "movie" that can be edited using the same process as you would use to edit a movie made with a video camera.

It'll take some time to figure out the nuances of creating screen recording-based videos. But this is where the fun and growth happens: in the doing!

Figure 58: ScreenFlow or PowerPoint can be used to make great screen capture movies

Step 4: EDIT YOUR VIDEO

Once you've finished recording your video, the next step is to edit your video, making it ready for uploading and syndication. For video blogs, the editing process should be simple and straightforward, with the goal of "getting in and out" as quickly and painlessly as possible. This "light editing" should involve little more than adjusting the intro and outro of your video, balancing sound, and ensuring the video is "encoded" or compressed into the best format (size and quality) for Web-based consumption.

To start editing a video, open up your video editing tool of choice and import the video file from your computer or camera. In some cases, you may be able to skip the editing process altogether, simply uploading video from your phone, camera, or computer right onto YouTube, Facebook, or another website, but I recommend you take the time to follow the four primary steps below:

1. **Trim intro and outro:** To make your videos look much more professional, trim off the first few seconds at the beginning and end of your videos, when you're turning on the camera, clearing your throat, or singing scales to get warmed up. ScreenFlow and Camtasia allow you to easily "trim" your videos to remove these unwanted pieces.

Figure 59: ScreenFlow and Camtasia make it easy to "trim" your video footage.

2. **Balance audio:** Even when using a lapel or computer microphone, your video might contain uneven or imbalanced audio. Even worse, you may notice background noise. Take the time to adjust the audio track for your video using your software's simple audio editing controls.

Figure 60: ScreenFlow's audio editing menu makes perfect sound quality easy to achieve.

3. **Add images and text:** Once you're comfortable with the basic functions of your editing software, you may want to add images and text to your videos. The addition of logos, title banners, or even calls to action such as a Web address or phone number can really make your videos look and perform better (see following figure).

Figure 61: Adding text and images can really make your videos STAND OUT.

4. **Encoding:** Encoding is ensuring a video is in its best format for consumption on the Web. It's important for your videos to be playable on most devices in high-quality, preferably HD, format.

The problem that most video producers who aren't tech-savvy make is not ensuring that videos are exported in the proper size and format. Since our video files pass through two or more separate tools before making it to our blog or YouTube Channel, we need to maintain consistency and ensure the final product is of the quality that we desire.

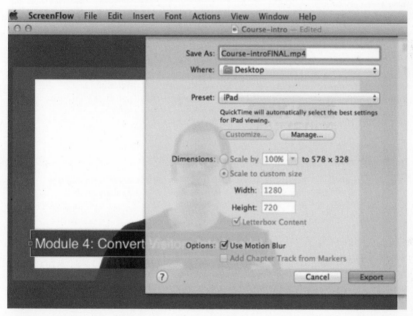

Figure 62: Encoding videos is the last but most important step in editing video.

Most video editing tools now have "preset" compression settings that do all the work for you. Just make sure the resolution of your video is at least 1280 x 720 (HD). This will ensure that your video plays on most devices in high-quality format.

RESOURCE: Vimeo's Guide to Video Compression
Vimeo has a great guide for encoding video (https://vimeo.com/help/compression) using just about every popular video editing application.

Once you've edited and encoded your video, save it to your desktop or location of your choice and you'll be ready to publish your video for all the world to see!

🎥 Video

Codec: H.264

A codec is the format in which your video will be encoded. Different codecs have different features and varying quality. For best results, we recommend using **H.264** (sometimes referred to as MP4).

Frame rate: 24, 25, or 30 FPS

If you know at which frame rate you shot, it is best to encode at that same frame rate. However, if it exceeds 30 FPS (frames per second), you should encode your video at half that frame rate. For example, if you shot 60 FPS, you should encode at 30 FPS. If you're uncertain what frame rate you shot at, set it to either "Current" or 30 FPS. If there is an option for **keyframes**, use the same value you used for frame rate.

Data rate: 2000 kbps (SD), 5000 kbps (HD)

This setting controls both the visual quality of the video and its file size. In most video editors, this is measured of kilobits per second (kbps). Use **2000 kbps for standard definition or 5000 kbps for high definition** video.

Resolution: 640x480 (SD), 1280x720 (HD)

Choose 640x480 for 4:3 SD video, 640x360 for 16:9 SD video, and 1280x720 or 1920x1080 for HD. If you have the option to control the pixel aspect ratio (not the display aspect ratio), make sure it's set to "1:1" or "1.00," sometimes referred to as "**square pixels.**"

Figure 63: Vimeo.com's online video compression guidelines

Step 5: PUBLISH YOUR VIDEO

Although many CMS systems allow you to upload videos directly, doing so requires you to host the large, space-consuming video file on your server, causing potential performance and bandwith issues. The better bet is to simply upload the video to YouTube, let them host the video, and embed it on your site.

How to Upload Your Video to YouTube

Uploading videos to YouTube requires that you follow a specific strategy for best results:

► Log in to YouTube.
► Click the "Upload" button.
► Select the file you want to upload.
► Perform the video SEO steps below.

Believe it or not, optimizing video content for online visibility is an art unto itself. Many geeks like VSEO (video search engine optimization). However, there's a short list of things you can easily do to gain 90 percent of the SEO benefits from your video files—even if you're not particularly a tech geek.

Many folks skip SEO steps when uploading videos. This usually results in lackluster performance in terms of visibility, traffic, and conversions. Video SEO is all about doing what it takes to ensure the largest possible number of your audience finds your videos. A part of this will be syndicating your video, but the SEO process starts on YouTube, right where your videos are uploaded.

While uploading your videos, follow these steps for video SEO:

► **Title:** Use the specific keywords this content is intended to target, while still factoring in compelling copy.
► **Description:** The description is simply a long-form text area used to describe the contents of the video. I recommend the following format when creating video descriptions:
  • **Website:** URL of the landing page you want visitors to go to
  • **Phone number:** used to generate calls and help Google match the video with your business
  • **Physical address:** your full business address, exactly as it's listed on your website and local business directories
  • **Main copy:** a unique description of the video content (do not paste from your website or other source), including your target keywords and a call to action

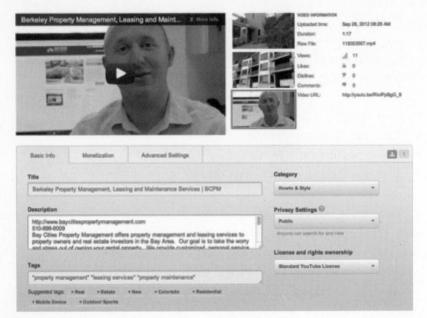

Figure 64: Basic settings for uploading a video to YouTube

▶ **Category:** Select the best category for your video, usually the simple category of "How-to & Style," as the options are fairly limited.

▶ **Tags:** Use your target search terms and location-based terms (e.g., "Boston Property Management"). One trick with tags is to search for YouTube videos that outrank yours for the same topic and keywords, then use the same tags they are using.

▶ **Localizing:** One of the most helpful yet lesser-known tools YouTube offers is the "Video Location" field. Using this feature attaches a specific location to your video—a good thing if your target audience is within a specific geographic area. To access this feature, click on "Advanced Settings" from the video editing screen (Figure 65).

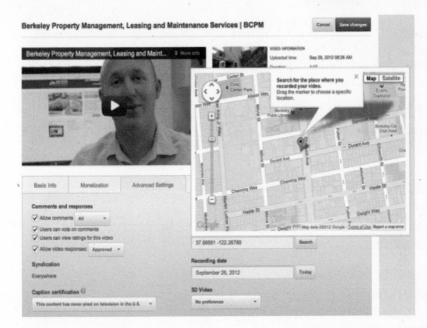

Figure 65: Don't forget to use the "Video Location" feature when uploading YouTube videos.

▶ **Adding a transcript:** As you can imagine, YouTube has a hard time extracting the content from video files (although this is rapidly changing). In order to get the most out of your YouTube videos, YouTube allows you to upload a transcript of your video. Doing so not only helps with SEO by adding Googlebot-friendly text to your video, it also helps make your content available to people with disabilities via closed-captioning. To add a transcript to your video, navigate to "captions" in the top navigation bar and click on "Upload caption file or transcript" (see Figure 66).

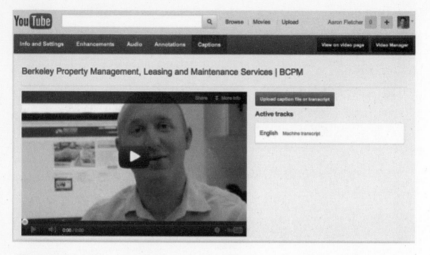

Berkeley Property Management, Leasing and Maintenance Services | BCPM

Figure 66: Adding a text transcript of your video is a surefire way to attract more visitors.

RESOURCE: **Save Tons of Time Using Video Transcription Services**
Creating a text transcript for each of your videos is essential not only for uploading on YouTube, but also for your blog and online marketing program in general. There are several extremely affordable and high-quality video transcription services on the Web:

▶ Speechpad (https://www.speechpad.com) is a popular site offering video transcription for $1.00 per word

▶ Fiverr (http://fiverr.com/) is a community of folks who will do just about anything for $5.00. I have found a few great sources for video transcription, my favorite of which is here: http://fiverr.com/transexpert/provide-quality-transcripts-for-any-10-minute-english-audio-or-video)

How to Add YouTube Videos to Your Site

To add a video to your website, copy the embed code from YouTube and paste it into the body of a blog post following the simple steps outlined on the following pages:

1. From the video page on YouTube, click on the "share" button, followed by the "embed" button. Select the size you want the video to be on y your site and copy the embed code provided (see figure below).

Figure 67: YouTube embed codes make posting videos on your site a snap.

2. Open a new or existing blog post. From the edit screen, be sure you're viewing the editor in HTML format (Figure 68). Next, paste the embed code into the body area and hit "publish." Your video should be live on your blog (Figure 69). Now all you need to do is add the text transcript and optimize your blog.

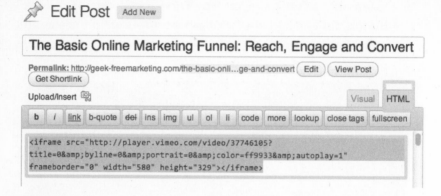

Figure 68: *Adding YouTube videos to your website or blog is a piece of cake using simple embed code.*

Figure 69: *Example of YouTube video embedded on my blog*

Add the Text Transcript to Your Site

The last step in publishing your video blog post is adding a transcript to your site. This will go a long way in helping search engines and visitors find and consume your content more easily. Once you have the text transcript created, paste it under the video on your blog post and shazam! You have a live video blog, without ever writing a word!

RESOURCE: Add a Video Site Map to Your Site
If you're using a WordPress site and publishing video blogs, the "Video SEO for WordPress" plugin (http://yoast.com/wordpress/video-seo/) does a bunch of technical stuff with your videos (creates an XML video site map, adds video to your RSS feeds, etc.) and helps your videos show up in search results as well instead of just the plain text showing up.

NEXT STEPS: Recycle and Syndicate Your Videos
From here, follow the same steps you followed for optimizing and syndicating your blog posts, covered in Chapters 10 and 11: syndicate your videos to all the major video sites and recycle your videos, publishing their content into any relevant form(s).

KEY CONCEPT: Use Quick Videos to Curate Content
A great way to produce engaging curated content is to use a quick video covering your feedback and comments. The next time you spot a highly valuable or newsworthy article, create a two- to three-minute video covering the key takeaways and publish the video, transcript, and original article (be sure to cite the source). These curation videos are a snap to create and go a long way toward reaching and engaging your audience with great content.

RESOURCE: A Blog a Day Makes "Gary V." a Huge Payday
Gary Vaynerchuk started Wine Library TV (http://tv.winelibrary.com) as a way to increase the online reach for his family's liquor store. Virtually every day, from 2006–2011, Gary made a daily video blog covering wine tasting notes, reviews, with some great humor and New York Jets fanfare sprinkled in. Vaynerchuk's commitment to producing content relevant to his target audience on a regular basis not only increased his family's business by nearly 1,000 percent, it also helped launch an entire new career as a marketing speaker, author, and consultant. His book

Crush It (http://crushitbook.com) went on to be a *New York Times* bestseller.

The bottom line: The best way to STAND OUT in your niche is to produce better content than your competitors, and more often!

Figure 70: Gary Vaynerchuk has had enormous success by releasing one video blog a day at Wine Library TV.

CHAPTER SUMMARY

Online video is the new frontier of content marketing, second to none in its ability to reach and engage your target audience online. Online video is quickly becoming a core component of savvy small business owners' content marketing strategies. If you act now and get over the "hum" of the learning curve and learn to make simple video blogs, you'll gain a distinct advantage over your less forward-thinking competitors.

Video marketing requires more than simply uploading a video blog to your website or YouTube channel. For maximum results, you must apply the STAND OUT Content Marketing strategy to your videos, following a clearly defined process, syndicating, recycling, and measuring the results of every video you create.

Have fun, be yourself, and get seen everywhere!

VIDEO RESOURCES

▶ ReelSEO (http://www.reelseo.com)
▶ Get Seen (http://stevegarfield.com)
▶ iPhone Video Hero (http://ivideohero.com)
▶ Tube Mogul (http://tubemogul.com)
▶ Web Video University (http://webvideouniversity.com)

CHAPTER CHECKLIST

✔ **Step 1: Select the Right Video Creation Tools**
  • Camera
  • Microphone
  • Lighting
  • Editing software
  • Optional equipment
✔ **Step 2: Create a Video Outline**
  • Headline
  • Introduction
  • Body (bullet points)
  • Summary
  • Call to action
✔ **Step 3: Produce Your Video**
  • Live action (video camera)
  • Screen recording

✔ **Step 4: Edit Your Video**
- Clip your intro and outro
- Balance the audio
- Add images and/or text
- Encode your video

✔ **Step 5: Publish Your Video**
- Upload your video to YouTube, optimized for SEO
- Publish your video on your website

✔ **Step 6: Syndicate Your Video to the Major Video Sites**

✔ **Step 7: Recycle Your Video**
- Articles
- Slideshare
- Infographics
- Audio and podcasts

PART FIVE

NEXT STEPS FOR

STAND OUT MARKETERS

THIRTEEN

GET MORE REFERRALS, REVIEWS, AND RENEWALS WITH NURTURE CAMPAIGNS

"Profit in business comes from repeat customers, customers that boast about your project or service, and that bring friends with them."

—*W. Edwards Deming*

While the primary goal of STAND OUT is to help you institute an effective online marketing strategy based on the online marketing funnel, I couldn't responsibly send you off into cyberspace without discussing lead nurturing.

As exciting as it will be to watch your site traffic, content engagement, and inbound leads numbers start to rapidly grow, it's how you handle these leads that determines the ultimate ROI of your marketing efforts. The process your business uses for managing inbound leads, opt-ins, and customer lists is critical to examine and optimize.

There is a great deal of profit to be made from implementing "nurture" campaigns—specific practices (email, direct mail, phone calls, or even sending gifts) in following up with your customers, past and present, to improve relationships and obtain customer reviews and referrals.

It's unfortunate that most business owners fail to view their clienteles' "lifetime value" when making marketing decisions, as it's so much more cost-effective (and usually more pleasurable) to keep an existing customer than to generate a working relationship with a new one.

When was the last time you went to a restaurant and were asked by the server to leave your email address or like them on Facebook in exchange for a coupon or free side of fries?

Think about it: say a customer spends $65 each time he visits his favorite restaurant, about once every two months. This adds up to around $390 per year. Let's assume the average patron maintains this bi-monthly dinner pattern for four years, before he moves out of town or picks a new favorite hot spot for pumpkin curry. The lifetime value for this customer would be over $1,500! By not measuring the long-term value of their clients, most small businesses who depend on repeat business are leaving thousands, if not tens of thousands, of dollars, on the table each month.

All such businesses would need to do is place value on building a list of customers to whom they can send emails and postcards. If just by sending each customer a coupon for a free haircut/meal/carpet cleaning or laser hair removal on her birthday, you could generate one or two additional visits and referrals per year, your sales would snowball!

Does your business have a customer referral program in place? How about a strategy for ensuring that your customers provide feedback on the important online reviews sites? And let's not forget the all-important renewals. What methods does your business use for staying in touch with customers and encouraging them to patronize your business more often?

These "Three Rs" of lead nurturing—Referrals, Reviews, and Renewals—are each important enough to demand their own strategies. And implementing these strategies is some of the most productive work you can do to grow your business.

LEAD NURTURING EXPLAINED

The majority of people who come to your website don't become leads, and the majority of leads don't become customers. For most websites a good conversion rate is 2–3 percent.

Sometimes, we place too much focus on where our next customer will come from and not enough on keeping in touch will all the folks who may have "raised their hands" by completing a lead form, calling our business, or opting in to a mailing list. This shortsighted approach results in many business owners missing out on the majority of sales opportunities.

Lead nurturing is the art of building a list of customers and prospects and following up with them on a regular basis. While there are complex lead nurturing strategies and tools out there, the process doesn't have to be complicated. Think of the power of simply sending your customers emails on their birthdays, or when you have a special or sale. Or how about putting a process in place to ask your new customers to write a quick online review or refer two to three friends to your business?

BENEFITS OF LEAD NURTURING

1. **Automate your marketing:** Since most nurturing programs can be executed using simple email marketing software, you can literally put your lead nurturing on auto-pilot, communicating with prospects and customers 24/7 without needing to be there.
2. **Save a ton of money:** Aside from a little set-up time and a small monthly fee for your email marketing software, nurture campaigns are extremely cheap to operate.
3. **Reduce dependency on Google:** Building your own database of subscribers yields security benefits by reducing your dependency on search engines. If Google decides to penalize your site for any reason, you'll have a means of reaching a portion of your audience yourself.
4. **Get more sales:** Nurture campaigns not only help increase repeat sales through consistent follow-up with customers, but they also provide a platform for obtaining revenue-generating referrals and reviews.

THE STAND OUT LEAD NURTURING PROCESS

Lead nurturing begins as soon as a phone rings or a Web form gets submitted. Whether your initial contact came from someone looking to buy now or from someone opting in to your subscriber list, you need to have a basic nurturing process in place for each new contact:

1. **Implement a lead intake process for hot leads.**
2. **Select an email marketing tool.**
3. **Set up a basic lead nurturing campaign.**
4. **Create a customer nurture campaign.**
5. **Follow email marketing best practices.**
6. **Measure and test against your email metrics.**

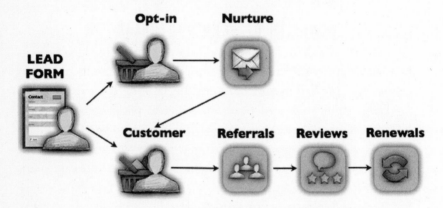

Figure 71: The STAND OUT Lead Nurturing Strategy

Step 1: IMPLEMENT AN INTAKE PROCESS FOR HOT LEADS

Hot leads come first. These are the folks who are contacting your business via phone, Web form, or some other method with immediate needs. These hot leads should obviously be priority number one for you and your staff. However, many small businesses fail to properly capitalize on these leads due to a lack of a clear intake process.

SOMETIMES THE FIRST IS THE BEST

More often than not, the early bird gets the worm when it comes to Web and phone leads. It's critical to treat leads like the golden opportunities they are and follow up as quickly as you can, if not immediately!

While I was working with one large silicon valley start-up, we did an analysis, modeling the outcomes of thousands of Web and phone leads, measuring their value based on a number of factors including follow-up time and which percentage were reached, engaged, and eventually became customers. You'll be astounded by the conclusions of the study:

▶ Phone leads must be answered in real time via a live person answering the phone who is trained to qualify the lead and schedule an appointment.

▶ Web leads should be contacted via phone and email within four hours of receipt (immediately is ideal).

▶ Leads that aren't immediately followed up with lose 50 percent of their value after four hours and 80 percent of their value after twenty-four hours.

You must ensure that everyone in your company values the importance of responding to and measuring inbound leads. If you can't answer calls or greet walk-ins in real time, train a staff member or outsource this to someone who can. Train whoever answers the phone on how to greet, screen, and obtain information from callers. If you run a retail or dining establishment, the same rules apply.

LEAD INTAKE PROCESS BEST PRACTICES

▶ **Document the lead intake process for your business.** This should include how phone and Web leads are routed, who follows up, and in what time frame. Also include how inbound leads are tracked. Create a simple lead intake process and train your staff.

▶ **Never let leads get answered by a machine or voicemail.** While I understand that many businesses are stretched thin in terms of staff, it's critical to have your phone leads answered by a real person. If you can't dedicate staff, use a service like AnswerConnect (http://www.answerconnect.com). For around $150 per month, you can have professional staff answer your calls and capture and email you leads.

▶ **Respond to Web leads within hours.** Web leads begin depreciating in value the minute your prospects hit "send" on your Web form. Make it a priority to respond immediately, preferably via phone, as doing so is much more personal than email.

▶ **Develop a script for inbound leads.** You don't need to turn your staff into telemarketers, but ensure that you train them on the main talking points and questions for converting leads into appointments, in-store visits, or whatever the next step in your sales funnel is. Also, train them to capture the prospect's contact info right off the bat.

▶ **Always add phone leads to your nurture campaigns.** Since many prospects will call rather than fill out a Web form, it's important that your staff is trained to add these contacts to your lead nurturing database (after receiving their permission). This way, even those prospects who don't buy right away will hear from you on a regular basis.

▶ **Share the results with your staff.** Make a point of discussing inbound lead metrics with your employees on a regular basis. This will not only help foster friendly competition, but it will also help you identify best practices and weak links in your lead intake process.

Establish your "hot leads" intake process as soon as you can. You can always expand on this as you get more feedback and identify new best practices.

Step 2: SELECT AN EMAIL MARKETING TOOL

If your business is in the early stages of online marketing, with little website traffic or content, lead nurturing may not seem like a priority. While this assertion may be true for the most part, it's critical to start building a subscriber/nurture list right away. Since all you need to do is choose an email marketing/list building service and slap an opt-in form on your site, it's worth doing as early as possible.

BASIC EMAIL MARKETING SOFTWARE

For most small businesses, basic email marketing software will work just fine. Each of the services listed here works the same way: you simply sign up, paying from $19 to $100 per month depending on the size of your list, create Web forms to capture leads on your site, and set up "sequences," or automated email campaigns. Any of the following four providers will work just fine:

▶ Aweber (http://www.aweber.com)
▶ MailChimp (http://mailchimp.com)
▶ Constant Contact (http://www.constantcontact.com/)
▶ Vertical Response (http://app.verticalresponse.com)

COMPLETE MARKETING AUTOMATION SYSTEMS

If you want to do more than simple email nurture campaigns, such as accept payments online, monitor your prospects' Web activity, and integrate direct mail and other "offline marketing" into your nurture programs, I recommend the following two providers:

▶ Infusionsoft (http://www.infusionsoft.com)
▶ Office Autopilot (http://officeautopilot.com)

If you're new to the world of lead nurturing or are on a tight budget, you'll be fine using one of the four basic services listed above. I use InfusionSoft and can't recommend it highly enough if you're more advanced in lead nurturing or need a more powerful solution.

Step 3: SET UP A BASIC LEAD NURTURING CAMPAIGN

There are two primary ways of sending email communications to your nurture list:

1. Email Broadcasts

Broadcasts are one-time emails sent to your whole database or segments of your list. The ability to reach your entire list at once makes broadcasts especially powerful for sales promotions, news, or events. Here are a few ideas you can use to generate broadcasts.

▶ **Content updates:** Part of your content syndication strategy involves sending content updates to your subscriber list. Each time you publish a new blog post or video, be sure to send an email with a link to your new content. In Google Analytics, you'll notice an uptick in "direct traffic" resulting from your subscribers.

▶ **Seasonal updates:** Email broadcasts work great for seasonal promotions and updates, holiday promotions, and events. If you get creative, you can come up with an offer to match every holiday or milestone throughout the year. With little effort, you could generate a dozen or more broadcasts to send to your contacts, one for each month.

▶ **Sales and specials:** Broadcasts work great for moving extra stock or filling slow periods in your business. Is your business exceptionally slow on Monday afternoons or during the month of August? Send your subscribers special promotions for coming in during these slow periods. For even better response, add urgency by doing a limited time or quantity offer ("Free _____ for the first 25 people who come in Monday").

2. Sequential Emails

Sequential mailings are a series of emails pre-set to get delivered over time, allowing you to keep in touch with your prospects for weeks, months, or even longer. Consult with your chosen email marketing provider to learn more about setting up campaigns.

Here are a few ideas for sequential mailings that have proven to be extremely effective:

▶ **The mini course:** With an "email mini-course," you would offer your visitors a series of articles or videos (top 5 lists) delivered over time. A chef could offer "5 Dinner Party Recipes to Dazzle Your Guests," sending those who opt in one recipe each week.

▶ **Case studies:** Nothing builds social proof with your audience like real-life examples of other customers finding happiness through the use of your products or services. Imagine how powerful it would be to load up five or six case studies and then email them out to your subscribers over time.

▶ **Drip offers:** With drip offers, you create a series of emails offering different products or services. If your business has more than one thing to offer, set up a long-term campaign that highlights different products or services over time.

▶ **Affiliate offers:** A mainstay for Internet marketers, affiliate offers are a great way to generate extra revenue. Affiliate marketing is the act of selling other companies' products and services for a commission. This is a great way to expose your audience to offerings that complement yours but that you don't offer directly. For example, if you run a Tahoe Bed & Breakfast, why not send your subscribers emails offering discounted ski packages, restaurant deals, or other services? Just be sure you only recommend businesses you have personally used and that you know will bring value to your audience.

▶ **The launch formula:** If you have a product launch, live event or other time-sensitive promotion, the launch formula will be extremely effective. Launch formula email sequences are a series of messages that lead up to an event or other specific time-sensitive purchase. For example, if you will be displaying your wares at a tradeshow or seminar, you could easily create a campaign to remind your audience of the upcoming event and build interest along the way. For more information on product launches, check out Jeff Walker's Product Launch Formula: http://www.productlaunchformula.com.

Step 4: CREATE A CUSTOMER NURTURE CAMPAIGN

As the old saying goes, "It's much easier to keep a customer than acquire a new one." If you recall from Chapter 9, it's important to measure the lifetime value of a customer (LCV). When you focus on this bigger picture in terms of revenue, you can spend more to acquire a customer. If your clients visit your place of business, offer incentives to join your email list. If you provide services elsewhere, add email fields to your invoices and implement staff incentives for email acquisition. You can even use direct mail to build your list, sending low-cost postcards with a special offer in exchange for opting in. Here are several ways to leverage your customer relationships:

Referrals

I have yet to encounter a stronger source of leads than customer referrals. When a customer recommends your business to a friend or colleague, a magical thing happens: You get to skip the first several steps of the online marketing funnel, as each recommendation comes pre-packaged with trust and authority. The best way to ask for referrals is to do so with class and sincerity. Just send your new client a brief and sincere message similar to this one:

SUBJECT LINE:
"Hi Jim, It's Aaron—I Have a Favor to Ask"

Dear Jim,

It's our great pleasure to have you as a new customer; we really hope you enjoy your new bicycle. We hope you found your experience with us to be exceptional and we look forward to serving you and your family for years to come. Please contact me on my personal line anytime if I can be of service in any way: 760-777-7777.

Secondly, I have a favor to ask. As you know, Gotham City Cyclery exists for one reason: we are extremely passionate about helping people live happy and healthier lives through the joy of riding bicycles, and we're always looking for more families like yours to help. If you have one or two friends you think would enjoy working with us as much as you have, we would be honored if you would help us spread the word.

To make this easy, I have included a link for three 10 percent off coupons for our store for you to hand out to anyone you wish. I've also included a 20 percent off coupon for you as a gesture of thanks for your time and consideration.

Thanks so much for your time, and keep riding!

Best,
Aaron

To set up a nurture campaign for client referrals, send two or three emails every week or so using this gentle but effective approach. If they don't respond the first time, send a reminder or two the next week. You'll be amazed at how much new business you can generate using this simple approach.

BEST PRACTICES FOR MORE REFERRALS

▶ **Ask right away.** The best time to ask for a client referral is right away, while your new customers are still excited, with your business fresh on their mind.

▶ **Make it easy.** Give your customers an easy way to create referrals, whether that means a link to a short referral form or a business reply card in the mail. Don't just ask for referrals and expect your customers to do all the work.

▶ **Provide incentives.** We're all driven by incentives, including gift cards and discounts. Use incentives to get referrals from your customers. Even if you send a gift card in advance, many of your customers will follow through out of a sense of reciprocity.

▶ **Combine online and offline.** As cost-effective as email can be, you might get better results when it comes to obtaining referrals using offline means such as postcards. Many marketers have foolishly abandoned direct mail in favor of all-digital means, but postcards can really cut through the ice and help your message STAND OUT.

▶ **Follow up immediately.** When you get a referral, treat it as your hottest lead, applying the same follow-up rules we discussed earlier.

▶ **Track your referral sources.** Make sure you measure your referral sources using your intake process and CRM or client database. You may find that one or two of your clients or other sources are lighting up the scoreboard with referrals, triggering you to reinforce their behavior with incentives.

► **Launch a referral program.** If you really want to crank up your referrals, go beyond your existing clients and launch your own referral or affiliate program. Any other business serving the same market you do could be a great source for referrals. For example, a carpet cleaner could partner with a landscaping company, painter, or furniture retailer, sending campaigns to each other's client lists for mutual gain.

KEY CONCEPT: Use List Segmentation to Target Your Campaigns

One of the common mistakes people make when first using email marketing and lead nurturing tools is placing all their contacts into one huge "bucket." It's important to segment your list into separate categories ("customers," "leads," "former customers"), allowing for targeted communications down the road. Most popular email marketing software programs accomplish this using "tags," which are easy to create and set up. Start with the following three list segments:

► **Master subscribers:** This would be everyone—both clients and prospects. Many times you'll want to send broadcasts to your entire database.

► **Leads:** This should include everyone on your list who has yet to purchase from you.

► **Customers:** This includes all the folks who have already purchased from you at least once.

Reviews

Depending on your reputation and point of view, online reviews sites have become one of the best or worst things to happen to small business owners. In our modern, connected world, people have become accustomed to reading and leaving reviews for everything. If you recall from Chapter 4, reviews are also a great sign of "social proof." Whether your customers are ecstatic, infuriated, or somewhere in between, you can expect to find reviews on your business. Search engines also view reviews as evidence of "trust."

How to Ask for Reviews

Just as with referrals, there's a good way and a bad way to ask for reviews. Instead of saying something like, "Please fill out a review, we really need more reviews for Google to like us!" use the same direct, service-based approach you would for referrals:

SUBJECT LINE:
"Hi Jim, Aaron Here—Please Tell Us How We're Doing"

Dear Jim,

Hello again! It's Aaron from Gotham City Cyclery. It's been a few weeks since you purchased your mountain bike and I hope you've found time to get on the trails and enjoy this great weather.

I am writing to gather some quick feedback about your experience with Gotham City, and your level of satisfaction with our customer service, pricing, and the bicycle itself. We place a great deal of emphasis on getting feedback from all of our customers, as this allows us to provide the best possible services, train our staff, and decide which bicycles to carry.

You're the type of customer we want to attract and your feedback would mean the world to us. To make it easy, I have included links to our reviews pages below. Please pick one or two and tell us how we're doing—good or bad, we appreciate your feedback:

▶ LINK TO YOUR HELP PAGE
▶ LINK TO YOUR GOOGLE+ PAGE
▶ LINK TO YOUR MERCHANT CIRCLE PAGE

Thanks,
Aaron

P.S. I really do appreciate your time. Once you've completed a review, I'll leave a free inner tube here at the shop for you to grab during your next visit.

Can you see how friendly and non-promotional this approach is? Once you view reviews sites as critical customer feedback channels, you'll find the process of getting more of them much easier.

TOP REVIEWS SITES

For your review acquisition program, stick with a short list of social sites and build from there. It's important to note that your niche might have separate, industry-specific directories that are great for reviews, such as Avvo. com and Lawyers.com for lawyers, and Caring.com for senior care providers. Start with the top three to four of the following established local directories:

- ▶ Google+ Local (https://plus.google.com/local)
- ▶ Yelp (http://www.yelp.com)
- ▶ Superpages (http://www.superpages.com)
- ▶ Yahoo Local Listings (http://listings.local.yahoo.com/overview.php)
- ▶ Merchant Circle (http://www.merchantcircle.com)
- ▶ Yellow Pages (http://www.yellowpages.com)
- ▶ City Search (http://www.citysearch.com/)

BEST PRACTICES FOR MANAGING ONLINE REVIEWS

- ▶ **Make it easy.** Send your clients a list of three specific sites on which you'd like them to post a review, making sure to link to the exact URL.
- ▶ **Never pay for reviews.** As previously mentioned, don't take shortcuts like using automated methods or paid reviews. Giving clients a gift or discount for their time, however, is fine.
- ▶ **Go beyond your client list.** One way to increase your review volume is to request reviews from prospects, associates, and other business contacts. People don't have to pay for your products or services to have an opinion or receive value from you. If you write a blog, your

subscribers may be inclined to comment on the value your content has brought them.

▶ **Respond to both good and bad reviews.** Make it a point to be engaged in your online reputation, commenting on and responding to reviews. Instead of trying to hide from or bury negative reviews, respond to the clients' concerns and engage in a discussion. Many times, negative reviews result in more new business than positive ones!

▶ **Monitor your reviews.** Use Google Alerts or a service like Review Trackers (http://www.reviewtrackers.com) to monitor your online reviews.

Renewals

Unless you run a funeral home, repeat business or customer renewals should be a cornerstone of your business and marketing plans. If you did no other marketing but launch a great customer renewals campaign, you'd likely see a dramatic increase in bottom line sales. Sometimes all your customers need is a gentle reminder that your business is right around the corner.

Whether your business has a very long sales cycle (tax accountant), or a very short one (coffee shop), it doesn't take much to communicate with customers on a regular basis, prompting them to patronize your business just a tad more often.

Many businesses approach renewals way too late in the game, contacting customers right before their services expire, or worse yet, after. The better approach is to stay in contact often, adding value to your customers' lives, maintaining your position of authority in their minds.

REASONS TO STAY IN TOUCH WITH CUSTOMERS

▶ **Content:** Just as with your nurture campaigns, your existing customers should be included in your email broadcast announcing new blog posts and videos, news, and other valuable content.

▶ **Birthdays:** As mentioned, make it a point to capture your customers' birthdays and send them a message, along with a gift or coupon as an expression of your gratitude for their business. These gifts aren't expenses, they're investments. For example, if a restaurant owner sends a coupon for a free birthday entrée, the customer will almost certainly bring one or more guests with her to the restaurant on her special night.

▶ **Service Reminders:** Using email campaigns to trigger renewals or service reminders can have a huge impact on your business. A carpet cleaner could send out six-month cleaning notices, or a nail salon might remind you that it's been two months since your last pedicure.

▶ **Surveys:** Use a tool like Survey Monkey (http://www.surveymonkey. com) to perform customer surveys covering a range of topics, including key challenges and strategies, general client satisfaction, and other poll topics. You can even publish the results to participants or create a blog post using what you've learned.

▶ **Just Because:** It's important to stay in touch as a human being, reaching out just to see how your customer is doing, what's new in his life, and whether or not he or she has any questions. This engagement will set you apart from your competitors and accomplish the prime goal of all marketing—establishing a bond between people.

KEY CONCEPT: Use Facebook to Reach Existing Customers

Your nurture campaigns can reach beyond your website and personal leads database. Social media sites like Facebook provide their own lead and customer nurturing ecosystems that can greatly enhance and supplement your email marketing efforts.

One great lead nurturing activity is to send messages to your Facebook fans and groups, following the same best practices listed in this chapter. You can place Facebook ads (https://www.facebook.com/advertising) targeted at only those who have "Liked" your business page. Here's a powerful use for this:

1. Offer an incentive to get your customers to like your page on Facebook. This can be done via electronic means (Web form or email) or in person ("Like us from your mobile phone for a free beer!").

2. Place an ad for a special promotion targeting only your followers. For example, if you're doing a Taco Tuesday special in your restaurant, you can place a display ad targeting only your followers within a specified distance from your business.

Step 5: FOLLOW EMAIL MARKETING BEST PRACTICES

Like a blog article, video, or online ad, your emails should be written with the online copywriting funnel in mind (Chapter 11). Use attention-grabbing headlines, engaging copy, and calls to action in every email message you send. Also, remember to be personal and concise with a basic format/structure, to contact regularly (once a week), to request permission from clients to be on your list, and to avoid spam filters by not including "spammy" keywords and links to questionable sites.

Step 6: MEASURE YOUR EMAIL METRICS

Your email marketing tool of choice should provide metrics related to each campaign and broadcast you send. The main metrics you want to pay attention to are:

▶ **Open rate:** the number/percentage of recipients who opened the email (this is a rough number, as some email opens won't be tracked based on the recipients' html settings). Aim for an open rate of 20 to 30 percent.

▶ **Click-through rates:** the number/percentage of the recipients who clicked on the link in your email. A good click-through rate is 8 to 15 percent.

▶ **Bounce rate:** the number/percentage of emails that bounced or failed to arrive in the recipients' inboxes. Shoot for a bounce rate of less than 2 percent.

▶ **Unsubscribes:** the number/percentage of recipients who opted out of your email campaign. You shouldn't get more than 1 percent unsubscribes.

▶ **Complaints:** the number/percentage of recipients who marked your message as spam. Aim for zero complaints.

Once you've sent your first few email campaigns, you should start testing different subject lines, messages, offers, and sending times, always trying to beat your best open and click-through rates.

EMAIL MARKETING RESOURCES:

For more on email marketing tips and best practices, check out:

▶ Chris Brogan (http://www.chrisbrogan.com)
▶ MarketingProfs email marketing course: (http://www.marketingprofsu.com/course/1283/email-marketing)
▶ The Ultimate List of Email SPAM Terms (http://blog.hubspot.com/blog/tabid/6307/bid/30684/The-Ultimate-List-of-Email-SPAM-Trigger-Words.aspx)

CHAPTER SUMMARY

In the end, marketing success is graded on a pass or fail system: either dollars came in or they didn't. By implementing a clearly defined intake process for "hot leads" and setting up nurture campaigns for leads and customers, you'll close the loop on your marketing systems, resulting in a growing and self-sustaining ecosystem of new referrals, reviews, and renewals.

CHAPTER CHECKLIST

✔ **Step 1: Implement an Intake Process for "Hot Leads"**
   • Document your intake process, including timing and script
   • Train your staff
   • Always have a human answer the phone
   • Share the results with your team
✔ **Step 2: Select an Email Marketing Tool**
✔ **Step 3: Set Up a Basic Lead Nurturing Campaign**
   • Broadcasts
   • Sequential emails

✔ **Step 4: Create a Customer Nurture Campaign**
- Referrals
- Reviews
- Renewals

✔ **Step 5: Follow Email Marketing Best Practices**
- Be personal
- Use a basic structure and format
- Test for the right frequency
- Only send with permission
- Avoid spam filters

✔ **Step 6: Measure and Test Your Email Metrics**
- Open rates
- Click-through rates
- Bounce rates
- Unsubscribes
- Complaints

FOURTEEN

BECOME A DIGITAL CITIZEN AND JOIN THE DISCUSSION

"Constant interactions with the community help you stay on target and up-to-date with latest trends. By actively participating in conversations, you are immersing yourself in the digital culture and soaking up valuable information."

—*Magdalena Georgieva, Blog.Hubspot.com*[8]

Once you've implemented the strategies in Parts 1–4, you'll have built a fully functioning lead-generation engine, combining the best tools and techniques for each phase of your marketing funnel. Your website is poised for reaching, engaging, and converting your target audience, and your STAND OUT Content Marketing Plan is in full effect, churning out tons of high-quality blogs and videos, and sending your message out into the far reaches of cyberspace!

Although you have a complete online marketing system in place, I want to point out a few additional notable tools, strategies, and resources to review and consider implementing in your business.

One of the most pivotal changes you'll make on the road to online success will be awarding yourself the title of "digital citizen," defined as "those who use the Internet regularly and effectively."[9]

My spin on digital citizenship is simple, with my "Three Cs":

▶ **Community:** Using the Internet as a tool for engaging with people in your industry, potential customers, and personal connections
▶ **Consumption:** Consuming online media for both personal and professional use

---

8 http://blog.hubspot.com/blog/tabid/6307/bid/4969/Be-a-Digital-Citizen-Not-a-Digital-Tourist.aspx?preview=true
9 http://en.wikipedia.org/wiki/Digital_citizen

▶ **Creation:** Creating (or curating) content on a regular basis

Becoming a digital citizen boils down to embracing technology as a tool to make our lives and businesses better, educating ourselves, having our voices heard, and communicating with others. You can't dabble in the online word, throwing up a decent website and waiting for the results to come. You have to embrace what the Internet is and what it means to your life and business.

According to an August 2011 study from Mashable (http://mashable.com/2011/09/30/wasting-time-on-facebook/), the average Facebook user spends eight hours per month on the site. Most of us are full-fledged cyber citizens in our personal lives; we just need to shift some of our Facebook interaction and YouTube kitten-video-watching hours to a more productive channel: online marketing. And that's exactly what Chapter 13 is all about—picking up and using a few useful, effective tools to help us increase our awareness and knowledge of the online landscape, specifically about the markets we intend to pull revenue from.

RSS READERS

If you're like me, you love to read your favorite morning paper. Whether daily or weekly, you look forward to opening up to your favorite sections, perhaps browsing the classifieds or maybe even dabbling in Sudoku.

Imagine if you had your own custom printing press—one that would allow you to pick exactly which topics, sections, and sources you would like to fill your paper. Picture how useful and interesting it would be to wake each morning to "Dan's Digital Daily Planet," an ultra-customized A.M. edition that contained pages-upon-pages of news that targeted your exact interests and nothing more.

Welcome to RSS readers! An RSS reader (which stands for "really simple syndication") is a way to receive updated content from sources you specify, all delivered to you in real time, categorized in a simple format, and viewable on any device.

This will save you tons of time because you will no longer need to go and visit each of your favorite sites, looking for new updates and content. With RSS, all of your content comes right to your virtual doorstep!

Great Sources for RSS Subscriptions

▶ **Competitors:** By adding your competitors' sites to your RSS feed, you'll receive an update every time they publish new content, providing insight into their content strategies, the quality of the content keywords that they're targeting, and the frequency with which they're targeting them.

▶ **Industry news and blogs:** Keeping abreast with what's happening in your marketplace and industry are paramount to your success.

▶ **Educational sites:** This category covers the umbrella of general online marketing knowledge, which can be broken down into SEO, Web design, social media, blogging, and copywriting, Web analytics, conversions, email marketing, and more. In each of these categories, there are several highly reputable websites publishing great FREE educational content daily.

▶ **News and entertainment:** No "digital morning paper" would be complete without news, financial information, horoscopes, and even comics. Now you can choose the best of the best and add them to your personal RSS Feed.

RESOURCE—Your RSS Starter Kit:
To get started on the right foot, subscribe to the following sites, each of which provide valuable and simple-to-understand content that you can put to immediate use:

▶ **Copyblogger** (http://www.copyblogger.com/blog/): for any small business blogger looking for tips related to content writing (from great headlines right on down to the call to action) and Internet marketing

▶ **Hubspot** (http://blog.hubspot.com/): publishes helpful content daily, spanning topics from how to set up your Facebook Timeline page to how to track your website conversions

▶ **MarketingProfs** (http://www.marketingprofs.com/): an "all-inclusive" small business marketing site that covers a wide variety of issues including branding and Web design

▶ **The Smart Passive Income Blog** (http://www.smartpassiveincome. com/): a goldmine for any business owner looking to build an audience through content marketing, with a great deal of helpful, immediately actionable how-to content

▶ **Geek-Free Marketing** (http://geek-freemarketing.com/): a very helpful resource for busy small business owners looking for actionable instructional content, minus the geek speak

How to Set Up Your RSS Reader

1. **Pick an RSS reader. There are hundreds of RSS readers available. Google Reader (http://www.google.com/reader) is extremely simple and integrates well with other Google and Gmail-related services.**

2. **Add sites to your RSS feed. Visit your favorite websites and click on the "RSS Subscribe" Icon (or copy the site's URL and add it to your reader manually). You'll immediately receive a "feed" from each of these sites whenever they add new content.**

3. **Read, share, or email content: Google Reader makes it super-easy to view, consume, save, share, or email content to your network of personal and business contacts.**

KEY CONCEPT: Consume Your News on the Go with Mobile RSS Apps
Once you get familiar with your new RSS reader, you'll likely want to access your latest feeds on the go. There are several apps available for the iPhone, iPad, and most other smartphone and tablet platforms. I recommend "Feedler RSS Reader." It's super-simple to set up (as are many other popular RSS apps)—just enter your Gmail log-in details and you'll be dialed in!

LEARN MORE—RSS Reader Details:
Watch this video explaining Google's RSS Reader: http://www.youtube.com/watch?v=VSPZ2Uu_X3Y

Darren Rowse of ProBlogger explains RSS readers in this article: http://www.problogger.net/what-is-rss/

GOOGLE ALERTS

Google Alerts is a free service that lets you track designated keywords mentioned on the Internet and sends you an email alert any time these terms show up on a newly published Web page.

Unlike RSS readers, which send feeds each time new content is published on sites you specify, Google Alerts notifies you each time a specific word or words you've chosen shows up on any site across the Web. For example, if you're a dry cleaner in Oakland, you can set an alert for the search term "Oakland dry cleaning" and receive an email each time Google finds a new site using this keyword. This is a great way to monitor your industry, competitors, and even your own brand. According to Google, business owners can use Google to:

▶ find out what is being said about their company or product
▶ monitor a developing news story
▶ keep up to date on a competitor or industry
▶ get the latest news on a celebrity or sports team
▶ find out what's being said about themselves (https://support.google.com/alerts/bin/answer.py?hl=en&answer=175925)

How to Set Up Google Alerts

1. **Log in to your Gmail account.**
2. **Go to http://www.google.com/alerts.**
3. **Pick the keywords you'd like to track and specify how often you want to be alerted (I recommend once per day), then wait for the results.**

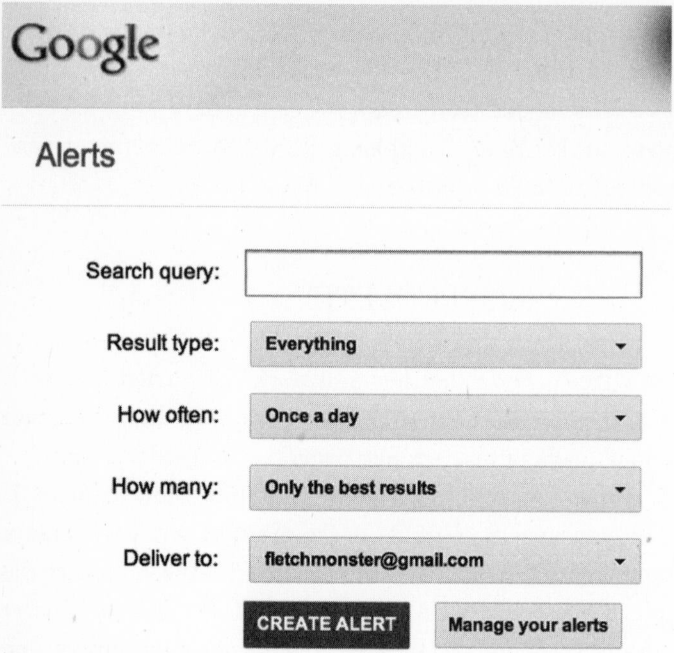

Google

Alerts

Search query:	[ ]
Result type:	Everything ▾
How often:	Once a day ▾
How many:	Only the best results ▾
Deliver to:	fletchmonster@gmail.com ▾
	CREATE ALERT Manage your alerts

Figure 72: Google Alerts notifies you when specified keywords appear on the Web.

KEY CONCEPT: Three Great Topics to Track Using Google Alerts
▶ Your company name and website address
▶ Your primary business category and city ("San Francisco Pizza")
▶ Your competitors' company/brand names and website addresses

PODCASTS, VIDEO, AND MULTIMEDIA SITES

The third mark of a digital citizen is the consumption of content in multiple formats.

YouTube

We've already discovered the power of YouTube and online video as an unparalleled form of content for reaching your audience. It only makes sense, then, that YouTube should serve as a primary channel for consuming content as well.

YouTube is a great site for learning virtually anything you need to know about online marketing, from updating your WordPress website to setting up a Google+ page for your business. Many find it easier to watch a video than to read through a 1,000-word article.

Podcasts

The term "podcast" was coined by Guardian reporter Ben Hammersley in 2004, when he described the act of using the iPod ("pod") to consume broadcasted media ("cast") (http://en.wikipedia.org/wiki/Podcast). According to PEW Research (http://stateofthemedia.org/2011/audio-essay/data-page/), there were over 90,000 podcasts published on the Web in 2012.

Podcasts are an invaluable source of education, resources, tools, and even motivation for small business owners. The ability to listen to podcasts on mobile devices makes them highly portable, allowing subscribers to consume content while on the go. I have spent many a commute, treadmill session, and baby/dog walk consuming great podcasts that have directly impacted my business.

An increasing number of podcasts are being published in video format as well, making the content that much more useful for those viewing on computers, tablets, or smartphones.

How to Get Started with Podcasts

To listen to podcasts, all you need to do is decide how and where you want to consume content:

▶ **On the original site of the podcaster:** Since iTunes and other podcast sites display a feed of podcasts directly from publishers' sites, you can consume podcasts directly from the source. You can also subscribe to most podcasts using your RSS reader.

Figure 73: ILoveMarketing.com's podcasts listed on their website

▶ **On mobile devices:** Using iTunes or another podcasting directory, you can search for and subscribe to podcasts of your liking and download the files to your iPhone, tablet, or other device. Each subscription you create will trigger iTunes to update your device(s) with the latest editions, saving you a great deal of time compared to updating your podcasts manually. If you're using an Android, there are several apps for listening to podcasts including DoggCatcher (http://www.doggcatcher.com) and Google Listen (http://www.androidcentral.com/tags/google-listen). All of these work the same way and are easy to install and use.

Podcasts ▸ Business ▸ Business News ▸ Dean Jackson & Joe Polish

I Love Marketing

▲	Name	Time	Released
1	I Love Marketing 088	1:16:49	9/27/12
2	I Love Marketing 87	1:05:16	9/21/12
3	I Love Marketing 086	1:15:53	9/12/12
4	I Love Marketing 85	1:09:51	9/8/12
5	I Love Marketing 084	2:06:59	8/28/12
6	I Love Marketing 83	1:07:31	8/20/12
7	I Love Marketing 82	1:08:45	8/13/12
8	I Love Marketing 081	1:09:08	8/9/12
9	I Love Marketing 080	1:07:36	8/9/12
10	I Love Marketing 079	1:10:23	7/23/12
11	I Love Marketing 078	1:08:55	7/16/12
12	I Love Marketing 077	1:07:34	7/9/12
13	I Love Marketing 076	1:04:36	7/2/12
14	I Love Marketing 075	1:01:20	7/2/12
15	I Love Marketing 074	1:06:44	6/16/12

I LOVE MARKET-ING DEAN JACKSON & JOE POLISH

Subscribe Free ▾

Category: Business News
Language: English

More From Dean Jacks...
Website

Links
Report a Concern

Figure 74: The I Love Marketing Podcast listed on iTunes

TOP PODCASTS FOR SMALL BUSINESS OWNERS

The following list contains small business podcasts that are chock-full of powerful content that you'll devour and put to immediate use. They're quite entertaining as well.

▶ **I Love Marketing** (http://ilovemarketing.com): This podcast, hosted by small business marketing experts Dean Jackson and Joe Polish, features a unique, systematic approach to education-based marketing that will help you take your business to the next level.

▶ **CopyBlogger Radio** (http://www.copyblogger.com/category/radio/): Copyblogger is my favorite resource for all things copywriting, blogging, and content marketing. Their well-produced podcast is insightful and includes many great interviews with renowned experts.

▶ **Small Business Big Marketing** (http://smallbusinessbigmarketing.com): This Australian-produced show from Tim Reed is a great resource for small business branding, social media, and other helpful content you can use today.

NICHE BLOGS, WEBSITES, AND FORUMS

One surefire way to build online authority and reach more of your audience is to engage them where they hang out. It's a paradigm shift for most small business owners new to the online marketing landscape to seek out like-minded folks, customers, and influencers. Remember, most of your target audience isn't hanging out on your site, they're engaging in social media discussion groups, forums, and blogs.

As a digital citizen, it's important to join the discussion and become a true member of the online culture with which you align your business with and from which you draw clientele. If your RSS feed leads you to an article or piece of content you find exceptional, tell the author with a quick blog comment. If you're on LinkedIn and you notice a question related to your area of expertise, answer it. If you stumble upon a negative review on Yelp for your business, respond to it.

▶ **Online Forums:** It's important to set aside time for online networking the same way you might do in "real life." Go out and join the forums centered on your topic. No matter how obscure your niche, there are likely one or more online forums dedicated to it.

- Do a Google search for "{Your Industry} forum" and notice which communities seem to be the largest and most active.
- Sign up for these forums and include a link to your website and use your top target keywords in your profile.
- Stay engaged, answering questions and adding to discussions online. Your contributions will certainly be noticed by potential clients, influencers, and/or business partners. A glance at your Google Analytics "referring sites" report will show traffic coming from these forums.

▶ **Social Media Groups:** Each major social media site has thousands of groups, spanning virtually every topic. Sign up for two to three of these and make a point of interacting on a regular basis. Answer questions, participate in healthy debates, and/or share content you think the community will find valuable.

- LinkedIn Groups(http://www.linkedin.com/search-fe/groupsearch)
- Facebook Groups (https://www.facebook.com/about/groups/)

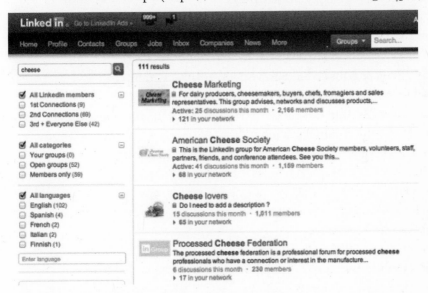

Figure 75: If the American Cheese Society LinkedIn group has over 1,000 members, it's likely that your niche has popular groups as well.

CHAPTER SUMMARY

Like any worthwhile pursuit, online marketing requires true dedication and commitment. By transforming yourself into a digital citizen who consumes and creates digital content, and engages in online communities and discussions, you'll gain insights, tools, relationships, and information unavailable to digital bystanders. Being a digital citizen doesn't mean spending countless hours in front of your computer—on the contrary, many of the tools listed in this chapter can save you a great deal of time and expose you to new efficiencies.

CHAPTER CHECKLIST

✔ **Step 1: Choose an RSS reader**
  - Subscribe to several sites you want to follow
✔ **Step 2: Set Up Google Alerts**
  - Your brand name
  - Your competitors
  - Your top target search terms
✔ **Step 3: Subscribe to Several YouTube Channels**
✔ **Step 4: Subscribe to Two to Three Podcasts**
✔ **Step 5: Join at Least Two Online Forums Devoted to Your Business Niche**
✔ **Step 6: Join Two to Three Social Media Groups**

CONCLUSION

You've come a long way, considering where you started from and how much new information you've digested and implemented. And if you're not there yet, don't worry. All that matters is that you continually move forward, following the framework and strategy outlined in these pages. The only way you can fail is either by quitting or never starting (the second of which you have already conquered by reading this book). I have laid out for you a specific, step-by-step plan for getting more clients and increasing your business by at least 20 percent in ninety days. But by now, you are armed with both the confidence and the necessary game plan to dwarf these figures.

Given the potential that online marketing has to distract and mislead small business owners, it's critical to keep it simple. Anything you do related to marketing should be viewed through the lens of your simple online marketing funnel:

- Does it *reach* my target audience using the right search terms and verbiage?
- Will it *engage* them with compelling copy that's focused on their questions and needs?
- Is it set up to *convert* them to take action and advance through the funnel?

The key is action.

I can't tell you how many times I hear business owners rationalize their plans to start blogging, making videos, or launching a WordPress site at a later date, "when the time is right." But *right now* is the perfect time to STAND OUT. If you remove all the technical gibberish and noise floating around the Web related to marketing and do nothing else but produce compelling content that speaks to the needs of your audience in your own passionate voice, you'll be much better off than most small business owners. The road to 10,000 visitors begins with a single keystroke.

At the core of the STAND OUT online marketing strategy lie two very powerful elements for long-term success: simplicity and action. Those are the two most important things to keep in mind as you implement your online marketing.

THE ROAD AHEAD

Throughout this book I have laid out a clear strategy that follows proven steps that countless small businesses have used to reach their audiences, become authorities, and achieve levels of growth and happiness beyond their wildest dreams! Like any worthwhile pursuit, marketing requires hard work, persistence, and dedication. Given how many different skill sets are required to master online marketing—SEO, copywriting, email marketing, conversion rate optimization, video creation, and social media, just to name a few—STAND OUT has set you on the right path to mastering these skills, while leaving behind the nonessential and ineffective tactics and strategies that relentlessly attempt to demand the attention of business owners.

What's important is that you maintain the right mindset, understanding that education-based marketing and content development together comprise the quickest and most sustainable path to becoming the authority in your niche. It's also important that you keep your passion alive as you continue down your road of learning, seeking new tools and knowledge related to online marketing and the art of finding and keeping clients.

The goal has never been to blend in with the pack. Your mission, should you choose to accept it, is to STAND OUT.

If you have any questions related to STAND OUT, want to interact with like-minded small business owners and entrepreneurs, or simply want to drop me a line and tell me how you're doing, I can be reached at http://geek-freemarketing.com.

Thank you for the valuable time and energy you've invested in reading this book.

NOTES

Introduction

- Internet use statistics are drawn from *The Huffington Post* (http://www. huffingtonpost.com/2010/06/22/Internet-usage-statistics_n_620946.html).
- Search engine marketshare figures from http://www.karmasnack.com/ about/search-engine-market-share/
- Timothy Ferriss, *The 4-Hour Workweek* (Crown Publishing Group, United States, April 2007)
- Timothy Ferriss, *The 4-Hour Body* (Crown Publishing Group, United States, December 2010)

Chapter 1

- "The aim of marketing is to know and understand the customer so well the product or service fits him and sells itself." Peter Drucker. Source: http://www. brainyquote.com/quotes/quotes/p/peterdruck154444.html
- Hans Christian Anderson, "The Emperor's New Clothes" (C.A. Reitzel, Denmark, April 1837)
- Michael E. Gerber, *The E-Myth: Why Most Small Businesses Don't Work and What to Do about It* (HarperCollins Publishers, Inc, New York, 1995)
- Michael Mastersen, *Ready, Fire, Aim* (John Wiley & Sons, Inc, New Jersey, 2008)
- Facebook is at more than a billion users per month and counting. Source: http://newsroom.fb.com/Key-Facts

- Owned by Google, YouTube is the second largest search engine in the world. Source: http://www.reelseo.com/youtube-search-engine-domination/
- Sun Tzu, *The Art of War* (Oxford University Press, New York, 1963) is a classic book on military strategies, many of which have been applied to business and marketing environments in countless works over the years.

Chapter 2

- "That's been one of my mantras—focus and simplicity. Simple can be harder than complex: You have to work hard to get your thinking clean to make it simple. But it's worth it in the end because once you get there, you can move mountains." From Steve Jobs, source: Business Week (http://www.businessweek.com/1998/21/b3579165.htm)
- According to Wikipedia, a funnel is ". . . a pipe with a wide, often conical mouth and a narrow stem." (http://en.wikipedia.org/wiki/Funnel)

Chapter 3

- The Marcus Sheridan quote "In today's information age of Marketing and Web 2.0, a company's website is the key to their entire business." cited from the website http://www.thesaleslion.com (http://www.thesaleslion.com/have-you-lost-the-keys-to-your-small-business/)
- "The history of the company website helped change the mindsets of business owners from the old 'outbound' style of marketing, focused on 'marketing disruptions' such as direct mail, sales calls and tradeshows, to the new "inbound" strategies which include content marketing, social media and search engine optimization." Brian Halligan, Dharmesh Shah and David Meerman Scott, *Inbound Marketing: Get Found Using Google, Social Media, and Blogs* (New Rules Social Media Series) (John Wiley & Sons Inc., New Jersey, 2010)
- SEOmoz's 12 Rules for Choosing the Right Domain Name: (http://www.seomoz.org/blog/how-to-choose-the-right-domain-name)
- What is a 301 Redirect and Why Should You Care?, http://blog.hubspot.com (http://blog.hubspot.com/blog/tabid/6307/bid/7430/What-is-a-301-Redirect-and-Why-Should-You-Care.aspx)
- HTML, http://en.Wikipedia.org, (http://en.wikipedia.org/wiki/HTML)
- WordPress, http://en.Wikipedia.org, (http://en.wikipedia.org/wiki/WordPress)
- How to Build a Blog in Less than 4 Minutes (and Write Your First Blog

Post), Pat Flynn, 2009, SmartPassiveIncome.com, http://youtube.com (http://youtu.be/wPwQvnar99w)

Chapter 4

- "Bad design is smoke, while good design is a mirror." Juan-Carlos Fernandez, (http://www.designsphere.info/2011/03/29/55-great-design-quotes/)
- Empathizing Color Psychology in Web Design. Source: http://www.1stwebdesigner.com, (http://www.1stwebdesigner.com/design/color-psychology-website-design/)
- "Don't make me think. I've been telling people for years that this is my first law of usability. And the more web pages I look at, the more convinced I become. It's the overriding principle—the ultimate tie breaker when deciding whether something works or doesn't in web design." Steve Krug, *Don't Make Me Think!: A Common Sense Approach to Web Usability* (New Riders, Berkeley, 2006)
- Web Design Trends: Testimonials Design, http://noupe.com, (http://www.noupe.com/how-tos/web-design-trends-testimonials-design.html)
- "Figure 2: Example of a "Facebook Fan Box" used on my blog" http://geek-freemarketing.com
- Sakkas, Cahn & Weiss, LLP makes good use of trust logos on their site (http://www.sakkascahn.com/)
- J. David Ford Construction (www.eastbayretrofit.com)
- "Social Proof Is the New Marketing," (http://techcrunch.com/2011/11/27/social-proof-why-people-like-to-follow-the-crowd/)
- Steve Krug, *Don't Make Me Think!: A Common Sense Approach to Web Usability* (New Riders, Berkeley, 2006)
- Susan M. Weinschenk, *Neuro Web Design: What Makes Them Click?* (New Riders, Berkeley, 2009)

Chapter 5

- "There's a fine line between fishing and just standing on the shore like an idiot." Steven Wright. Source: http://brainyquote.com (http://www.brainyquote.com/quotes/quotes/s/stevenwrig105995.html#xY7OwzqRIfGBH2I5.99)
- According to businessdictionary.com, a call to action (CTA) is defined as, "Words that urge the reader, listener, or viewer of a sales promotion message to take an immediate action, such as 'Write Now,' 'Call Now,' or (on Internet) 'Click Here.' A retail advertisement or commercial without a call-to-action is

considered incomplete and ineffective." (http://www.businessdictionary.com/definition/call-to-action.html)

• 5 Real-Life Examples of Fantastic Calls to Action. Source: http://blog.hubspot.com/blog/tabid/6307/bid/30691/5-Real-Life-Examples-of-Fantastic-Calls-to-Action.aspx)

• "Managing Plugins." Source: http://codex.wordpress.org/Managing_Plugins

• AdWords Help, "Check and Understand Quality Score." Source: http://support.google.com/adwords/bin/answer.py?hl=en&answer=2454010.

• "How Google's 'Content Experiments' Can Simplify Website Testing," Entrepreneur, Jonathan Blum and Anthony Mowl, June 7, 2012, http://www.entrepreneur.com/blog/223724

Chapter 6

• "If it isn't on Google, it doesn't exist.", Jimmy Wales (http://www.brainyquote.com/quotes/quotes/j/jimmywales450088.html)

• Google owns 70 percent of the global search market, with over three billion searches each day and annual sales exceeding $10 billion. By The Numbers: Twitter Vs. Facebook Vs. Google Buzz, http://searchengineland.com. Source: http://searchengineland.com/by-the-numbers-twitter-vs-facebook-vs-google-buzz-36709.

• Figure 10: The first organic listing on Google gets 53 percent of clicks. Source: Search Engine Watch http://searchenginewatch.com/article/2215868/53-of-Organic-Search-Clicks-Go-to-First-Link-Study.

• What percentage of all search is local? http://quora.com (http://www.quora.com/What-percentage-of-all-search-is-local

• "According to Netcraft, there are around 644,275,754 active websites on the Internet," March 2012 Web Survey, http://news.netcraft.com (http://news.netcraft.com/archives/2012/03/05/march-2012-web-server-survey.html)

Chapter 7

• "If you don't get noticed, you don't have anything. You just have to be noticed, but the art is in getting noticed naturally, without screaming or without tricks." Leo Burnett, "Get Noticed and Get Busy" (http://www.ortho2.com/otherResources/consultants/Bray/Bray-GetNoticedAndGetBusy.pdf)

• "The Periodic Table of Seo Ranking Factors." Source: http://

searchengineland.com (http://searchengineland.com/seotable)

• "The Long Tail," by Chris Anderson, *Wired* magazine, Issue 12.10, published October 2004 (http://www.wired.com/wired/archive/12.10/tail.html)

• "The following article by Matt Bailey describes the long tail quite well" from the article "Keyword Strategies - The Long Tail" August 16, 2005, http://www.searchengineguide.com/matt-bailey/keyword-strategies-the-long-tail.php

• B2B Long Tail SEO figure. Source: http://www.elliance.com (http://www.elliance.com/aha/infographics/seo-factors.aspx)

• Google Analytics (GA) is a "free service offered by Google that generates detailed statistics about the visitors to a website" (Wikipedia: http://en.wikipedia.org/wiki/Google_Analytics)

• "RESOURCE: Using Webmaster Tools Like an SEO" http://youtu.be/tQQmq9X5lQw, Maile Ohye, January, 2011

• Rand Fishkin's "Local SEO Checklist for New Sites," Aaron Wheeler, SEOmoz, October 2011 http://seomoz.com (http://www.seomoz.org/blog/local-seo-checklist-for-new-sites-whiteboard-friday)

• David Mihm's Local Search Ranking Factors, http://www.davidmihm.com (http://www.davidmihm.com/local-search-ranking-factors.shtml)

• Mobile Growth Stats & Mobile Web Tips to Start Marketing, http://searchenginewatch.com (http://searchenginewatch.com/article/2120678/Mobile-Growth-Stats-Mobile-Web-Tips-to-Start-Marketing)

• Authorship Markup and Web Search (http://googlewebmastercentral.blogspot.com/2011/06/authorship-markup-and-web-search.html)

• The Definitive Guide to Google Authorship Markup: (http://searchengineland.com/the-definitive-guide-to-google-authorship-markup-123218)

Chapter 8

• Zig Ziglar's quote "If you go looking for a friend, you're going to find they're very scarce. If you go out to be a friend, you'll find them everywhere" cited from the *Forbes* article "Zig Ziglar: 10 Quotes That Can Change Your Life," http://www.forbes.com (http://www.forbes.com/sites/kevinkruse/2012/11/28/zig-ziglar-10-quotes-that-can-change-your-life/)

• "article directory," Wikipedia, http://en.wikipedia.org/wiki/Article_directory

• Mashable's list of "20+ Free Press Release Sites" (http://mashable.com/2007/10/20/press-releases/)

• Great Article: How to Use the Modern Press Release (http://www.copyblogger.com/how-to-use-the-modern-press-release/)

- Article: How to Write a Press Release That Gets Attention: (http://www. problogger.net/archives/2010/12/12/how-to-write-a-press-release-that-gets-attention/)
- Video: PrWEB in Plain English: Vocus, September 2007 (http://www. youtube.com/watch?v=1YB74txAaTc)

Chapter 9

- Karl Pearson's quote: "That which is measured improves. That which is measured and reported improves exponentially." Cited from http://english. stackexchange.com (http://english.stackexchange.com/questions/14952/that-which-is-measured-improves)

Chapter 10

- The quote "Think like a publisher, not a marketer" from David Meerman Scott cited from http://stadiastudio.com (http://www.stadiastudio.com/tip/socialmedia/"think-publisher-not-marketer"—david-meerman-scott)
- "You no longer need to spend tons of money interrupting your potential customers. Instead you need to create remarkable content, optimize that content, publish the content, market the content, and measure what is working and what is not working. A savvy inbound marketer is half traditional marketer and half content creation factory." Shaw and Halligan, *Inbound Marketing* (Wiley, 2010)
- " . . . graphic visual representations of information, data or knowledge" from the article "Infographics" (Wikipedia: http://en.wikipedia.org/wiki/Infographics)
- "Dog Owners vs. Cat Owners" (http://editorial.designtaxi.com/news-dogvscat1207/1.png)
- "Syndication: to publish simultaneously, or supply for simultaneous publication, in a number of newspapers or other periodicals in different places" dictionary.com (http://dictionary.reference.com/browse/syndicate)

Chapter 11

- "Where the Internet is about availability of information, blogging is about making information creation available to anyone." George Siemens, The Art of Blogging (http://www.elearnspace.org/Articles/blogging_part_2.htm)
- Figure 48: Right at Home uses clearly defined blog categories.

- Tag Clouds allow users to find content related to common keywords (http://en.wikipedia.org/wiki/Tag_cloudhttp://wikipedia.com)
- "Be yourself, everyone else is taken." This quote from Oscar Wilde (http://www.goodreads.com/quotes/19884-be-yourself-everyone-else-is-already-taken)
- "Your readers should be so compelled to read your copy that they cannot stop reading until they read all of it as if sliding down a slippery slide" (Joseph Sugarman, *The AdWeek Copywriting Handbook,* John Wiley & Sons: Hoboken, NJ, 2006).
- How to Write Headlines That Work, Brian Clark, Copyblogger.com (http://www.copyblogger.com/how-to-write-headlines-that-work/)

Chapter 12

- "Internet video is now 40 percent of consumer Internet traffic, and will reach 62 percent by the end of 2015, not including the amount of video exchanged through P2P file sharing. The sum of all forms of video (TV, video on demand [VoD], Internet, and P2P) will continue to be approximately 90 percent of global consumer traffic by 2015." Cisco white paper, June 1 (http://www.cisco.com/en/US/prod/sanity/white_paper_c11-481360_test.html)
- http://youtu.be/La4JR-bYtns, Chadisms, December 2011
- http://youtu.be/Z4UeametC-w, MissNutritionistTV, April 2012
- iPhone Video Hero (http://ivideohero.com) is a great online course that costs $97. This video course demonstrates how to make video using the iPhone from start to finish, all in a very straightforward, step-by-step process.
- Video Lighting Basics - Three Point Lighting (http://www.youtube.com/watch?v=AcMX1RcNRYA, videomaker, 11, 2008)
- Figure 56: Rand Fishkin of SEOmoz.org uses a whiteboard to create great video content." . . . permits the photographer to view through the lens and hence see exactly what will be captured, contrary to viewfinder cameras where the image could be significantly different from what will be captured" (Wikipedia: http://en.wikipedia.org/wiki/Digital_single-lens_reflex_camera).
- The following is a great overview of basic video lighting from mediacollege.com (http://www.mediacollege.com/lighting/three-point/)
- "The rule of thirds: "a 'rule of thumb' or guideline which applies to the process of composing visual images such as paintings, photographs and designs. [1] The guideline proposes that an image should be imagined as divided into nine equal parts by two equally-spaced horizontal lines and two equally-spaced vertical lines, and that important compositional elements should be placed along

these lines or their intersections.[2] Proponents of the technique claim that aligning a subject with these points creates more tension, energy and interest in the composition than simply centering the subject would" (http://en.wikipedia.org/wiki/Rule_of_thirds).

• Figure 58: ScreenFlow or PowerPoint can be used to make great screen capture movies. Source: "Facebook Landing Page (on TIMELINE)" (http://www.youtube.com/watch?v=27QnH7XpOW0)

• Vimeo.com's online video compression guidelines can be found at https://vimeo.com/help/faq/vimeo_plus

• Fiverr (http://fiverr.com/) is a community of folks who will do just about anything for $5.00. I have found a few great sources for video transcription, my favorite of which is here: http://fiverr.com/transexpert/provide-quality-transcripts-for-any-10-minute-english-audio-or-video)

• Gary Vaynerchuk started Wine Library TV (http://tv.winelibrary.com) as a way to increase the online reach for his family's liquor store. Virtually every day, from 2006–2011, Gary made a daily video blog covering wine tasting notes, reviews, with some great humor and New York Jets fanfare sprinkled in. Vaynerchuk's commitment to producing content relevant to his target audience on a regular basis not only increased his family's business by nearly 1,000 percent, it also helped launch an entire new career as a marketing speaker, author, and consultant. His book *Crush It* (http://crushitbook.com) went on to be a *New York Times* bestseller (HarperCollins, New York, 2009).

Chapter 13

• "Profit in business comes from repeat customers, customers that boast about your project or service, and that bring friends with them." W. Edwards Deming cites from Brainyquote.com (http://www.brainyquote.com/quotes/quotes/w/wedwardsd131224.html)

• The Ultimate List of Email SPAM Terms (http://blog.hubspot.com/blog/tabid/6307/bid/30684/The-Ultimate-List-of-Email-SPAM-Trigger-Words.aspx)

• According to PEW Research (http://stateofthemedia.org/2011/audio-essay/data-page/), there were over 90,000 podcasts published on the Web in 2012

Chapter 14

• "Constant interactions with the community help you stay on target and up-to-date with latest trends. By actively participating in conversations, you are immersing yourself in the digital culture and soaking up valuable information." Authored by Magdalena Georgieva, Blog.Hubspot.com (http://blog.hubspot.com/blog/tabid/6307/bid/4969/be-a-digital-citizen-not-a-digital-tourist.aspx)

• Watch this video explaining Google's RSS Reader: http://www.youtube.com/watch?v=VSPZ2Uu_X3Y, Google, August 2008

• Darren Rowse of ProBlogger explains RSS readers in this article: http://www.problogger.net/what-is-rss/

• "The term 'podcast' was coined by Guardian reporter Ben Hammersley in 2004" from the Wikipedia article "podcast," http://en.wikipedia.org/wiki/Podcast

INDEX